RENEWALS 458-4574

DATE DUE

GAYLORD			PRINTED IN U.S.A.

NONGOVERNMENTS

Kumarian Press Books on International Development

Selected Titles

Nongovernments: NGOs and the
Political Development of the
Third World
Julie Fisher

Beyond the Magic Bullet:
NGO Performance and
Accountability in the
Post–Cold War World
*Michael Edwards and
David Hulme, editors*

The Two Faces of Civil Society:
NGOs and Politics in Africa
Stephen N. Ndegwa

Achieving Broad-Based
Sustainable Development:
Governance, Environment, and
Growth with Equity
*James H. Weaver, Michael T. Rock,
and Kenneth Kusterer*

Promises Not Kept:
The Betrayal of Social Change in
the Third World, Third Edition
John Isbister

Getting to the 21st Century:
Voluntary Action and the
Global Agenda
David C. Korten

Democratizing Development:
The Role of Voluntary
Organizations
John Clark

Intermediary NGOs:
The Supporting Link in
Grassroots Development
Thomas F. Carroll

NONGOVERNMENTS

NGOs and the Political Development of the Third World

Julie Fisher

Kumarian Press

To my parents, David and Frances Hawkins,
who have never wavered in their support
for my eclectic, sometimes erratic journey

Nongovernments: NGOs and the Political Development of the Third World

Published 1998 in the United States of America by Kumarian Press, Inc.,
14 Oakwood Avenue, West Hartford, Connecticut 06119-2127 USA.

Production supervised by Jenna Dixon
Copyedited by Linda Lotz   Proofread by Beth Richards
Typeset by CompuDesign
Index prepared by Nomi J. Waldman

The text of this book is set in 9.5/12.5 Adobe Melior.
The display type is Adobe Syntax.

Printed in the United States of America on acid-free paper by
BookCrafters. Text printed with soy-based ink.

PRINTED WITH
SOY INK.

♾ The paper used in this publication meets the minimum
requirements of the American National Standard for
Information Sciences—Permanence of Paper for Printed
Library Materials, ANSI Z39.48-1984.

Library of Congress Cataloging-in-Publication Data
Fisher, Julie, 1941–
    Nongovernments : NGOs and the political development of the Third World /
Julie Fisher.
        p.   cm. — (Kumarian Press books on international development)
    Includes bibliographical references and index.
    ISBN 1-56549-075-4 (cloth : alk. paper) — ISBN 1-56549-074-6 (paper : alk. paper)
    1. Non-governmental organizations—Developing countries. 2. Sustainable
development—Developing countries. 3. Democracy—Developing countries.
I. Title. II. Series.
HC59.7.F545   1997
338.9'009172'4—dc21   97-14228

07 06 05 04 03 02 01 00 99 98   10 9 8 7 6 5 4 3 2 1
                                        1st Printing 1998

Contents

Foreword

—Jeremy Rifkin

The global economy is undergoing a fundamental transformation in the nature of work brought on by the new technologies of the Information Age revolution. These profound technological and economic changes will force every country to rethink long-held assumptions about the nature of politics and citizenship.

At the heart of this historic shift are sophisticated computers, robotics, telecommunications, and other Information Age technologies that are fast replacing human beings, especially in the manufacturing sector. Automated technologies have been reducing the need for human labor in every manufacturing category. By the year 2020 less than 2 percent of the entire global workforce will still be engaged in factory work. Over the next quarter century we will see the virtual elimination of the blue-collar, mass assembly-line worker from the production process.

Acknowledging that both the manufacturing and service sectors are quickly reengineering their infrastructures and automating their production processes, many mainstream economists and politicians have pinned their hopes on new job opportunities along the information superhighway and in cyberspace. Although the "knowledge sector" will create some new jobs, they will be too few to absorb the millions of workers displaced by the new technologies. That's because the knowledge sector is, by nature, an elite and not a mass workforce. Indeed, the shift from mass to elite labor is what distinguishes work in the Information Age from that in the Industrial Age. With near-workerless factories and virtual companies already looming on the horizon, every nation will have to grapple with the question of what to do with the millions of people whose labor will be needed less, or not at all, in an evermore automated global economy.

Jeremy Rifkin is the author of *The End of Work: The Decline of the Global Labor Force and the Dawn of the Post-Market Era.* He is president of the Foundation on Economic Trends in Washington, D.C.

Julie Fisher's book captures the new role nongovernmental organizations are playing in addressing this issue. The civil society is playing an increasingly important social and economic role in nations around the world. People are creating new institutions at both the local and national levels to provide for needs that are not being met by either the marketplace or the public sector.

Today, NGOs are serving millions of citizens in scores of countries. Their reach and scope often eclipse both the private and public sector, touching and affecting the lives of every citizen, often more profoundly than the forces of the marketplace or the agencies and bureaucracies of government.

Expanding the role of NGOs in socioeconomic development requires that we rethink our notion of politics. While politicians traditionally divide society into a polar spectrum running from the marketplace, on the right, to the government, on the left, it is more accurate to think of society as a three-legged stool made up of the market sector, government sector, and civil sector. The first leg creates market capital, the second leg creates public capital, and the third leg creates social capital. In the old scheme of things, finding the proper balance between the market and government dominated political discussion. In the new scheme, finding a balance between the market, government, and civil sectors becomes paramount. Thinking of society as creating three types of capital—market capital, public capital, and social capital—opens up new possibilities for reconceptualizing both the social contract and the meaning of work in the coming era.

The key to a genuine attempt to recast the political landscape will depend on the political will to increase the clout and elevate the profile of the civil society, making it an equal player with both the marketplace and government. But since the nongovernmental sector relies on both the market and government for its survival and well-being, its future will depend, in large part, on the creation of a new political force that can make demands on both the market and government sectors to pump some of the vast financial gains of the new Information Age economy into the creation of social capital and the restoration of civil life around the world.

The potential for a new third force in political life exists but has not yet been galvanized into a mainstream social movement. It consists of the millions of citizens who give of their time each week serving in the many NGOs that make up the sprawling civil society. These individuals already understand the importance of creating social capital in their own neighborhoods and communities.

Up to now, however, the millions of people who either volunteer or work in this sector have not seen themselves as part of a potentially powerful constituency—one that, if politicized, could help reshape the national agenda in every country. Participants in the civil society come from every race and ethnic background, and from every class and walk of life. The one thing they share is a belief in the importance of service to the community and the creation of social capital. If that powerful shared value can be transformed into a sense of common purpose and identity, we could redraw the political map. Mobilizing these millions of people into a broad-based social movement that can make tough demands on both the market and public sectors will be the critical test of the new politics of social capital.

The ever-deepening problem of rising productivity in the face of declining wages, vanishing jobs, and poverty is likely to be one of the defining issues in every country in the years ahead as the global economy makes the tumultuous transition out of the Industrial Age and into the Information Age. The growing social unrest and increasing political destabilization arising from this historic shift in the way the world does work is forcing activists of every stripe and persuasion, as well as politicians and political parties, to search for a "new center" that speaks to the concerns and aspirations of a majority of the electorate. The conventional political discussion continues to take place along the polar spectrum of marketplace versus government—a playing field that becomes increasingly limited in addressing the magnitude of the challenges and opportunities that exist in this new age. As Fisher suggests, redirecting the political debate to a tripartite model with the civil society in the center between the market and government spheres fundamentally changes the nature of political discourse, opening up the possibility of re-envisioning the body politic, the economy, and the nature of work and society in wholly new ways in the coming century.

Preface

Years ago, when I was in graduate school, I was required to read a great deal of "modernization" theory. I remember being uncomfortable with the idea that developed countries were considered so advanced. One of my earliest memories was the terrible poverty in the alley behind our apartment on Rhode Island Avenue in Washington, D.C. And I wondered whether something might be lost in the modernization of traditional societies. Another early memory was my maternal grandfather, wrapped in his *Taraoumara* blanket, eating his morning eggs with Tabasco and lemon juice, and telling me stories of his years in northern Mexico. Later, as a teenager, when I lived in Mexico with my parents, I felt welcomed—indeed overwhelmed—by the warmth of the people and the beauty of their traditions. I was further inoculated against the underdeveloped-developed dichotomy by my lively anthropology professor at Pomona College, Charles Leslie.

There was one corner of modernization theory that fascinated me, however, and that was the subject of "political development." As much as I loved Mexico, I couldn't help being aware that its political system, while promoting industrialization, was perpetuating poverty. I retained this fascination, even as my successors in graduate school were reading dependency theory and being taught that the idea of political development was naive and ethnocentric. My doctoral dissertation, written over the course of five years as I coordinated the naps of two little boys and hired afternoon baby-sitters, dealt with neighborhood organizations in the Latin American squatter settlements. Maybe, I remember thinking, democracy was still possible, at least on a local level.

During four years working with Philip Coombs on a major study of global education trends, I became aware that, at least in Thailand, Indonesia, and Sri Lanka, there were intemediary nonprofit organizations that worked with grassroots organizations. In 1982, shortly after my first husband died unexpectedly, I immersed myself in teaching comparative politics and a senior seminar of my own design at Connecticut College. I called it "The Politics of Third World Development," and I spent some time returning to the political development literature and focusing on the political role of grassroots organizations.

After a field evaluation of Save the Children's women's program in Colombia in 1986, I attended a meeting of the Latin American Studies Association in Boston. There I met the late Mario Padrón, an influential leader of the global as well as the Peruvian nongovernmental organization (NGO) movement, and Brian Smith, who, in a panel presentation, asserted that there were at least seven or eight thousand intermediary NGOs in the Third World working with grassroots organizations. Suddenly, everything came together, and I decided to learn all I could about this new global phenomenon. Along the way, I gained professional support from the Program on Non-Profit Organizations (PONPO) at Yale and confirmation from the work of others. As Robert Berg wrote almost ten years ago, "Something is happening out there."

My research, carried out between consulting jobs, finally led to the publication of *The Road from Rio: Sustainable Development and the Nongovernmental Movement in the Third World* in 1993. That book was what David Cooperrider calls an "appreciative inquiry," an attempt to understand the who, what, and where questions. Yet I continued to research the larger issues of how NGOs are impacting politics, governance, civil society, and democratization, as well as sustainable development.

The result is this second book, which could not have been written without the support of many people. My husband and consulting partner, Richard Peck, first inspired me to undertake this long scholarly journey and read, reread, and edited the manuscript more times than either of us cares to remember. Many thanks as well to my father, David Hawkins, who read and commented on the entire manuscript with the keen judgment of a philosopher. My son, Tom Fisher, was great at pinpointing trouble spots, and I tested many ideas with my other son, Scott. My stepdaughter, Linda Peck, was a continual source of guidance on computers. My colleagues at PONPO—Peter Hall, John Simon, Brad Gray, Lisa Berlinger, and Dick Magat—were both supportive and challenging. Many thanks also to Karen Refsbeck and Pam Greene for continual encouragement. David Bronkema, Adil Najam, Eric Sievers, Iman Ghazallah, and Celia Kl amath—all John D. Rockefeller fellows at PONPO—inspired me with both their intellect and their excitement about the subject. Thanks also to biologist Bob Wyman, who twice asked me to help teach a course on international population issues at Yale, enabling me to get to know students such as Liza Grandia, who is now working in Guatemala to use NGOs to extend family planning to the Peten region.

1

NGOs, Civil Society, and Political Development

■ There is no central committee: each committee is central.
—Brazilian Citizen's Campaign

■ We have it in our power to begin the world again.
—Thomas Paine

SINCE THE RIO CONFERENCE in June 1992, the global community has haltingly inched along the "steep and rocky path" of sustainable development.[1] Rio not only increased global awareness of the need to develop without destroying the resources needed for future development but also stimulated international debate about the relationships among poverty, population, and environmental degradation.

Two stories in the *New York Times* of July 13, 1993, symbolize the enormous gap separating the mindless destruction of natural resources from the promise of sustainable development. Hinunangan, on the Philippine island of Leyte, was once a rich tropical ecosystem of tall trees, bamboo, monkeys, wild boar, ducks, and ostriches. Because of the rapacious deforestation of valuable hardwoods, most wildlife is now extinct, water is in short supply, and even the basic rice crop is threatened. Hawaii, in contrast, has a laboratory and a commercial park complex that use differentials in seawater temperature to produce electric power and desalinated water. Its economic spin-offs include fruit, vegetables, commercial fish, and lobster.

Implementing a sustainable development project—be it a technologically sophisticated laboratory or a simple program such as planting fruit trees or teaching women to read—is never easy, as thousands of indigenous nongovernmental organizations (NGOs) in the Third World have already learned. Yet the complexities of implementing locally sustainable

1

development are dwarfed by the magnitude of the political and institutional changes needed at the local, national, and international levels to halt the gradual destruction of the global ecosystem.

Fortunately, the emergence of indigenous NGOs over the last three decades is a positive addition to the political mix in the Third World. Indeed, NGOs strengthen the institutions of civil society that mediate between the individual and the state, both on their own and in conjunction with governments. This, in turn, can promote increased governmental responsiveness and accountability.

This book is about the growing political and technical capacities of Third World, or "Southern," NGOs and their relationships with their governments. More specifically, I deal with NGOs' ability to contribute to environmentally sustainable development in their relationships with governments and how these relationships may become politically sustainable as well. Political sustainability depends on the roles that NGOs play in strengthening civil society and on their ability, in interacting with governments, to contribute to increasing governmental responsiveness and accountability at both the local and the national levels.

The rise of Third World NGOs has coincided with the increasing inability of the nation-state to muddle through as it confronts the long-term consequences of its own ignorance, corruption, and lack of accountability. At the same time, international networking among national NGOs from all parts of the globe and the proliferation of international NGOs (INGOs) have coincided with the post–Cold War emergence of an international community continually confounded by intertwined and intractable crises at the national level. Violence and ethnic conflict in some countries dominate the global media, but the underlying poverty-environment-population crisis dominates the news in many more places.

These three horsemen of the global apocalypse—poverty, environmental degradation, and population growth—are clearly interrelated, yet the directions of causality are complex and multidimensional. Overpopulation leads to deforestation or soil exhaustion, which leads to increasing poverty. Increasing poverty leads to migration to more remote areas, where the cycle begins again. Landlessness, an absence of opportunities for women, and a lack of hope that children will survive provide little incentive for the success of family planning. And environmental destruction by outside interests can increase poverty, even if the people and the environment have coexisted for generations.

Deforestation, for example, is fueled by both greed and need. Japanese timber companies have ruthlessly destroyed tropical ecosystems in Asia in their quest for profits. Governments have shortsightedly joined in this destructive frenzy in their efforts to pay off mounting debt burdens, and their lack of accountability only accelerates the tendency to choose the quick buck rather than sustainable development.[2] But once a tropical forest is "opened up" by timber companies or governments, deforestation is propelled by growing numbers of desperately poor people who may have no other means to survive.

On a deeper, even more troubling level, there are those who question whether we have already exceeded the earth's carrying capacity. Rees (1996, 207), for example, uses the concept of "ecological footprint" to show that it is the developed countries that are already "over-populated in ecological terms—they could not sustain themselves at current material standards if forced by changing circumstances to live on their remaining endowments of domestic natural capital. This is hardly a good model for the rest of the world to follow."[3]

Thus, if sustainable development is to be implemented on a large scale, massive political change will be required everywhere. There are some politically encouraging signs. In the United States, despite the mixed environmental record of many major multinational corporations, President Clinton reversed the Bush administration's refusal to sign the mandatory provisions of the treaty to stabilize greenhouse gases. The Clinton administration also reversed the long-standing "Mexico City" policy, which placed restrictions on U.S. foreign assistance to population and family planning NGOs in the Third World. And democratization is visible in some Third World and formerly communist transitional countries, despite the lapse into violence and civil war in others.

Despite such encouraging trends, most governments lack the means, to say nothing of the will, to confront democratization and sustainable development. Indeed, there are those who argue that human beings have already sown the seeds of their own destruction and are incapable of political adaptation to the magnitude of the global challenge. Perhaps the road from Rio is, quite literally, impassable.

There are, however, signposts along this road, although they are rarely erected by governments. They are being painted not only by visionary scientists and industrialists in the developed countries but also by thousands of Third World NGOs. There are also "roads less traveled" in the Third World that may intersect with existing ways of progressing that have become impassable. Yet the signposts and alternative paths emerging in Third World countries are largely ignored by a public and world media that continue to disregard the ominous causes of the global environmental crisis while focusing on its dramatic, short-run symptoms.

I wrote *The Road from Rio: Sustainable Development and the Nongovernmental Movement in the Third World* to illuminate the signposts that are being painstakingly constructed out of sheer necessity by hundreds of thousands of professionals and millions of common people in Asia, Africa, and Latin America. *The Road from Rio* was written as an

Figure 1.1   Third World NGOs: GROs, GRSOs, and Their Networks

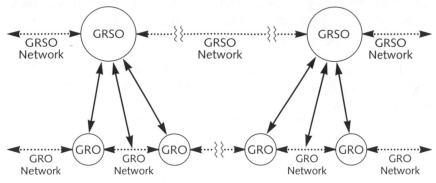

appreciative inquiry into the organizational ingenuity increasingly required for people to survive and improve their lives in the Third World.[4] If it did nothing else, I am gratified that the book was described by one reviewer as "[exploding] two especially pernicious myths about sustainable development: that the concept was invented by the Brundtland Commission report of 1987 and that how to put this difficult goal into practice is not yet known" (Levy 1994, 26).

One of the signposts along the road to sustainable development is a historically unprecedented partnership between intellectual elites and the common people. This partnership defines two major types of NGOs in the Third World—member-serving grassroots organizations (GROs) based in local communities, and nationally or regionally based development assistance organizations called grassroots support organizations (GRSOs) (see Figure 1.1). GRSOs are usually staffed by professionals who channel international funds to GROs and help communities other than their own to develop. In addition to these vertical connections between GROs and GRSOs, there are two other types of NGOs in the Third World defined by their horizontal connections with each other—GRO networks linking local communities to one another, and networks of GRSOs.

That these two types of NGOs, tied to each other, should have emerged at the same time, independently, all over Asia, Africa, and Latin America is nothing short of remarkable. Third World professionals have been creating GRSOs and building ties to traditional and newly organized groups at the local level for some thirty years. Yet this historic and cross-nationally similar response to increasing impoverishment was not only unanticipated by their Northern colleagues; it is, to this day, largely unappreciated by most Northern academics, to say nothing of mainstream policy makers. This worldwide expansion of civil society, now also occurring in transitional countries, is bound to be consequential, although not in ways that we can easily predict.

This chapter, divided into five sections, begins with background information on these four broad types of NGOs—GROs, GRO networks, GRSOs, and GRSO networks. The second section, which explores the meaning of civil society, is followed by an exploration of the multiple roles that NGOs play in creating, strengthening, and sustaining it. Since civil society is a static concept, however, that cannot encompass dynamic interactions with governments, the fourth section of the chapter resurrects the concept of political development, elaborated in the 1960s and academically discredited *before* NGOs began to proliferate throughout the developing and transitional countries. Although political development is far from inevitable, when it does occur, it takes place in the political commons between government and civil society. Contrasts are also drawn between the concepts of political development and democratization, even though democratization may be indicative of political development. The concluding section of the chapter provides an outline of the rest of the book.

The Nongovernmental Movement in the Third World

The term NGO has many different meanings. Some observers use it to mean all nongovernmental organizations everywhere, including Northern NGOs (NNGOs) based in one developed country that operate internationally, international NGOs (INGOs) or networks based in three or more countries, Southern NGOs from the Third World, and many other kinds of nonprofit organizations throughout the world. The term also has numerous culturally specific meanings. In Western Europe, it generally means nonprofit organizations that are active internationally.[5] In the transitional countries of Europe and the former Soviet Union, it tends to mean all charitable and nonprofit organizations.

In the Third World, the term NGO generally refers to organizations involved in development, broadly defined. Hospitals, charitable organizations, and universities are usually called voluntary or nonprofit organizations rather than NGOs.[6] Although some observers of the Third World use the term NGO to mean only intermediary or grassroots support organizations, all four types of NGOs are involved in sustainable development, and many individual organizations interact with governments. This section first explores GROs and their horizontal connections with one another in GRO networks. Next, the focus is on GRSOs and their vertical connections with GROs, as well as their horizontal connections with one another in GRSO networks. The section concludes with a discussion of how NGOs are "scaling out," or extending their reach to include more people.

GROs and GRO Networks

There are probably over 200,000 GROs in Asia, Africa, and Latin America, defined as locally based membership organizations that work to develop their own communities.[7] Although many GROs have been promoted and stimulated by GRSOs, they have also become more active on their own. Faced with the combined deterioration of their environment and the increasing impoverishment of the 1980s, and sustained by the gradual liberation of women, both traditional and newly created GROs are organizing horizontal networks among themselves. Although many GROs face frustration and failure, there is an immense field-based body of evidence that GROs are the sine qua non of effective and sustainable development. In the slums of Orangi, near Karachi, Pakistan, for example, lane committees provide self-help sewerage and water with little outside help to over 100,000 people (Uphoff 1993, 617).

A majority of GROs are nonprofit organizations. The two most common types of GROs are local development associations (LDAs), such as village councils or neighborhood associations that represent an entire community, and interest associations (IAs), such as women's clubs or irrigators organizations that represent particular groups within a community.[8] A third type of GRO—including borrowers groups, pre-cooperatives, and cooperatives—may make profits. Cooperatives can have a major impact on developing their own communities, yet they clearly differ from nonprofit GROs, as well as from private businesses without members.[9]

Regional or horizontal GRO networks link local community organizations in three different ways. First are the formal umbrella networks that link individual GROs such as cooperatives, LDAs, and IAs. Second are the informal economic networks tied together by barter arrangements that can widen local markets and build a vested interest in regional collaboration. Third are the amorphous grassroots social movements that increasingly focus on environmental concerns; they may or may not be based on individual GROs. For example, the Inter-Ethnic Association for the Development of the Peruvian Jungle (AIDESEP), organized in 1980, unites GROs representing two-thirds of the 300,000 indigenous peoples that live there. In some cases, GRO networks become self-supporting and create GRSOs from below by hiring their own expertise. The Committee for Development Action, a regional training center in Senegal, links three different ethnic groups and sixteen villages and is funded by a percentage of profits from a communal field (Pradervand 1990).

Although there is an enormous amount of development activity and institution building bubbling up from below, the right mix and quality of outside technical assistance and self-reliance are not easy to determine.

And even self-reliance can degenerate into self-serving behavior. Unfortunately, one large Senegalese peasant federation is already "generating bureaucrats," according to Pradervand (1990, 171). Yet GRO networks help scale up impact, are "more accountable to local people than any other development institution" (Bebbington 1993, 286), and are often in the forefront of understanding the connections between poverty and environmental degradation, if not yet the population issue.[10] Moreover, horizontal linkages between GROs seem to have an additive impact on both participation and equality (Fisher 1993, chap. 2).

GRSOs and GRSO Networks

The proliferation of GRSOs began in the late 1960s. On the supply side, there was an increased availability of official and voluntary foreign assistance. On the demand side, these new resources provided idealistic young professionals, who had benefited from widespread governmental investment in universities in the 1960s, with protection from political repression; a means to express their genuine commitment to the poor; and an alternative to unemployment, dead-end government jobs, or migration to the developed countries. In response, these Third World baby boomers created thousands GRSOs concerned with development, environment, the role of women, and primary health care that work in partnership with GROs.

The most obvious long-term consequence of this phenomenon is that there are now at least 50,000 active GRSOs in the Third World (Fisher 1993, 80–94; United Nations Development Programme 1993, 86). Although there are few data on the birth and death rates of GRSOs, their numbers continue to increase, and Schneider's (1985) estimate that GRSOs were reaching over a hundred million people in the Third World could safely be tripled by 1996 (Fisher 1993, 93–5). A second, striking fact is how similar these organizations are in Bolivia, Botswana, or Bangladesh.[11] Yet what is truly extraordinary about these organizations is that in all but a few Third World countries throughout the world, this coincidence of education and idealism has continued to be nourished by grassroots ties. Indeed, the idea and practices of grassroots support have spread to vastly different types of organizations. Although a small group of professionals that obtains foreign support and begins to work with one or more GROs is the most typical pattern, other organizations are adding grassroots support to their repertoires without necessarily giving up other functions. GRSOs, in other words, turn up in unexpected places such as hospitals, universities, churches, nonprofit theater groups, and, particularly in Latin America, private research centers.[12]

In their core activities, GRSOs confront what David Korten (1983, 220) called the "central paradox" of development—influencing people to build capacity to act on their own behalf. Because this paradox is based on an unequal power relationship, the autonomy as well as the accountability of GRSOs ultimately depend on their success in empowering ordinary people at the grassroots level.

GROs and GRSOs do, however, have some particular comparative advantages in relation to empowerment that complement one another. According to an Inter-American Foundation study of the organizations it has funded, GRSOs have the capacity for "organizational, economic or technological innovation, as well as for rapid response to unforeseen opportunities. Yet membership organizations (GROs) have the potential (albeit often unrealized) to have a much deeper, and potentially more far-reaching social impact" (Fox and Butler 1987, 4). In fact, a strikingly consistent theme of *The Road from Rio* is GROs' strong impact on the continual rethinking and reassessment that are typical of many GRSOs. GRSOs may, therefore, have the greatest grassroots development impact by providing services that strengthen GROs as membership organizations. In some cases, they encourage GROs that would not otherwise have done so to organize networks. GRSOs also link GROs to the outside world while protecting them from it. For example, Bolivian GRSOs have helped unemployed tin miners cope with structural adjustment policies by organizing food-buying cooperatives.

Even though GRSOs that concentrate on environmental issues have proliferated rapidly in the last ten years, it has become more difficult to define the boundary between poverty-focused and environment-focused organizations. A wide perusal of recent accounts of GRSO activity reveals a kind of branching out to every conceivable sector related to environmentally sustainable development:

- The Brazilian Association of Canoeing and Ecology (ABRACE) in Amazonia is using river trips on canoes to dramatize the plight of the rain forest and to provide preventive health care and medical assistance (IRED 1987, 22; *Brundtland Bulletin* 1990, 41).

- In Costa Rica, CEFEMINA helps women build housing around common courtyard gardens of edible, endangered plant species.

- In Bangladesh, the Nature Conservation Movement is training an endangered species of otter to chase fish into nets.

Apart from such dramatic examples of sustainable development, most GRSOs invest in human capital, which is generally the least environmentally destructive form of development. Despite the attention to sustainable development, however, far fewer GRSOs concentrate on the population issue than on poverty or environmental deterioration.

There are, of course, some corrupt organizations, and others that siphon off donor funding without cultivating strong grassroots ties.[13] Nonetheless, GRSOs have a generally positive reputation. At the very least, they contribute to an overall growth of the independent sector (see Box 1.1) At best, they help strengthen democratic decision making at the grassroots or even the national level of society. Women's professional associations seem to be particularly suited to integrating middle-class and low-income members at the national level, and in some countries they are mobilizing vast numbers of highly qualified volunteer professionals. In Bangladesh, for example, a national association of women lawyers organized a project that traveled to 68,000 villages to teach millions of women (and men) their basic legal rights. Still at issue in terms of the sustainability of GRSOs, however, is whether the thousands of remarkable individuals who created them, beginning in the early 1970s, are training others to take their places.

In addition to building linkages with GROs, GRSOs are uniting with one another, both formally and informally. Both formal and informal networks may be multisectoral or may focus more narrowly on one development sector. And they may be regional or national in geographic focus.

Formal umbrella organizations of GRSOs usually have written constitutions or bylaws, hold annual meetings, and represent GRSOs as a group in negotiations with governments and international donors. Although they often assist their member organizations through management training or bulk purchases, formal networks are not generally involved in grassroots support. This often means that they are less insulated than individual GRSOs from the bureaucratic diversion provided by foreign financial support. Financial dispersion from the international to the national level does not inevitably cascade down to GRSOs and GROs. The availability of funding can also lead to competition instead of collaboration among GRSOs.

GRSOs in informal networks are more likely than those in formal networks to interact with one another in the field, and they may provide grassroots support as a group. The two most common types of informal networks are service networks and support movements. Service networks may be large or small, but they are consistently homogeneous, involving mainly GRSOs and perhaps one other member of a different type, such as a foundation. Service networks enable GRSOs to exchange and promote one another's professional capacities. In Honduras, for example, Agua Para el Pueblo works with both GROs and other GRSOs to coordinate agronomy and aquaculture, so that completed water systems can be used immediately (Fisher 1993, 143). Support movements, in contrast, are large, heterogeneous, often amorphous systems of communication that include

---

Box 1.1   The Independent, Voluntary, Third, or Nonprofit Sector?

Once the government and private business sectors are defined, scholars argue about what to call everything else. The term *voluntary sector* tends to imply the use of volunteers. The term *third sector* coined by Nielsen (1979) is confusing unless one already knows that government is the first sector and business the second. Although the term *nonprofit sector* is useful for the developed countries, it does not encompass the complex organizational reality of the Third World today. Cooperatives, for example, promote projects benefiting an entire community, in addition to making profits for their members. Therefore, I use the term *independent sector.*

GRSOs, universities, charities, GROs, and some individuals, such as journalists or professors interested in grassroots development.

Scaling Out

Networks at both the grassroots and grassroots support levels not only enhance the sustainability of individual organizations but also help address the difficult challenge of scaling out the reach of sustainable development.[14] According to Khan (1991), the 20,000 or more GROs with ties to Proshika, a large Bangladeshi GRSO, proliferated because village leaders visited other villages where groups were already organizing. Given the spread of GRO and GRSO networks, it is obvious that hundreds of thousands of activists understand the need for an impact on wider systems. Moreover, the idea of networking, even particular forms of networking, has itself become contagious. For example, the Six S Association, which began in Burkina Faso, is promoting indigenous GRO networks reaching over half a million people in Chad, the Gambia, Guinea Bissau, Mali, Mauritania, Niger, Senegal, and Togo.

Since it has become nearly impossible in many countries for individuals to advance themselves, they have begun to organize collectively in ways that both predate and postdate industrial bureaucracies. To be sure, individual GROs and GRSOs can become sources of privilege and patronage for the few, yet the linkages among NGOs, coupled with the computer revolution, provide enormously enhanced capabilities for implementing sustainable development and for creating paths to change that may violate Robert Michels's ([1915] 1959) "iron law of oligarchy." Although Michels's theory has, understandably, conditioned the thinking of at least three generations of societal observers, there is evidence that the link between "human nature" and oligarchic behavior is not always inevitable.[15]

The powerful potential connections among political, social, and sustainable economic development are being pursued consciously, if not always simultaneously, by NGO activists. They possess a remarkably widespread commitment to the idea that political empowerment from below can untie the negative connections among ignorance, malnutrition, inequality, and powerlessness that now sustain poverty. Political and institutional sustainability ultimately depends, however, on NGOs' impact on civil society and the ways in which NGOs and the state interact to promote both environmentally and politically sustainable development.

What Is Civil Society?

Interest in the concept of civil society is not new. John Locke wrote about its role in protecting property rights, and Antonio Gramsci described it in terms of autonomous institutions that may either support or challenge state power. Yet the proliferation of NGOs throughout the world has spurred interest in what Michael Walzer called "the space of uncoerced human association" (1991, 293). In Latin America during the 1970s, intellectuals who were reacting against Marxism as well as right-wing dictatorship began to write about *sociedad civil*.[16] During the 1980s, the term *civil society* reappeared in the writings of central and eastern European dissidents as they tried to carve out an understanding of social process that could stand in opposition to the state, while being broader and more humane than the market.

Although Walzer's definition provides a good beginning for discussions of civil society, debate continues about what civil society means.[17] Some observers, building on classical political theory, include the for-profit as well as the independent sectors in their definitions.[18] In a landmark book on recent Spanish history, Victor Perez Diaz (1993, 56), for example, defines civil society as "markets, associations, and a sphere of public debate." There are, in fact, three good reasons for expanding the definition of civil society beyond the independent sector.

The first is that businesses as well as nonprofit organizations help mediate between the citizen and the state. The second is that markets and associations are often more than unrelated members of the same civil society. Just as the craftsmen's guilds formed in northern Italy a thousand years ago were economic in character, NGOs as diverse as the Grameen Bank in Bangladesh and the Foundation for Economic and Social Initiative in Poland are promoting for-profit enterprises.[19] Poverty-focused NGOs also work to promote credit and technical assistance for microenterprises and informal economic activity throughout the world.

The third reason is that the for-profit sector promotes nonprofit organizations in some countries. In Bombay, India, for example, a Ford Foundation study of thirty-six companies revealed that they had contributed $7.1 million to their own development projects and in donations to other agencies (Sen 1994, 9).[20] In South Africa, the business sector was, until recently, the major financial backer and provider of technical assistance to NGOs (Lee 1992, 97).[21]

Whereas it is relatively easy to include a growing informal sector of microentrepreneurs in civil society, there are difficulties with including large multinational corporations. Indeed, as Korten (1995, 124) argues, "It has become a matter of pride and principle for corporate executives to proclaim that their firms have grown beyond any national interest." He points out that although "multinationals" can take on many national identities, the trend is toward transnationalism, "which involves the integration of a firm's global operations around vertically integrated supplier networks" (125).

The importance of what Perez Diaz calls the "sphere of public debate" to civil society is clearly understood by GROs in the Philippines that use large community blackboards as local newspapers. Newspaper readership is one of four indicators used by Putnam (1993a) in contrasting the strength of civil society in northern Italy with its weakness in the south. Even partially independent media can help a country move from deferential to autonomous, active civility.

Moreover, in the Third World, NGOs are only part of the independent sector, even though other kinds of voluntary organizations, such as churches and universities, are, as noted earlier, increasingly acquiring grassroots support capabilities. The tendency to equate civil society and NGOs limits our understanding of a broad process of interaction among different types of organizations. Much independent-sector research has emerged from advocacy and may not always acknowledge bureaucratization or self-serving behavior. Voluntary organizations, just like governments, businesses, and other forms of human interaction, can destroy the independent grassroots initiatives that constitute social capital.[22]

Yet what is undeniable is that NGOs, because of their rapid proliferation, are the vanguard of civil society in most of the Third World, as well as in the transitional countries of Europe and the former Soviet Union.[23] In the Third World, NGOs promote civil society in six major ways. These are explored in the next section.

NGOs and Civil Society

The strength of civil society is roughly related to the sheer number of functioning intermediary organizations between the citizen and the state. Within the independent sector, these include everything from strictly civic associations, such as athletic teams, to NGOs that are trying to develop their communities or promote social change. Bebbington and Farrington (1993, 205) consider this to be the most important role of NGOs: "Rather than democratizing development NGOs may better be seen as steps towards organizational pluralism."[24] Similarly, in contrasting the strength of the "civic community" in northern and southern Italy, Putnam (1993a) used data on organizations of all types—including choral societies and sports clubs—as a key indicator.

Yet NGO proliferation over the last thirty years has played a second, more specific role in nurturing sustainable development and viable civil societies in the Third World. The large number of GRSOs that focus on microenterprise development are building a vested interest in their work among the members of GROs. Since vested interests usually help sustain *inequitable* institutions, creating vested interests among the poor may be an equally powerful way to promote the institutional sustainability not only of microenterprises and cooperatives but also of the village councils or women's group that support such income strategies on a local level.

A third, more targeted role for NGOs is to promote political rights and civil liberties. There are now an estimated 4,000 to 5,000 indigenous human rights organizations at the most political end of the NGO spectrum in the Third World, ranging from national chapters of Amnesty International to professional associations of lawyers or journalists (Fisher 1993, 104–5).[25] According to Welch (1995, 3) they now exist in most African countries, "unlike the situation barely a decade ago."[26]

Some human rights NGOs have already had a disproportionate impact on national dialogue, if not democratization, as Waltz's (1995, 193) study of six human rights groups in Morocco, Tunisia, and Algeria shows. Indeed, Waltz argues that by challenging the rules of the political games in North Africa, these few organizations are already performing a "metapolitical" as opposed to a "relational" function.[27] In Tunisia, for example, during the Bourguiba regime, the League of Human Rights (LTDH) was "the first politically independent organization that [the government] had allowed to exist, and its exemplary behavior was a dilemma for the regime. Violating human rights principles it allegedly supported and repressing the LTDH were equally damnable (Waltz 1995, 137–8). Even in Algeria, where the human rights movement has been largely silenced by the violence and chaos that have gripped the country since 1992, "the idea of human rights . . . has not entirely disappeared from what political discourse yet remains" (Waltz 1995, 144).

Other human rights organizations have begun to expand beyond their original goal of protecting political dissidents by collaborating with GRSOs or by acquiring their own grassroots support capabilities:

- In Cambodia, where there were almost no NGOs even ten years ago, a small women's rights organization called Ponleu Khmer has become an active player in the national human rights dialogue. Ponleu Khmer has also helped organize an NGO network that includes GRSOs.[28]

- In Brazil, an ad hoc coalition of NGOs prepared a plan to ensure grassroots feedback on the new constitution being drafted.

- In Nigeria, a group of lawyers mobilized a group of human rights and other NGOs working with prisoners and successfully challenged the authority of prison administrators opposed to reforms (Sandberg 1994b, 12).

- In the Philippines, an NGO network called the National Citizens Movement for Free Elections (NAMFREL) played a major role in observing elections, did a parallel quick count of the vote, and helped unmask widespread fraud.[29]

In Asia, this democratization of the human rights movement centers on the rights of the poor to have access to sustainable natural resources threatened by deforestation or other environmental disasters (Fisher 1993, 105). For instance, an NGO established by the Indonesian Lawyers Association has thirteen regional branches and a human rights budget of $1.5 million. Among its 150 yearly litigations with a "structural or public impact" are those focusing on environmental threats to local communities (Theunis 1992, 249).

Just as human rights organizations have begun to fight for the rights of the poor, GRSOs that focus on sustainable development are increasingly concerned with human rights and political liberties, either in collaboration with human rights organizations or on their own.

- In Colombia, a GRSO network called the Foro Nacional por Colombia initiated a national campaign challenging "restricted democracy" (Theunis 1992, 179).

- In Bangladesh in 1989, the largest women's network in the country, Bangladesh Mahila Parishad, organized a national conference of 30,000 to demand a democratic political system (*DAWN Informs* [1989], no. 7/8, 6). By 1991 the Bangladeshi Coordinating Council for Human Rights (CCHR), a network of human rights, development, and environmental organizations, was holding seminars for journalists and used 2,000 of its members to observe the parliamentary elections.[30]

In Africa, by the end of the 1980s, GRSOs and grassroots economic networks were providing a "recruiting ground" for protest against post-colonial autocracies. Sometimes, NGOs are only semiconscious of this political role. NGOs in Kenya, for example, do not necessarily see themselves as enhancing democracy; rather, they understand that democracy would allow them to operate more freely (Ndegwa 1996, 53).

This increased interest in democracy and human rights in Africa is simultaneously operating at an international level.[31] The GERDESS network in West Africa, for example, includes election monitoring (Bratton 1994a, 6). The African partners of IRED (Development Innovations and Networks, located in Geneva) are also active politically. In March 1995, a regional conference of fifty IRED partners was held in Burkina Faso to strengthen ties among GRSOs, human rights organizations, and governments. This was followed two months later by a workshop of GRSOs and human rights organizations in Niger on conflict prevention and management (Doulaye Maiga 1995, 16; Fisher forthcoming).

A fourth way in which NGOs strengthen civil society is by focusing on bottom-up democratization. Ndegwa's (1996) study of civil society in Kenya shows that the Undugu Society helps empower local communities and allows grassroots clients to confront the state, even though Undugu itself avoids the kinds of protests over political repression carried out by other Kenyan NGOs such as the Greenbelt Movement. Even in Yemen, where the government matches every independent grassroots activity with a competing effort or the establishment of another government-organized NGO (GONNGO), an autonomous "civil society is in the making" (Carapico 1995, 83). And in Nigeria, the government-organized Centre for Democratic Studies provided a haven for intellectuals, helped several human rights organizations develop, and took the "leading role in monitoring the aborted 1993 presidential elections" before falling from government favor (Welch 1995, 239–40).

Grassroots organizing and bottom-up democratization are increasingly being combined with both national and local networking.[32] When President Fernando Collar de Mello of Brazil was implicated in a corruption scandal in 1992, 900 GRSOs, professional associations of lawyers and journalists, student associations, church agencies, and GROs organized the

Movimento Pela Ética na Política, which petitioned Congress to investigate Collar. Local committees organized street demonstrations throughout Brazil, which led to his impeachment. The behind-the-scenes organizer was ABONG, the Associacao Brasileira de ONGs (Garrison and Landim 1995, 40).

What is most striking about vertical as well as horizontal NGO networking is the contrast between authoritarian political superstructures in most countries and innovative cooperation among NGOs. Although GRO and GRSO networks harken back to traditional, deeply rooted cultural practices, they also provide the expanding space needed to enlarge and strengthen civil society.[33]

There is also a spillover effect among NGO activists at both the grassroots and grassroots support levels that can strengthen civil society. In Argentina, NGOs working to empower AIDS patients have begun to work on the problem of the "disappeared" and to challenge government accountability more generally.[34] In Costa Rica, local health committees working on infant mortality and its connection to poverty began to demand that the government promote the creation of more jobs. Indeed, international support for participatory community projects sponsored by the World Health Organization (WHO) and the United Nations Children's Fund (UNICEF) in Costa Rica was withdrawn because officials from a number of countries feared that community participation would lead to political instability (L. Morgan 1990).

The fifth vanguard role played by NGOs, described earlier, is to influence other voluntary organizations. Churches in Africa are establishing community outreach activities, and hospitals in many parts of the world are setting up preventive health care clinics in neighboring villages. Autonomous university programs and research institutes not based on membership bring high-level talent to the process of sustainable development, enriched by their contacts with GROs. Thus, GRSOs are increasingly influential within the broader independent sector.

Sixth, as noted earlier, GROs and GRSOs are at the crux of the relationship between the for-profit and independent or nonprofit sectors of civil society. By focusing on microenterprise development, NGOs broaden the ownership of capital, a connection that has the potential to challenge governments, because the habits of participation and empowerment necessitated by creating a business feed back into the political system. In Colombia, for example, members of women's clubs who created their own microenterprises became the first women to participate in meetings of village councils (Fisher 1986).[35]

This proliferation of GRSOs promoting enterprise development has been able to build on the dynamism of the informal for-profit sector in many countries. In *The Other Path*, Hernando de Soto (1989) shows how low-income entrepreneurs in Peru overcame daunting bureaucratic and political obstacles to create microenterprises. This convergence between NGOs and informal for-profit enterprises offers some promise for building a different model of society from that found in the developed countries, since profits generated within this new nonprofit–for-profit nexus are invested in public as well as private goods and services.

To be sure, there is nothing foreordained about the strengthening of civil society through the activities of NGOs. Islamic extremists "have destroyed the civil society that was emerging in the Sudan from 1985 to 1989 [and the] National Islamic Front regime has made it hard to restore a wide range of social, religious, political and economic institutions" (Lesch 1995, 71).[36] Yet as the vanguard of civil society in the Third World, NGOs not only enlarge its available space but also help create and enlarge the political commons where state and civil society, broadly defined, interact. Because civil society is not a dynamic concept, however, it is helpful to view this enlarged political commons as the arena for political development.

Political Development

There was a period during the 1960s when political development, conventionally defined as "changes in political structures and attitudes accompanying and supportive of modernization," was as hot a topic in political science as civil society is today (Bertsch, Clark, and Wood 1982, 530). The arena for this school of thought was the Committee on Comparative Politics of the Social Science Research Council. By the 1970s, however, interest in political development had been eclipsed by "realistic" approaches to Third World politics built on dependency theory, corporatism, and descriptions of bureaucratic authoritarianism stemming from democratic reversals in Latin America.[37] Many graduate students in political science are familiar only with the critics of political development who argued that the approach was "ethnocentric, naively optimistic, and failing to recognise the political implications of economic dependence upon the West" (Randall and Theobald 1985, 33).[38] Those who back off from discussing the topic may also do so because it is insufficiently empirical or because apparent progress toward more open political systems is so often reversed.[39] Strangely enough, no one avoids the term *economic development*, although it is equally reversible and uneven, and its empirical measurement is contentious.

Ironically, both the rise and fall of political development theory took place before NGOs began to proliferate throughout the developing and transitional worlds. There is, therefore, an obvious need to reexamine this school of thought. For one thing, the trendy concept of civil society, promoted by rising interest in NGO proliferation, does not encompass interactions with government over time.

A second reason for reexamining the concept is that *political development* has a broader societal, if not political, meaning than democratization. Democratization, defined by O'Donnell and Schmitter (1986, 8) as "the progressive extension of the citizenship principle to encompass a wider range of eligible participants and a wider scope of domains in which collective choice among equals or their representatives can make binding decisions on all," is useful for describing electoral reforms, increasing partisan competition, the expansion of human rights, or the enhanced capacities of municipal governments. Political development, however, encompasses such indicators of democratization without being limited to them. As Desmond King argues, "There is a significant tradition of state intervention built around the idea of citizenship for which there is no real equivalent to underpin voluntary activity" (cited in Hamilton 1994, 17). Moreover, as a concept, political development tends to focus on open interactive processes between state and civil society, rather than on particular types of political systems. The term *democratization* still carries a whiff of Western (or Northern) imposition, despite recent democratic advances in Latin America and elsewhere and an increasing recognition that the indigenous roots of democracy are stronger than a previous generation of scholars had assumed. Despite the universality of certain basic values, such as freedom from the knock at the door or abhorrence of torture, a Northern lens may not only be resented, it can also distort political reality by ignoring democratic traditions such as village assemblies, as well as the emergence of NGOs.

A third reason to reexamine political development is that the concept can provide a theoretical meeting ground for those who specialize in Third World politics and those who work in Third World development. Just as political scientists have overlooked the institutions of development, development practitioners in the United States and Europe only began to ask questions about the impact of development projects on governmental policies or political systems in the late 1980s.[40]

Overcoming the "Syncratic" Alliance

Despite the charges of naivete later levied against them, some of those who first focused on political development were acutely aware of the political barriers to change. A. F. K. Organski (1965), for example, described what he called a "syncratic" alliance between traditional rural aristocracies and industrial elites as the major factor that had to be overcome for political development to take place in the Third World.

This explanation of the barriers to political development should not be understood as an all-inclusive theory. There is much that it does not explain. In some countries, the military becomes a third party to this alliance, even though officers may be of humble origin and may even replace agrarian elites. Yet just as the inclusion of the English yeomanry in the seventeenth century set the stage for the rise of Parliament and widening of the franchise, so also are political monopolies in the Third World being challenged—by civil wars and ethnic violence, as well as by democratization and the rise of NGOs. The concept of power monopolies also helps unlock the complex relationship between politics and development and defines the political limits that constrain even the more complex and industrialized of the developing countries. The breakup of the syncratic coalition is, therefore, a necessary, albeit insufficient, condition for sustainable political and socioeconomic development.

To be sure, there are some countries, such as Costa Rica, where historical accidents have weakened the syncratic alliance or prevented it from emerging at all. In other countries, Marxist revolutions replaced the syncratic alliance with new power monopolies. In a few others, such as Venezuela under Romulo Betancourt (1958–63), exceptional leaders undermined the syncratic coalition while strengthening democratic institutions. However, since most Third World countries lack both favorable historical circumstances and exceptional leadership, the proliferation of NGOs may provide the only possible, albeit long-term, way of undermining power monopolies. Indeed, the gradual undermining of narrow political monopolies by an expanded civil society has the potential for a more profound impact on sustainable development than did the accidental weakening or deliberate destruction of ruling elites in some countries in the past, even though NGOs may be co-opted by governments.

The dilemma, in other words, is how to weigh the evidence of power creation from below, which has largely occurred since the 1960s, against the leaden mass of social and economic privilege maintained by political repression. Although political monopolies are enormously resilient, many parts of the developing world seem to be poised between the persistence of old power structures and the development of new organizations that are not yet able to challenge them effectively. A number of case studies demonstrate that empowerment of the poor can loosen the grip of local elites such as landowners and moneylenders, and such attempts are increasing. Yet NGOs may have to race ahead just to stay even with the increasing absolute numbers of poor people (see Box 1.2).

Box 1.2   Population Growth

Although the latest United Nations data indicate that the net addition to global population probably peaked at 87 million between 1985 and 1990 (due to declining fertility in Latin America and parts of Asia), the populations of sub-Saharan Africa and parts of South Asia are still expanding enough to double their populations in one generation. Because increasing numbers of people are entering their childbearing years throughout the Third World, global population continued to increase by an estimated 81 million people a year between 1990 and 1995. Over 90 percent of this growth was concentrated in the Third World. According to the UN's medium variant projections, the population of the less developed regions alone will exceed 8 billion by 2050, when these regions will still be adding an estimated 46 million people a year to the world's population. This compares with a projected population of 1.16 billion in the developed regions by the year 2050—approximately the same as the figure today—and a net annual decline of over 2 million a year. (*Source:* United Nations 1996.)

Organski's theory of the syncratic alliance is also relevant to discussions about the political systems within which NGOs must operate. A major cause of political instability, according to Kohli (1986), is elite competition. Yet, as Organski pointed out, it is what elites *agree* on, rather than what Kohli (1986, 176) calls "the need to explore the conditions for elite consensus," that is the crux of the political dilemma in the Third World. Even where elites contend violently with one another, as in the Colombian civil war in the late 1940s, both sides have a tacit understanding that other players are excluded. On the other side of the argument about elites are those who focus on competition among them as the most obvious driving force behind the push for democracy, and who therefore tend to exclude other actors such as NGOs.[41]

The problem with these two competing versions of the elite model of Third World politics is not that they are wrong; power monopolies are, after all, the problem to be overcome. The problem with elite models is that they are incomplete. It is as if a sharply but narrowly focused look at one part of reality allows one to ignore what is going on in one's peripheral vision. Although some political scientists have long recognized the importance of local politics and grassroots organizations in the Third World (Booth and Seligson 1979c), and although democracy has become professionally respectable, the democratic sea change and the explosion in writings about Third World NGOs have only recently begun to influence experts on political change, political parties, or military factions in a given country. Barkan (1994, 89), for example, describes what he calls a "permutation" of the modernization–political development paradigm as placing "less emphasis on central institutions and the elites that control them than the original formulation of three decades ago and more emphasis on how organized interests in society seek to establish linkages with the state to make it more responsive."

This is partly because the NGO explosion is a relatively recent development. In the mid-1970s, when Huntington and Nelson (1976, 36) wrote that "the choices on participation strategies are essentially choices of the elite," they were accurately depicting Third World reality.[42] Moreover, GROs do not usually resemble the more obviously political interest groups or labor unions, which were the focus of earlier interest in autonomous intermediate institutions.[43] And the political activities of GRSOs, particularly the promotion of bottom-up empowerment, are sometimes less obvious than those of political parties or unions. Thus, the proliferation of NGOs and their interactions with governments both challenge the ethnocentrism of the original political development theorists and resurrect some of their more stimulating, if forgotten, theoretical insights. As Wiarda (1989–90, 78) points out, the political development theorists may have been only prematurely optimistic.

Defining Political Development

Both the top-down shift toward democracy in some countries and the growth of civil society are indicators of positive political change that *may or may not be sustained and strengthened in the long run.* Is what we are seeing political development, even if it must still overcome enormous odds, and even if it may be reversed in the future? Because earlier political development theorists were concerned primarily with the capacity of the state, there is a need for a new working definition of the process (Ndegwa 1996, 15).[44] What I next explore are five theoretical requirements for a working definition of political development that builds on the contributions of earlier theorists, takes account of the newly empowered representatives of civil society throughout the world, and includes connections with macrolevel change. I define political development as *an interactive, public decision-making and learning process, within and between government and civil society, based on power creation and dispersion. This process leads to increasing individual and group autonomy from below and more responsiveness from above.* In quest of this definition of political development I reasoned that:

1. *A definition of political development should not equate the process with the goal.*[45] One example of this kind of faulty reasoning is the

idea that political development occurs when modernizers come to power (Kautsky 1972). Using the same reasoning, Berger and Novak (1985) define political development as "liberation from tyranny," an event easily reversed if it is not built on the more gradual growth of civil society. The broader goals of political development—autonomy of intermediate institutions and governmental responsiveness—are clearly distinct from the process of interaction that can lead to them.

2. *A definition of political development should be based on an expanded understanding of political systems that encompasses civil society.* Although Western democratic values are often deemed inapplicable to Third World conditions, Western political concepts are sometimes applied unthinkingly. In particular, the concept of the political system is often implicitly equated, particularly in popular writing, with government and opposition.[46] Hirschman (1984, 181) explains this by quoting a historian of the French Revolution, Francois Furet, who writes of the "strange consensus [stemming from the Revolution] according to which any aspiration to social change implies, for *all* groups (on the Left and Right) the prior seizure of the central power of the state. . . . Perhaps it is this heritage that is being questioned today." As Binder (1986, 18) points out, "it must take a special sort of ideological naivete to persist in the belief that strengthening the state in a developing system will lead, in general, to increasing political freedom."[47]

It is what happens outside governments and political parties, however, that leads them to become more inclusive. In Peru, for example, the confluence of members of different political parties within GRSOs has led to dialogue, communication, and concentration on practical political inclusion strategies (Padrón 1988b, 58).

Most academic definitions of political systems are, in fact, broad enough to include civil society. Bertsch, Clark, and Wood (1982, 530), for example, argue that political systems, as "distinguished from the narrower concept of government, . . . incorporate all individuals and institutions involved in the political process visualized as interacting systematically."[48] Political systems include not only the government and those opposition figures who manage to function in some countries but also subnational and national institutions of all kinds that relate to public decision making. And public decision making includes not only all authoritative governmental decisions but also political participation, defined by Booth and Seligson (1979a, 6) as "behavior influencing or attempting to influence the distribution of public goods . . . [which] can be supplied by governments or by local communities themselves."[49]

That public decision making includes participation has been recognized by Meyer (1996), who suggests that participation in politics or in local development should be viewed as the functional equivalent of efficiency in economics. Some of the earlier political development theorists, however, mentioned participation mainly in relation to government's capacity to cope with it. Jaguaribe (1973, 148–151), for example, gives most of his attention to the government's capability to adapt and mobilize people politically.[50]

In contrast to these statists, dependency theorists have tended to treat politics as a variable that is dependent on socioeconomic development for the poorest people in a society. Gamer (1982, 11), for example, defines political development as "broadening the social base of the political system and increasing the percentage of the populace experiencing stable personal environments." He argues that change cannot occur within governments, because they depend on both a paternalistic social system and an exploitative international economy. Although this approach can be a useful way of understanding the impact of multinationals within Third World countries, it discounts at the outset autonomous organizing from below and changes in particular government bureaucracies. As Apter (1987, 29) points out, dependency theory "loses the ability to see transforming strategies available to those inside a society . . . [and adopts an] outsider's view even when practiced by insiders."

The dilemma of what to include within political systems and therefore in the political development arena should be resolved in favor of political participation, but not against the increasing competence and adaptation of the state. It is in the *interaction between the two* that theory must focus, and some theorists recognized this even before the worldwide proliferation of NGOs. Hirschman (1963, 230), for example, argued that "political development could . . . be described in terms of the emergence of a wide diversity of mechanisms and leverages, from elections to lobbying by pressure groups, through which individuals and groups can compel policy-makers to pay attention to their problems." Almond and Powell (1966) defined it as an increase in subsystem autonomy, role differentiation, and secularization. More recently, Apter (1987, 18) wrote: "Political development denotes regimes, state systems, and political systems whose institutional functions, evolving along with developmental equity, will require greater participation and elite accountability." The expanded definition of the arena of politics and participation developed here strengthens rather than challenges this theoretical tradition.

3. *The concept of political development should be based on an open acknowledgment of the value of institutional autonomy and its relationship to democratic values, broadly defined.* In reaction to the justifications for authoritarianism and in response to the resurgence of democracy, some U.S. observers of the Third World began to question so-called value-free research more than ten years ago (Duncan 1983). For their part, Latin American political scientists began to acknowledge that

opposition to U.S. foreign policy had sometimes blinded them to the virtues of liberal democratic political systems and that there was a need to formulate new ideas, that melded redistributive social goals with democratic institutions.[51]

Indeed, the mass demonstrations in the streets of Port-au-Prince, Manila, Rangoon, or, more recently, Indonesia suggest that the commitment to democratic values may be more widespread than many had imagined. Values such as individual freedom—to organize a labor union or a local development association, for example—are a functionally effective means of creating or dispersing political power within a wide range of political systems, particularly if power is defined as the ability to influence the behavior of others in a local, provincial (state), or national political context.[52] For example, some dictatorships, described in Chapter 2, allow local organizations to operate while continuing to suppress more obvious opposition at the national level.

Of course, the political reality of the Third World includes both the power and potential of democratic ideals and the resilient and seemingly infinite abilities of power elites or ethnic rivals to resist them. In north-eastern Brazil, large landowners have been known to shoot sharecroppers who do nothing more than plant fruit trees to improve their families' diets. The Argentine military regime in power during the late 1970s was able, despite the country's high educational level, to suppress all but what O'Donnell (1986, 261) describes as the "oblique horizontal voice." And this terrible picture would not be complete without acknowledging the recent ethnic genocide in Rwanda, the rural terrorism of the Khmer Rouge in Cambodia, and the killings of peasants and aid workers by the Shining Path in Peru.

Another way of approaching the relationship between values and the autonomy of intermediate institutions is found in discussions of pluralism and corporatism (Binder 1986). Pluralism is usually defined as a condition in which many distinct groups with conflicting interests compete for power (Bianchi 1986). As a functional term, *pluralism*, like *civil society*, is less obviously tied to Western values than is *democracy*. However, the keystone of pluralism is autonomy, since corporatist systems can also lead to increasing numbers of intermediate institutions.[53] Despite the reasonably clear theoretical distinction between corporatism and pluralism, there are few modern examples of pure corporatism (see, however, Box 1.3), and contrasts between the two are often more evident within countries than between them.

So the real world is complex, and autonomous structures are hardly inevitable. Yet in recognizing the need for honest value judgments, more observers seem to be saying that democracy provides a more hospitable climate for human advancement than does dictatorship, autonomous

---

Box 1.3 Corporatism in Action

When Pinochet took over the Chilean government in 1973, the mothers clubs established under the Frei regime underwent a complete change. Democratic structures were replaced by an administrative hierarchy under Pinochet's wife. Members (230,000 by 1983) produced crafts sold in special shops and were indoctrinated in military ideology by an army of 6,000 volunteers, mostly wives of army officers, who wore red uniforms. The basic philosophy of the program was that the truly patriotic mother submits herself to the *pater familias* and the *pater patria*. According to Schuurman and Heer (1992, 37), the ideology of this movement has survived the return to democracy and still presents difficulties for the women's movement in Chile.

---

political participation represents an advance over mobilized demonstrations, and pluralist structures represent an advance over corporatist ones. There is nothing foreordained about any of these changes, but it is important that political leaders, grassroots activists, and development professionals, as well as theorists, recognize and consciously build on them when they do occur.

Moreover, this value recognition has its roots in classical political theory, which used the word *state* as a broader concept than *government*. The state or broader polity "conditioned relations within government and opposition." A value commitment "provides a place of importance to social developments which at any one time lie outside of government and its stable inner circle of support and opposition."[54]

4. *A definition of political development should be based on both the centrality of power and the interaction of the state and civil society.* Because power has been so jealously monopolized by the few at the top in the Third World, the concept of political development needs to include empowerment from below, the increasing need for governments to develop and disperse new kinds of power to attack urgent issues, and the learning that occurs when these two processes interact.[55] This proposed sequence, which is often messy, contrasts with those political development–modernization theorists, such as Huntington (1968), who suggested that the state first had to accumulate and centralize power and capacity before it could expand its "reach" and, finally, be able to decentralize power.[56]

Processes of empowerment, although extremely uneven, may be initiated either by governments or by the institutions of civil society. Indeed, empowerment from below may be the only possible "growth pole" for political development, unless a country is possessed of unusual leadership. The most difficult question is whether first steps lead to second and third steps, as a kind of self-sustaining process focused on the interface between the state and civil society. Although empowerment has become the common language of NGOs throughout the Third World (Clark 1991; Fisher 1993), the kind of NGO-government connections described in Chapters 3, 4, and 5 are not yet everyday occurrences, and they tend to influence portions of bureaucracies rather than presidents or parliaments. Nonetheless, NGO-government interactions can alter the quantity and quality of power relationships in ways that illuminate the practicality of new ideas.

Of course, the long-term political impact of the growth of civil society may vary dramatically within the Third World, and empowerment from below can also be suppressed or co-opted from above. It may seem that the dispersion of power by politicians, particularly dictatorial ones, is a contradiction in terms. Why should any Third World governments, most of which use coercive means to remain in power, respond positively to pressures from development organizations that do not threaten them as directly as revolutionary movements do?

One possible answer is that these governments find it in their interest to reach out to civil society as they realize that the capacity to repress is unequal to the capacity to govern, and that they lack the ability to direct economic and social change. Indeed, governmental attempts to concentrate rather than disperse power are becoming increasingly counterproductive, for three reasons. First, governments are being challenged by the overwhelming nature of the poverty-environment-population crisis. Second, they are simultaneously subject to growing demands for human rights and political liberties. Third, governments are confronting the creation of power from below. Paradoxically, as GROs and GRSOs demand that government disperse its power, they challenge the very concept of dispersion, which implies a finite amount of power to be guarded and doled out.[57]

If governments do begin to respond to NGO pressures (the likelihood of which is examined in subsequent chapters), it is because a positive response will give them what they have lacked—the power to promote sustainable development. Esman and Uphoff (1984, 123) point out that if the goals of GROs and governments are compatible, increased power at the local level will enhance the government's ability to achieve its objective. When GROs, for example, are used to help train preventive health care workers, the pursuit of the power to influence development becomes a win-win game. Political capacity, as both the cause and the consequence of linkages between elite and mass, is a difficult concept because of its circularity, but it offers the *possibility* of change over the long run (Esman and Uphoff 1984).[58]

Probability is more difficult to assess or predict, as subsequent chapters show. Empowerment from below, as extensive as it is in some countries, should not necessarily be treated as a kind of quantitative indicator for positive change. Not only do political contexts differ, but NGO proliferation and networking may be undermined by population growth. As development organizations encompass more and more people, they may also exclude more and more and be unable to achieve the kind of critical organizational mass needed to transform their societies.

5. *Finally, an understanding of political development needs to describe the content and not just the structure of this interaction between state and society.* One of the major conclusions of *The Road from Rio* was that horizontal networking per se was linked to positive development outcomes. Similarly, in this volume I demonstrate that vertical connections between NGOs and governments can help reform politics and promote sustainable development policies. Interactive structures, in other words, provide the opportunity for qualitative changes in content. But whether, how, and what people learn as a result of such interactions is more complex.

Some types of bottom-up–top-down interactions are obviously *not* indicators of political development. A grassroots ethnic group, for example, could conspire with individuals in government to suppress a rival nationality. The violent interactions between the Peruvian government and the Shining Path guerrillas tended to reverse much of the progress achieved by Peruvian NGOs in their relationships with local and municipal governments. Defining what kind of interactions do constitute political development is more difficult, but several observers have shed some light on the issue.

One relevant theory of positive interactive learning was developed by Stephen Brown, a mathematics teacher, who was not writing about political development at all.[59] Brown (1984, 14) argues that "we have much to learn about the role of dialogue in problem solving" and that dialogue enhances the chance that people who are trying to solve a problem will (1) realize that they have been asking the wrong questions, (2) return to discuss and explore the more general situation behind the problem, (3) re-pose or reformulate the problem in a different way, and (4) begin to work on problem solution. If we think about this methodology in relation to the problems of the Third World, then poverty and inequality are the endemic *situations* that need to be jointly explored in order for reformulated and more specific *problems and solutions* to emerge. And the most creative efforts of NGOs seem to have been the result of just such a process.

A second contributor to the content of bottom-up–top-down interaction is Denis Goulet (1986). His remarkable discussion of the interaction of technical, political, and ethical rationalities in development decision making is based on the planning process for the Itaparica Dam in Brazil. Goulet describes how three groups—technicians, members of a GRO, and politicians—had to negotiate with and learn from one another rather than impose their own solutions. The government technicians argued that the soil near the new dam would not be sufficiently fertile to allow people to live along its shore. To deal with this argument, the GRO representing the people who would have to be relocated hired its own agronomists and economists and, "armed with their expert advice," got the technicians to accept a GRO proposal as the basis for negotiating relocation and compensation that reflected "the local organization's normative view of what was just." The third group—the politicians in the local mayor's association—saw itself as "moderate and constructive in providing a forum for all parties to meet and compromise" (Goulet 1986, 307–8). Although Goulet discusses several other Brazilian examples with more problematic results, he concludes: "Ultimately, the issue is how technological reasons will discourse with politics and ethics. Can the logic of efficiency join the logic of power and the logic of virtue in a holy alliance that produces genuine development? . . . The nature of this discourse in gestation may well give shape to development's most vital decisions" (Goulet 1986, 315).

In other words, political development begins when previously excluded groups, organized into associations, enter the arena and enhance the dimensions available for problem posing (in Brown's terms) and solving. GRSOs play a key role in this process by helping to empower and bring grassroots actors to the attention of governments. The impact of the NGO relationship with government depends in part on the relationships that develop between GROs and GRSOs. As I show in Chapter 3, NGOs of all types with strong grassroots ties tend to have greater autonomy and, therefore, greater impact on governments. In addition, the governments themselves gain autonomy and impact through ties with the grassroots.

A third group of contributors, the crisis theorists, have dealt with the content of interaction on a more macro level. They argue that poverty, environmental degradation, and political violence have produced a desire to participate, interact, learn, ask new questions, define manageable problems, and work out innovative solutions. O'Donnell and Schmitter (1986), for example, argue that more democracy is the only solution for the contradiction between the demand for political participation and the need for administrative autonomy. And Binder (1986, 33) argues:

> The solution to crises entails learning from the experience of others, acknowledgement of error, courage to change, willingness to know oneself. . . . Since emancipation of the self and of the collectivity cannot be separated, development learning and rational adaptation are all linked to democratization."[60]

Since there are obvious difficulties with including the qualitative complexity of this fifth requirement in the definition of political development, the words *interactive learning* should be considered a kind of inadequate shorthand for the above discussion. To repeat my proposed definition: Political development can be defined as an interactive public decision-making and learning process, within and between government and civil society, based on power creation and dispersion. This process leads to increasing individual and group autonomy from below and more responsiveness from above. This definition does not confuse the process with the goal. It includes both governmental and participatory decision making and is therefore based on an expanded view of political systems. It contains an explicit preference for autonomous intermediate institutions and democratic values. However, as I show in subsequent chapters, the autonomy of intermediate structures and their potential impact on government structures are not necessarily dependent on Western models of democracy. Finally, it is based on the centrality of power and focuses on an interactive learning process between bottom-up and top-down that creates and disperses power.

The circularity in this definition—that is, empowerment from below creates autonomy, and autonomy permits further empowerment—is inherent in any attempt to describe the complexities of the real political world. It is also what permits political development to continue, without ensuring that it will do so. Attempts to define political development need to focus on process recognition but need not—indeed, should not—imply that change is inevitable. It is a process that may start and be derailed, especially if civil society is only incipient or fragile. It may not be occurring even temporarily in some countries. Nor does it say anything about the pace of change, but focuses instead on how to recognize it when there is evidence that it is occurring. This definition of political development can encompass both top-down democratic reforms and mass demonstrations. But it also suggests that governmental reforms and expressions of democratic fervor can be easily reversed if they are not built on a process of institutionalization from below that confronts governments with more than an immediate crisis of reestablishing order. Burma, for example, despite the obvious popular desire for democracy, has neither a well-organized opposition party nor the kind of rapidly developing independent sector that is emerging in so many other countries. Finally, because civil society includes markets and a sphere of public debate, this definition of political development also encompasses the emergence of such institutions as an independent press, new businesses, and labor unions.

The purpose of this book is to present the considerable evidence that the cultivation of civil society, propelled by NGOs, can contribute to political development in the Third World. Self-sustaining political development is problematic at best. Yet when and if it occurs, even fitfully, and only in local spaces, it is likely to be based on the quality of power relationships and the quality of problem posing and solving as measured by interactions with those most directly affected. Given the dimensions of the crises already confronting the Third World, the long-term impact of NGO proliferation is hard to envision. What is already evident is the impact of this quiet revolution on grassroots politics. People organizing their own communities are supported by GRSOs that "have made the political choice for social change and justice, but have also chosen democracy; thus the importance they assign to notions such as self-government and democracy in their relations with the popular sectors" (Velarde 1988, 17). As a kind of entering wedge, this process can get going in many communities despite the dominant monopolies of political power that constrain development. The economic and social impact of NGOs is, therefore, likely to be indirect. Often it has more immediate influence on subnational governments than it does at the national level (see Chapter 5).

NGOs are, in part, the product of the very system that they now challenge. Although narrow political coalitions continue to exclude the public from decision making in the Third World, the last thirty years have witnessed, in addition to the rise of NGOs, an unprecedented expansion of mass education and the creation of an educated middle class. The failure of governments to even begin to meet the escalating challenges of sustainable development has vastly enhanced awareness of the widening gap between the desperate reality of the poor and what educated people believe to be possible. But it has also opened up unprecedented opportunities for NGOs not just to replace governments but to protest against them, influence them, and collaborate with them—in short, to radically alter the way that people in most of the world are governed. There is also evidence, explored in Chapter 2, that the powers that be in some countries may be willing to adapt intelligently to an NGO challenge that does not threaten them as immediately and directly as revolutionary movements have done in the past.

Nongovernments is organized so that the impact of NGO–government relationships on political empowerment and sustainable development can be viewed from a number of different vantage points. Chapter 2 explores the national government side of NGO–government interactions and deals with a remaining problem with any political development definition: by focusing on process, it cannot simultaneously focus on political context. For pragmatic reasons, I have argued that autonomous participation that creates new sources of power represents an advance over participation controlled from above and that a definition of political development should be functional rather than being tied to particular liberal democratic institutions. Yet, as I show in Chapter 2, democratic institutions may be the end result of the process or will almost certainly help it along if they already exist. Chapter 2 begins with the range of governmental policies toward NGOs, including some geographic contrasts. The chapter then explores two major factors that influence government policies toward NGOs—national political contexts, as defined by type of regime, degree of stability, political culture, and state capacity; and managerial reforms within governments. Political context also has an indirect influence on NGO proliferation.

Organizational autonomy, one of the key elements in the definition of political development (and the subject of Chapter 3), turns out to be the single most powerful factor determining the impact of NGOs on governments, in terms of their influence on both sustainable development policies and democratization. Chapter 3 begins with a discussion of autonomy and accountability and then explores seven keys to autonomy: internal commitment, financial diversification, strong grassroots ties, technical expertise, managerial capacity, strategic knowledge about development, and staff experience in training government professionals.

Chapter 4 focuses on the strategies NGOs use to influence national governments. Most NGOs pursue both sustainable development and democratization, at least in its bottom-up form. The chapter explores three strategies—isolation, advocacy, and cooperation—that GROs, GRSOs, and their networks use to achieve these goals in their contacts with governments. The cooperation discussion deals with the impact of government ties on extending the reach of development efforts.

Chapter 5 uses decentralization as a lens for focusing on the relationships between subnational governments at both the local and provincial or state levels. The chapter begins with a discussion of the impact of the deconcentration of national government officials to local areas. It then deals with devolution—pushed down by national government to subnational governments or NGOs, or pulled down by NGOs.

These strands are woven together in Chapter 6, which explores the political development commons shared by state and civil society in relation to the political context in which it is located. Despite the apparent democratization trends in the Third World, which are explored in this chapter, formidable political structures block both political development and solutions to the population-environment-poverty crisis. Chapter 6 concludes with policy recommendations for overcoming these barriers and advancing this dual challenge.

Notes

1. The analogy was coined by Stephen Schmidheing, a Swiss entrepreneur and founder of the Business Council for Sustainable Development. (See Smith 1992, 75.)
2. Robert Deacon of the University of California at Santa Barbara examined the political and environmental records of 120 countries. The twenty high-deforestation countries (those losing 10 percent or more of their forest cover between 1980 and 1985) are three times as likely to have military governments, four times as likely to have political assassinations, and twice as likely to experience general strikes, riots, revolutions, and regime changes. (See "Spectrum" in *Environment* magazine, November 1994, 21.)
3. The "ecological footprint" of the Netherlands, for example, is much larger than the country itself. Indeed, the Dutch require a land area fourteen to fifteen times larger than their country to support current domestic consumption levels. Economic analysis, based on money flows, is, Rees (1996) argues, particularly unsuited to understanding physical resource flows and transformations.
4. For a discussion of the concept of appreciative inquiry, see Cooperrider and Srivastva 1987, 129–69.
5. In the United States, such organizations are generally called private voluntary organizations or PVOs.
6. They may also be fundamentally different from GRSOs in their grassroots relationships. Islamic associations in Egypt, for example, have some charitable functions and work in villages or urban neighborhoods, but in contrast to most GRSOs, they have "replaced the traditional authority and control of local notables and bosses. . . . The religious networks make no effort to recruit local leaders onto their councils of administration, which consist exclusively of their own members" (Zubaida 1992, 9).
7. Although they also exist in the Middle East, they have proliferated less rapidly than in the rest of the Third World and are more likely to be focused on religious or other traditional purposes than on development. (See Fisher 1993, 25.)
8. See Esman and Uphoff (1984) for more on this distinction.
9. Members of pre-cooperatives may not receive a strictly monetary profit, but they clearly receive an individual benefit from pooling their labor.
10. The quote pertains to networks or federations in Chimborazo, Ecuador, but is typical of many other areas.
11. There are, however, areas such as Burma and parts of the Middle East and Africa where GRSOs are sparse or nonexistent (see Fisher 1993, 80–94). However, some countries of the Middle East, such as Jordan and the West Bank, have large and growing numbers of charitable organizations, including GRSOs that focus on community organizing and empowerment.
12. Whether or not private research centers are involved in grassroots research and support, they often become policy advocates on the issues that concern NGOs more generally. (See Levy 1996, chap. 5.)

13. Brian Smith (1990), for example, who did his research in the early 1980s, found that many Colombian organizations tended to utilize foreign funding without empowering the poor. And Clarke (1995, 70) found that in the Philippines, "phantom NGOs" have been established as tax shelters.
14. For more on networking and sustainability, see Fisher 1993, 70–2, 150–9, 199–202, 207–10.
15. For more on this topic, see Fisher 1994a.
16. Waltz (1995, 135) points out that, beginning in the mid-1970s, human rights activists in Morocco, Tunisia, and Algeria had to struggle against the predominant intellectual view in their countries that human rights was a "bourgeois notion and dangerously American."
17. Indeed, Peter Hall, a historian of the U.S. nonprofit sector, contends that connections of all types among the three sectors constitute civil society (personal conversation, December 10, 1996).
18. See Hamilton's (1994, 20–1) discussion of this. He argues that "for many people, their often justified distaste for commerce has led them to draw moats around philanthropy."
19. For a discussion of what has been called the "nursemaid" function of nonprofits promoting for-profit activity, see Abzug and Webb 1996.
20. Obviously, both international NGOs and multinational corporations can impact civil society in a given country. But I have excluded these as a means of limiting the scope of the inquiry to the national level. As national civil societies become stronger, the impact of international institutions may even decrease.
21. Jeppe, Theron, and Van Baalen (1992, 98) point out that South African businesses have provided both legal and accounting assistance to NGOs.
22. See Putnam 1995, 71. Whether or not one should make the same argument about separatist movements remains in doubt. Some separatist organizations in Africa are involved in violence. (See Welch 1995, 107–139.)
23. As Bebbington and Farrington (1993, 11) argue, NGOs are part of civil society, but they also work to strengthen the other institutions of civil society.
24. Welch (1995, 294) argues that the general strength of civil society is more important than the level of economic development to the emergence of human rights NGOs.
25. Livezey (1988, 135–6) argues that this has not occurred entirely in isolation. The International League for Human Rights "stands out for its affiliates program, particularly because of its efforts to enable the organizations of the Third World to operate effectively within the United Nations Human Rights Systems."
26. See also Welch 1995, 34, n. 1.
27. Waltz (1995, 34) attributes the impact of these organizations to "moral claims, international support and tactical choices." In 1983, a group of professionals from across the Middle East established the Arab Organization of Human Rights, Tunis became the headquarters for the Arab-African Institute for Human Rights, and Amnesty International groups were established in Tunisia and Algeria.

The terms *metapolitics* and *relational politics* are borrowed and adapted from Krasner (1985). Relational politics describes players within an established political context, whereas metapolitics describes effort to change political rules or alter the political context.

28. The group did this with the support of PACT, a consortium of U.S. private voluntary organizations.

29. After a 1990 Washington seminar with NAMFREL and similar groups from Paraguay and Bulgaria, the Haitian Association for Free Elections was created.

30. Philip Gain, conversation at the conference on Beyond Boundaries: Issues in American and Asian Environmental Activism, Asia Society, New York, April 24–26, 1991.

31. This national and international political role is not without historical precedent. According to Livezey (1988, 28–9), since the first half of the seventeenth century, when the Elizabethan charity acts first coordinated private philanthropy, voluntary organizations have consistently served as "a major source of innovation toward the increased standing of persons in relation to states." The Puritans created the first modern organizations for political dissent, and then the Quakers, Levelers, and other radicals acted for explicitly egalitarian and revolutionary change. International organizations, organized as early as the 1680s by the Freemasons and the financiers, also represented alternatives to state power. Later movements, such as the antislavery societies in Britain and the United States, are subsequent examples of this tradition.

32. Scherer-Warren (1995, 170, 178–9), a Brazilian NGO observer, points out that GRSOs still want to be referred to as popular organizations, when they are actually networking with and supporting them. She argues that they should be more transparent about their real identity as mediators, thereby making it easier to define their micro and macro transformative roles.

33. Ironically, in the United States, the cultural ethic of competition, so useful in the private economic sphere, may make broad-based cooperation among social change organizations more difficult than in the Third World.

34. These findings came from a Panos Institute Study (Allison and Macinko 1993, 24).

35. I did an evaluation of this project for Save the Children.

36. Putnam (1993a, 8) argues that social inequities may be "embedded in social capital" and can endanger individual liberties.

37. Barkan (1994, 87) points out that the critics of modernization theory (including political development) have attacked three of its assumptions: the idea that development is an internal societal process; the notion that viable political rule and economic performance reinforce each other; and the belief that the exercise of predictable, legitimate political authority is "associated with democratic rule" or at least with political accountability.

38. For an excellent skeptical assessment of these critics, see Wiarda (1989–90). Wiarda argues that political development is worth resurrecting. See also Ruttan (1991) for a description of the role of the Social Science Research Council and subsequent reactions to it.

39. For an interesting attempt to graph, if not quantify, political development, see Ruttan (1991). He asks, "What is it that grows in the process of political development?" and then argues that "political development has

advanced a) if the amount of power available to a society grows with no worsening of the distribution of power; or b) if the distribution of power has become more equal, with no decline in the amount of power available to a society" (277).

40. Among those who have asked such questions are Dichter (1986a) and Annis (1987 and subsequent writings). Curiously, some of those who have again become interested in political development seem detached from the Third World itself. Chilton (1988), for example, deals with political development mainly as a historical concept.

41. Typical of comments, at least in the mid-1980s, was that by Clapham (1985, 81): "A very great deal of politics is concerned with the activities of a very small number of people. True of almost any form of politics, this is especially so in the Third World states where institutions linking the mass of the population with political action are weak or nonexistent." Binder (1986, 12), who is more aware than Clapham of the development literature, nevertheless argues that the "call for unlimited participation in the Third World is a gross distortion of what the United States was actually like." He argues that "rational, secular elites" would be compromised by the indiscriminate expansion of participation. Binder is a Middle Eastern specialist, and his comments seem more relevant to that region than to the rest of the Third World.

42. Huntington and Nelson correctly foresaw that by stimulating self-help activity, politicians could help community organizations make more effective demands on government.

43. Even Bossert (1986, 314, 330), who correctly criticizes the dependency theorists for viewing the lower classes in Latin America as an "undifferentiated mass," can nonetheless write about the "enduring weakness of the lower-class groups in the new democracies," because he focuses on obviously political groups. Yet even overtly political groups are stronger than he assumes in some countries. Baloyra and Martz (1979) argue that rural voters are more politically active in Venezuela than urban ones, regardless of socioeconomic level. Political anthropologists, in contrast, have long recognized politically relevant organizations at the local level. Swartz (1968), for example, argues in favor of a definition of politics based on public goals rather than on government or its functional equivalent. Political anthropology has often been concerned with situations in which authority is in doubt. Barnes (1968, 107) describes how African village councils adjudicate disputes and mediate power struggles.

44. Huntington (1968, 1) best exemplifies the concern with state capacity when he begins *Political Order in Changing Societies*: with "The most important political distinction among countries concerns not their form of government but their degree of government."

45. Chilton (1988, 8) sets this out as a requirement.

46. See, for example, Huntington 1965, 386–430.

47. As Sheth (1983, 19) notes, the real concern of many semipolitical action groups in India is social transformation, not the "capture of state power."

48. Latin American theorists have recently favored the concept of civil society over an expanded definition of the political system. Munck (1990, 38), for example, argues that only autonomous civil society as a whole can avoid

the opposite pitfalls of government co-option versus isolated autonomous organizations with little influence on societal change. Since the "organizational revolution" (growth of NGOs) is of "recent vintage . . . it is only now being tested for survivability." What is needed, he explains, is "not a linear extension of citizenship, but a reformulation of the concept."

49. Uphoff (1986b, 60) uses the concept of "jointness of consumption" to define public goods and concludes that "the more jointness that exists the more public is the good and the more reason there is for LA [local administration] or LG [local government] to be responsible for the infrastructure providing it." Similarly, Cohen and Uphoff (1980, 214) define participation as "denoting the involvement of a significant number of persons in situations or actions which enhance their well-being, e.g., their income, security or self-esteem." However, effective local administration or government may not exist or may represent interests opposed to the public good.

50. Binder et al. (1971) equate political development with the system's ability to cope with five crises—legitimacy, identity, participation, penetration, and distribution—without recognizing that participation is part of the broader political system.

51. These views emerged during discussions with Latin Americans attending the 1986 Latin American Studies Association meeting.

52. Ilchman and Uphoff (1969, 33) used an alternative definition of power: "the ability to generate political capital and increase its productivity."

53. Past definitions of political development have not always made these distinctions explicit. Pye (1966), for example, defined political development in terms of equality (mass participation of any kind) without clearly stating that autonomous participation represented an advance over mobilized participation. In addition to participation, equality of political recruitment, and a secular and rational governmental approach to policy and efficiency, he includes the "differentiation and specialization" of political structures. This description could apply to corporatist as well as pluralist institutions. The point is not that more specialized corporate structures are irrelevant to the process, but only that they should not be equated with autonomous institutions.

54. The quote is from a letter written to me by my father, David Hawkins. He pointed out to me that John Dewey also addresses this topic explicitly in *The Public and Its Problems*. Dewey, writing in the 1920s, was concerned with the "eclipse of the public," although not with societies in which the public had never been part of the polity.

55. Despite Talcott Parsons's apparently narrower definition of power as an instrument enabling agents to alter the behavior of other agents, he also viewed power as a resource that could be expanded. See Ruttan (1991), for a discussion on Parsons and on power as the measure of political development. For a recent contributor to discussions about power relationships and civil society, see Macdonald (1997), who focuses on the political role of NGOs in Nicaragua and Costa Rica.

56. I am indebted to Claude Welch, who reviewed an earlier draft of the manuscript, for pointing out this contrast, which is in large measure a product of the changes that have occurred in the Third World since 1968. In

describing the gaps between rich and poor in the Third World, for example, Huntington (1968, 135) argues that "as in seventeenth-century Europe these gaps can *only* be overcome by the creation of powerful, centralized authority in government" (emphasis added), even though accumulation of power has rarely led directly to its wider distribution. In contrast, while using this sequence to describe Kemal Ataturk's reforms in Turkey in the 1920s, Huntington (1968, 357) acknowledges the contrast with Latin America, where "the broadening of political participation was not a brake on social change but a prerequisite to such change."

57. This does not mean that growing governmental capacity should exclude the ability to moderate or influence nonstate actors. (See Huntington 1968, 21.)

58. Swartz (1968, 14) describes how the Lapps in Norway made demands on the government. Their success made more Lapps willing to participate, which was used by the Lapp leaders to make further demands. Swartz calls this a "generative cycle" affecting the repertoires of both Lapps and government officials, providing both with new moral and jural principles as well as educational and economic resources. Note the similarity of this argument to that of Goulet (1986).

59. Brown (1984, 14) also deals with Kohlberg's structures of moral reasoning and the feminist critique of them developed by Carol Gilligan to support teaching mathematics in terms of "purpose, situation specificity, and people connectedness."

60. The crisis theorists have tended to focus on redemocratization and mass demonstrations in Latin America and elsewhere. They also focus specifically on the "middle sectors," but their approach is equally relevant to discussions of the role of NGOs.

2

Government Policies Toward NGOs: Political Context and the Growth of Civil Society

■ Power comes from the people
But where does it go?
And how does it happen
That it gets to such a place?
— Vladimir Vysotsky (the late Soviet popular singer)

DO GOVERNMENTS LEARN from nongovernmental organizations (NGOs)? The answer to this question depends on the behavior of both sides. This chapter, which focuses on the impact of governments on NGOs, begins with a discussion of government policies toward NGOs, which range from repressive to mutually beneficial relationships. The remainder of the chapter focuses on a number of factors that help determine government policies toward NGOs, beginning with an exploration of differences in NGO–government relationships in Asia, Africa, and Latin America. Yet geographic differences have less explanatory value than the direct and indirect impact of the broader political context, which is covered in the third section. Governments may be autocratic or democratic, stable or unstable; they may be subject to strong political cultures or traditions, and they may differ from one another in their ability to implement policy. Any of these contextual variables can directly affect policies toward NGOs. Yet context also has an indirect effect on government policies toward NGOs by influencing NGO proliferation. As increasing numbers of NGOs contribute to the emergence of stronger civil societies, governments face a changing political context, which forces them to reevaluate previous policies toward NGOs. Governments also reexamine policies toward NGOs because of changes they make in their own management.

The Range of Government Policy

A look at governmental responses to the growth of NGOs reveals a wide range of reactions and policies. At the most repressive end of the spectrum are governments that are fearful of NGO activity; indeed, some political leaders assume that nongovernmental means antigovernmental (Theunis 1992, 249). Most Middle Eastern governments tend to be suspicious of NGOs and often subject them to political surveillance.[1] In Singapore, leaders of grassroots support organizations (GRSOs) have faced arrest and imprisonment. The Kenyan government was closing down GRSOs in 1995 while creating government-organized NGOs (GONGOs) oriented toward the official party.[2] However, certain regimes may come to fear even GRSOs that they have created.

More subtle forms of repression against the independent sector have occurred as it has grown in power and influence. In Bangladesh in the late 1980s, for example, no development project could be initiated without forty official signatures, and NGO registration often took six months or longer. Both governmental and opposition political leaders have been known to accuse GRSO leaders of being agents of the communists or the U.S. Central Intelligence Agency, depending on the source of the accusation (Riker 1995b, 107).[3]

Subtle harassment may not represent a governmentwide policy; indeed, it is often limited to particular ministries or departments. In India, for example, many departments and autonomous agencies of the government are cooperating actively with NGOs. Yet other officials, apparently not in agreement with this policy, have denied registration to NGOs under the Foreign Contributions Regulation Act:

> The visit of intelligence officers to the doors of voluntary agencies has become almost a regular phenomenon now. If you apply for a [foreign] grant you have to receive them; if they want to inquire into the use of your grant, they visit you. [Another] form of harassment is to label false charges against voluntary agencies and their leaders. . . . This has been the experience of voluntary agencies working in tribal areas (Tandon 1987, 9).

Yet policies adopted by key ministries or departments can affect overall policies. Indian tax law, for example, requires NGOs to keep a budget surplus for the final six months of the year, presenting most organizations with serious cash-flow problems. In addition, the fiscal years prescribed in the tax code and the Foreign Contributions Act are different, so NGOs often have to file two sets of reports (McCarthy 1989, 16).[4] Even worse, the tax commissioner is legally allowed to appoint representatives to NGO boards of directors.

On the plus side, such schizophrenic policies can show up within extremely repressive regimes. In Kenya, NGO harassment coexists with cooperative policies, such as those that link the Ministry of Health to GRSOs throughout the country (Allison and Macinko 1993, 46). In the Philippines, despite the uneven treatment of NGOs, the military and a group of GRSOs have developed CODE-NGO, a liaison mechanism that, according to one GRSO leader, "allows us to resolve conflicts early" (Constantino-David 1992, 146). Repressive regimes may also harbor individuals with more positive attitudes toward NGOs. Although the Mengistu Haile Mariam regime in Ethiopia was "remarkably successful" in controlling NGOs, one commissioner "[strayed] from Mengistu's leash" and developed more positive relationships (Hovde 1992, 9).

A second, less harmful, governmental approach has been to ignore NGOs. From the time that GRSOs began to emerge in the early 1970s until the mid-1980s, this was probably the most common governmental response. For example, in Bolivia, successive regimes jailed leaders of opposition parties but allowed GROs and GRSOs to proliferate without interference. Ignoring NGOs is often less a deliberate policy than a symptom of what Gunnar Myrdahl (1970) called the "soft state," incapable of carrying out any kind of coherent public policy.

As NGOs have proliferated and become more politically active, however, governments have found it increasingly difficult to ignore them. The Malian government, for example, which was originally permissive toward NGOs, later tightened its policies through such measures as delays in tax exemptions (Johnson and Johnson 1990, 68). Yet even if political leaders of the "soft state" are increasingly likely to notice NGOs and formulate NGO policies, they remain, in many cases, unable to implement them. In Uganda, all NGOs are expected to register with the prime minister's office, present their project proposals, and receive an official endorsement for their correspondence with foreign donors. Yet the NGO office in the prime minister's office has few resources, no office equipment, and only one officer and one clerk (Gariyo 1996, 163).

A third general policy approach is co-optation, often caused by what Anheier (1994, 141) calls the tension between the need for more resources and the desire to control NGOs. Attempts to control GRSOs may take the form of subtle bribery, as in Tamil Nadu, where the social welfare board regularly gives small grants to GRSOs for "furnishings" (Moen 1991, 83–4). In other countries, such as Sri Lanka, governments try to preempt GRSOs by building their own ties to GROs (Riker 1995b, 112). Governments also try to divide GRSOs by the selective involvement of favored ones in government programs and policies (Tandon 1989a, 1).[5] In Egypt, for example, there are "cozy relationships between Islamic associations and government officials" (Zubaida 1992, 7).[6] Perhaps the most common approach, however, is for governments to create their own GRSOs, called GONGOs or government-run and -inspired NGOs (GRINGOs). In Zimbabwe, where most GRSOs struggle for years to get government approval to function at all, the Child Survival and Development Foundation, headed by the president's wife, is able to receive donations from foreign companies that cannot repatriate profits and need tax write-offs.[7]

Such close partnerships may be mutually beneficial. This is particularly true in the case of large environmental organizations with strong foreign ties. In Costa Rica, for example, the Fundación Neotropica and the National Parks Foundation buy land, transfer it to the government, pay park rangers, and channel foreign donations to the national parks (Livernash 1992, 20; see also Meyer 1995).

The state may also try to co-opt GROs, sometimes by creating its own local organizations. In Mexico, the official Party of Revolutionary Institutions (PRI) has a long history of making it difficult for autonomous organizations to maintain their character. After the leader of an independent taxi collective in Mexico City was murdered in 1986, drivers were required to support the PRI's taxi group just to get driving permits.

However, maintaining state control of GROs may not always be possible over the long run (Fisher 1993, chap. 2). The 1985 Mexico City earthquake created, by all accounts, what is close to a critical mass of autonomous GROs, impossible for any bureaucracy to track, let alone dominate. Sometimes governments attempting to co-opt local organizations inadvertently promote GRO autonomy. In Lima, once the federal government started distributing subsidized food to their own GROs, autonomous community kitchens demanded and received similar support (Barrig 1990).[8]

A fourth general policy approach is for the state to take advantage of, but not necessarily attempt to control NGOs or to learn from them. Obviously, there are financial reasons for this. As Bebbington and Farrington (1993, 204) point out, "participation [is] being grudgingly offered because [governments] can no longer finance patronage." In Nicaragua under the Sandinistas, more than one-third of the country's foreign exchange came from donations to NGOs.[9] Yet governments may also be tempted to kill the geese that lay the golden eggs. Prior to the North American Free Trade Agreement (NAFTA) negotiations, the Mexican government taxed NGOs so heavily that potential international donors were becoming reluctant to contribute.[10]

Another reason for passive acceptance of NGOs is the need to enhance government legitimacy. In Mexico, President Salinas de Gortari gave NGOs increased latitude in order to legitimate himself internationally, a strategy that probably backfired from the narrow political point of view, since NGO numbers and influence have grown (Stevenson 1994). Yet the political advantages of allowing NGOs to obtain foreign support can be considerable. Fruhling (1985, 59) argues that during the Pinochet dictatorship in Chile, GRSOs weakened potential government opposition when they obtained grants from the Ford Foundation.

Still another reason that governments may take advantage of NGOs is for military or security purposes. GRSOs generally lack a parochial ideology, so their resources are less likely than those of the government to be the target of ethnic and tribal rivalries (Hyden 1987, 86). GROs also be may be used as bulwarks against a guerrilla uprising. For instance, autonomous GROs promoting local security in Peru's highland villages were officially tolerated during the Shining Path uprising because they blocked the rebels' influence (Durning 1989, 79).

A final reason is that governments may be unable to make major reforms without NGO support. Rood (1992) argues that NGOs in the Philippines help provide the government with insulation from socioeconomic elites. And Clarke (1995) points out that the Philippine Department of Health needs NGO allies to overcome the Catholic Church's opposition to family planning. In addition, the Department of Health has problems recruiting young doctors for rural areas because of low government pay. "For many rural doctors, NGOs have become a lifeline, and NGOs now supplement doctors' salaries (by as much as three times the government salary) or provide equipment and medicine" (Clarke 1995, 89).

A fifth general government policy is for the state and NGOs to cooperate and learn from each other in an autonomous partnership, which may be either ad hoc in nature or systemwide. Cooperation is sometimes the result of other kinds of NGO–government contacts. A network of Sri Lankan NGOs called the Environmental Congress initially adopted a confrontational style in its relations with government. But when the government was receptive to the Congress's environmental complaints and dropped plans for a major project, confrontation yielded to a more constructive dialogue (Clarke 1995, 595).

Ad hoc arrangements, as discussed in Chapter 4, are often initiated by NGOs. However, governments also initiate field cooperation, especially when it does not challenge existing power monopolies. Since ad hoc cooperation has occurred in countries as politically diverse as India, Togo, Bolivia, Mexico, the Philippines, Jordan, Egypt, and Uganda, it is not inevitably linked to democratization. In some cases, the state acts as a "reference point" through which GROs and GRSOs can relate to one another; in other cases, GRSOs train government extension workers (Finquelievich 1987, 3–27).

Budget pressures are one of the factors pushing governments into the ad hoc use of NGOs for policy implementation. This is particularly true in Africa, where NGOs, despite their relatively weak advocacy record, are increasingly able to hook governments into joint projects by proposing to lower costs or to reach more people without increasing costs.[11] Whether or not low costs are based on reality in Africa or Latin America, there is considerable evidence from Asia that supports this much-touted NGO advantage (Fisher 1993, 163–4). In the Ciamis district of Indonesia, NGOs in charge of a government agricultural project were able to construct terraces at one-twelfth the cost of solo implementation by the government and improve 48,000 hectares of farmland, compared with the 4,000 hectares originally planned (Uphoff 1993, 617). In India, NGOs that have implemented government programs in certain villages "have done a remarkably more efficient and effective job" than government agencies working alone in similar villages (Tandon 1989b, 17).[12]

There are even cases of governments acknowledging that entire programs would simply be better run by development organizations under subcontracting arrangements. The Sri Lankan government turned over the implementation of the national day-care program to NGOs and incorporated the 125 existing government centers into the 2,300 centers that Sarvodaya Shramadana, a large GRSO, had created. This approach becomes, in itself, a policy change, yet it may have less potential than field collaboration for cross-fertilization and learning (Fernandez 1987, 46). Unless GRSOs are careful to share information and administrative capacities, they may take over and replace whatever service delivery capability the government possesses, and "there may be little state left on which to make claims" (Farrington and Bebbington 1993, 193). As leaders of a Chilean health organization complained, "Half of our medication goes to fill government health system prescriptions, to make up for basic medication the government health system lacks" (Downs and Solimano 1989, 203).

Related to cost control are the economic strictures imposed by structural adjustment.[13] The Bolivian government has, for example, included NGOs in its Social Emergency Fund (FES), which is designed to lessen some of the negative social impact of structural adjustment policies.[14] Even the Guatemalan and Honduran governments have begun working with NGOs to cushion the shock of recession resulting from structural adjustment (Williams 1990, 32). Structural adjustment in Latin America has also led to trimmer bureaucracies and decentralization, which make government more accesible to NGOs (Farrington and Bebbington 1993, 124).

Structural adjustment policies may, however, widen the gap in agricultural development objectives between NGOs and governments and inhibit closer collaboration, according to Farrington and Bebbington (1993, 190). Moreover, any collaboration may be short term, since compensatory policies may be held hostage by the wider policy environment. In Lima, a child development project run by an NGO received support from Gloria Helfer, the minister of education, yet structural adjustment cuts made it impossible for her to continue in office (see Dawson 1993, 412).

Ad hoc field cooperation may also be promoted by single ministries or autonomous agencies, despite overall government indifference or hostility. In Bolivia, for example, where some regimes have viewed NGOs as part of the opposition, the Instituto Politécnico Tomás Katari has had a contract with the Ministry of Health since the 1970s to implement health programs and policies in Chayanta. In 1976, Chayanta had one doctor for 120,000 people, but by 1990 it had a modern hospital, five medical posts, thirty-two sanitary posts, and eighteen health programs, including one that had vaccinated 15,000 children (Barrios in Toranzo Roca 1992, 49). Also in Bolivia, the Department of Technical Transfer of the Center for Tropical Research (CIAT) links agricultural research and extension carried out by GRSOs to producer organizations and private companies in the Santa Cruz region. Not only do staff move freely between various NGOs and CIAT, but as an autonomous government agency, CIAT is at least partially protected from political interference (Farrington and Bebbington 1993, 124).

Systemwide policies favoring cooperation with NGOs are not common. However, cooperative processes that included NGOs were present at the creation of an independent Namibia in 1991. At that time there were no operating procedures for NGO–government cooperation, the National Planning Commission and the Education Ministry were more favorable to NGOs than were other ministries still dominated by whites, and the NGOs themselves were politically divided into supporters of the new SWAPO government and its opposition. The unprecedented cooperation between state and civil society—fostered by rewards and sanctions designed by foreign donors, local planners, and NGOs—won the government legitimacy from a suspicious population in the first two years of independence (Sandberg and Martin 1994).[15]

Perhaps the most dramatic and systemwide cooperative policy was initiated by the Christian Democratic administration in Chile, elected in 1990. The Chilean National Institute of Agricultural Research established fifty Centers for Adjustment and Transfer of Technology (CATTs) corresponding to agroecological zones; local committees that included NGOs were designated to advise and oversee the activities of the CATTs (Farrington and Bebbington 1993, 143–7). The new regime also hired many NGO leaders. Although some had left the government in frustration by the end of the first year, many professionals still working for GRSOs in 1995 were taking leaves of absence to work temporarily in government (Loveman 1991; 1995, 139). Moreover, the Chilean model has begun to spread; the undersecretary of international cooperation in Chile and the Ministries of Foreign Affairs in Brazil and Argentina have exchanged information about international funding for the sustainable development projects of NGOs.[16]

Unfortunately, whether governments cooperate on an ad hoc or systematic basis with NGOs, they are generally unwilling or unable to undertake up-front research on NGO projects to find out who is doing what where, much less to evaluate success or failure in relation to possible field collaboration (Johnson and Johnson 1990, 117; Sandberg 1994a, 14). Nor do governments or NGOs usually track the combined environmental or developmental impacts of joint projects. When research does receive government support, it may be misdirected. In Bangladesh, for example, government studies based on conventionally defined rates of economic return are used to justify delays in the approval of grants to GRSOs, to monitor GRSOs through the Planning Commission, and to continue to pay large government subsidies to rural elites. Most of these studies conveniently ignore the low repayment rates of these subsidies, in contrast to the high repayment rates and vast reach of GRSOs such as the Bangladesh Rural Advancement Committee (BRAC) or the Grameen Bank that provide loans to the poor (Sanyal 1991).

Because even successful cooperation with governments can deflect GRSOs from their grassroots constituencies, it is important to examine the organizational patterns of government-initiated relationships with NGOs (Clark 1995, 599). Sandberg (1994b, 21, 26) identifies five possible organizational patterns: ad hoc connections, a single coordinating office, diffused responsibility for NGO coordination through every ministry, a decentralized approach through local governments, and a method she describes as "coordination through multiple stratified focus points." The latter method can accommodate diversity and preserve NGO flexibility more effectively than even friendly, fully coordinated government policies toward NGOs. A national NGO office within a government, for example, could assist NGOs with donors or proposals; however, it would not be in charge of NGO policies unless a problem could not be solved at a lower level.[17] This would be a particularly useful strategy for big populous countries such as Nigeria or Brazil, where there are too many NGOs for the government to track or coordinate.

Regional Contrasts in Policies Toward NGOs

Relationships between NGOs and governments in the Third World clearly differ from those in the developed countries. In the United States, for example, Salamon (1987) points out that voluntary organizations emerged during the nineteenth century, when charity and paternalism were predominant social values. It was only later that government made the provision of services a right rather than a privilege and assumed responsibility for some of the groups and problems that charities could not or did not deal with.

In the Third World, the rise of NGOs has strengthened and enlarged the independent sector at a different historical moment. Indeed, NGOs are founded as a result of governmental failure to address precisely those areas where governments have historically held a comparative advantage in Europe and the United States. Moreover, GRSOs are being established not by wealthy elites but by intellectuals and professionals.

It is more difficult to generalize about regional contrasts in the relationship between governments and NGOs within the Third World. There are many differences within Latin America, Asia, and Africa, but there are also some general differences among regions.

Latin America

Civil society in Latin America is more consistently autonomous in relation to the state than it is in Africa or Asia. One reason for this is that even before the NGO explosion, Latin American political systems were broad and heterogeneous. A generation ago, governments were buffeted by the demands of the middle class.[18] Now they must also confront a number of new interest groups, including NGOs. This means that even if governments want to control or repress NGOs, the very strength of civil society—including NGOs, private businesses, and labor unions— makes it more difficult for them to do so in Latin America than in Africa or Asia.

NGO political power is a function of the coincidence of growing NGO capacity and the continuing inability of Latin American governments to provide basic services or implement development policies. Now these "weakly institutionalized" states, pushed by international forces advocating structural adjustment and privatization, have turned to NGOs as a way of avoiding worsening poverty and social unrest.[19] The Bolivian Social Emergency Fund, for example, channeled $14 million through GRSOs between 1986 and 1991.[20]

The Bolivian situation also illustrates how government policies are being shaped by government interaction with NGOs. In 1990, when the government tried to register NGOs and define their obligations, long negotiations led to a reduction in a proposed tax on nonprofit organizations from 10 percent to 1 percent of their annual budgets. And although it did not renounce its "right" to shut down NGOs, the government did agree to provide three years' notice (Toranzo Roca 1992, 10, 39, 49).

More dramatically, Latin American NGOs have helped reshape the political systems within which they operate. Even under the military dictatorships that emerged in Brazil, Chile, and Argentina during the 1960s and 1970s, NGOs were carving out "political space" not available to opposition political parties. This was possible, in part, because most NGOs are nonpartisan.[21] Indeed, where major parties represent the upper and upper-middle classes, as in Colombia, being partisan would negate the commitment of GRSOs to the poor. As Miguel Fajardo, program director of a Colombian NGO, put it, "The political power of organized peasants is greater than any party. Parties are nominal national entities, but at the local level do not represent the people" (Brian Smith 1990, 244).[22]

Sometimes, of course, NGOs' ability to act independently may be eroded. During the Sandinista period in Nicaragua, for example, NGOs gradually lost their ability to intercede with the government and became less and less likely to act independently. According to Sollis (1995, 531), "as NGOs became instruments of government policy, they failed to realize how much humanitarian assistance was part of the government's counterinsurgency and pacification strategy."

In addition, the impact of NGOs may be diluted by the political strength of more traditional countervailing groups. Peasant organizations in Honduras, for example, have historically had more impact on agrarian reform policies and have been allowed to operate more freely than have Salvadoran peasant organizations, because landowners in El Salvador have traditionally exerted stronger countervailing political pressures on the government (Ickes 1983, 17). A Salvadoran GRSO called FUNDASAL developed a rural self-help model over more than a decade, but the government had little interest in using it on a larger scale, because it would have built up the power of autonomous peasant organizations (Stein 1990).

Asia

Unlike Latin America, NGO–government relationships in Asia are "largely determined by the government and its agencies" (Tandon 1989a, 28). According to Tandon (1989a, 116–7), this is true whether ties to governments are dependent, adversarial, repressive, or collaborative. Even when governments ignore NGOs, the withdrawal of recognition and legitimacy can be a powerful policy in itself. This situation is perhaps most extreme in China, where there are only a handful of NGOs (see Box 2.1).

In recent years, however, Asian governments have increasingly recognized the advantages of cooperative, if not always collaborative, development strategies. Acceptance of NGOs grew during the 1980s because of their international support and their capacity to deliver services. In fact,

---

Box 2.1   China—A Special Case

After the 1949 communist takeover in China, NGOs that had challenged feudal lords and the Kuomintang government were turned into organs of the new government. By 1986, however, the Chinese government was allowing European NGOs into the country. And in 1989, recognizing the extreme poverty of many of its rural citizens, the government helped found the Foundation for Underdeveloped Regions in China (FURC).

FURC is not an autonomous NGO; indeed, it is composed of a mixture of government and party officials, as well as a handful of private citizens. Nor did the government consider reviving rural cooperatives once the communes were abandoned, even though, according to Serrano (1994), they "could have provided a solid basis for the NGO resurrection." Indeed, the government "has been omnipresent and overbearing for four decades and has left virtually no room for private voluntary organizations" (276).

---

where governments lack resources, as in Cambodia or the Pacific islands, they are often eager to have NGOs as development partners. In Bangladesh, government acceptance of NGOs increased because a child survival program reached 85,000 villages. Elsewhere, line ministries such as Population and Environment in Indonesia and the Central Planning Commission in India assign liaison officers to work with GRSOs. And in Sri Lanka, the government has actually promoted the accountability of elite-dominated GROs by encouraging competition with other GROs over the allocation of resources (Howe 1986).

Cooperation has also tended to lessen burdensome government policies toward NGOs. Registration procedures have become simpler, according to 80 percent of the respondents to a 1992 survey of forty Asian GRSOs from Bangladesh, Pakistan, Indonesia, the Philippines, and India. Bangladesh has helped NGOs receive foreign aid more quickly by creating "one-stop" service through the NGO Affairs Bureau and the Foreign Donation Voluntary Activity Ordinance (Allison and Kak 1992, 164–5).[23] The Philippine government has been promoting an "enabling environment for NGOs" since 1986; even the Bureau of Internal Revenue has become supportive of NGOs (Riker 1995b, 116; Allison and Kak 1992, 164). In India, the Kudal Commission, set up to examine allegations about missing funds in Gandhian GRSOs, was dissolved in 1987 after a successful campaign against it (Sen 1994, 9). In Nepal, a critique of proposed regulatory legislation by NGOs led the government to curtail the power of a national council in charge of regulating NGOs, although its approval is still required for foreign grants (Fernandez 1987, 43).

Yet this generally rosy Asian picture conceals as much as it reveals. Other Asian governments may be relying more and more on co-optation, under cover of NGO-friendly policies (Heyzer 1995, 11). For example, some Indian observers contend that the Council for the Advancement of People's Action and Rural Technology (CAPART) has co-opted much of the original community development and cooperative movement and that NGOs have little real influence on its policies, despite their representation on its board (Verma and Menon 1993, 331; see Box 2.2). Among the barriers to interactive collaboration cited by respondents to the 1992 five-country survey were lack of funding, bureaucratic rigidity, and delays in processing applications. Some GRSO respondents felt that government attitudes were often negative. The Pakistani government, according to the responses of NGO leaders, is simply "not very helpful" (Allison and Kak 1992, 165).[24]

Moreover, as noted earlier, NGO policies in Asia are more likely than policies in Africa or Latin America to be schizophrenic. Although the Malaysian government has used NGO ties to provide services to isolated rural areas, GRSO leaders active in the environmental movement were arrested in 1987, along with a number of opposition political figures.[25] Security departments in Bangladesh, Sri Lanka, India, Nepal, and Singapore consider GRSOs to be a threat. As a result, NGOs in South Asia, except for the Philippines, have become wary of advocacy and confrontation (Holloway 1989b, 8). Even in the Philippines, where the health department achieved credibility by consistently seeking out NGOs with strong community ties, the military has continued to harass health programs run by religious NGOs (Goertzen 1991, 23).

Some governments engage in accusations against particular NGOs through the media. In Sri Lanka, the government initiated a media campaign against Sarvodaya, fueled by the NGO's presence in 10,000 villages and the government's envy over an annual budget larger than that of the Ministry of Rural Development (Tandon 1989a, 13). In Bangladesh, government-sponsored articles in the media led to the temporary closure of ADAB, the major umbrella organization of NGOs, although the government subsequently backed down and agreed to increase development partnerships with NGOs (Tandon 1993, 203).

Africa

Relationships between governments and NGOs are particularly difficult to assess in sub-Saharan Africa, although some observers have categorized state–NGO relationships by types of regimes. Although only a few countries are listed in each category, these observers argue that African

---

Box 2.2 Continuing Government Control in India

During the 1980s, the Foreign Contributions (Regulation) Act was used to deny hundreds of NGOs registration or remove existing registrations without cause. Demands were made for huge tax arrears, followed by repeated visits from government inspectors. In tribal areas, false charges were made that leaders were trying to convert people to Islam or Christianity.

Although the Eighth Development Plan, initiated in 1992, is based on a national grid of NGOs and only the 134 NGOs receiving large foreign donations have to register, other NGO projects still require bureaucratic approval. Bilateral funding distributed to NGOs through CAPART makes it easier for the government to control their activities. The Income Tax Act gives concessions to boarding schools and hospitals but not to NGOs engaged in development. NGOs also have to pay heavy federal and state taxes on for-profit activities, purportedly to ensure that nonprofit organizations do not restrict the growth of the private sector. (*Sources:* Fernandez 1987, 43–5; Verma and Menon 1993, 327, 331; interview with Siddhartha Sen, August 26, 1996; Farrington and Bebbington 1993, 53; Society for Participatory Research in Asia 1991, 46; Allison and Kak 1992, 165; Salamon and Anheier 1994, 94.)

---

dictatorships generally repress NGOs, single-party states such as Zimbabwe and Kenya accept service-provider NGOs but tend to restrain those promoting empowerment, and multiparty democracies have a "sweet and sour" relationship with NGOs (Tandon 1989a, 11).[26]

Perhaps the only safe generalization about Africa is that by the mid-1990s, most governments were more aware of NGOs than they had been ten years earlier. One reason for the lack of awareness in the 1980s was that NGOs maintained a low profile. Hyden (1983) argued that NGOs avoided questioning authority, because political criticism was both risky and foreign to African cultural tradition. Nonetheless, some governments were already disbanding GRSOs, as in the case of the Ruvuma Development Association in Tanzania (Hyden 1983, 122; see also Chapter 4). In Niger, GRSO leaders call government officials "inscrutable and demanding" because of elaborate registration requirements (Johnson and Johnson 1990, 25).

Since the late 1980s, however, governments have increasingly tried to co-opt large, successful GRSOs, while leaving the small, less successful ones alone (Glagow and Evers 1986). Co-optation provides governments with positive publicity and allows GRSOs to work in rural areas while distancing them from advocacy in capital cities. In fact, Fowler (1990, 40) argues that tens of thousands of official administrative units throughout Africa provide governments with "camouflaged opportunities to control and manipulate NGO activities." In Kenya, for example, the government responded to the growth of women's groups by subsidizing Maendeleo Ua Wanawake, a rural development NGO originally created by European women during the colonial period. Its expenditures have to be authorized by the local administrator of the district to ensure against "splinter groups" using the money (Wanyande 1987, 99).

Attempts to control NGOs are frequently justified by the need to ride herd on foreign contacts, even though international NGOs are sometimes better treated by governments than are indigenous organizations.[27] The Sudanese and Kenyan governments have used the supposed abuse of duty-free imports to deregister GRSOs. The same justification was used in 1989 by a Ugandan regime that required all NGOs to reregister and banned NGOs' use of radios to communicate with field projects (Bennett 1995, 96). Such policies tend to be reinforced by official international donors that require NGOs to obtain government approval before they will provide support (Anheier 1987; Bratton 1989; Schneider 1985; Fowler 1990).

Foreign financial support also fuels government suspicions, despite the countervailing desire to take financial advantage of NGOs. In Kenya, for example, NGOs provide the largest single source of foreign exchange. Although the Water Development Ministry relies on NGOs for 90 percent of its services, and the Health Ministry for about 50 percent, the foreign support for these projects goes directly to NGOs. "First, this is an irritatingly large bundle of money that leaders cannot get their hands on. Second, it does leave the country worryingly vulnerable to donor caprice. Third, it makes it difficult for technocrats to plan, never quite being able to estimate what may happen."[28]

Because foreign financial support also provides NGOs with the potential for independence from the government, their very existence challenges the idea that sovereignty rests with the regime, not with the people. As soon as African NGOs raise issues of political legitimacy and human rights, they draw rapid fire almost everywhere, even though, as Barkan (1994, 111) points out, a growing number of African political leaders have begun to realize that the state should become more accountable. The Public Law Institute in Kenya, the Legal Resource Centers in Tanzania, the Legal Advice Centers in Zimbabwe, and the Law Societies and Catholic Peace and Justice Commissions in other countries often confront the state on human rights issues. The Catholic Commission for Peace and Justice in Zimbabwe, for example, faced governmental repression after it complained about abuses by Korean-trained army units.

GRSOs that engage in participatory consciousness-raising in rural areas provoke particularly negative reactions. In 1983, the Christian Development Education Service of the Catholic Church in Kenya was disbanded under official pressure because it engaged in leadership training for rural groups (Fowler 1990, 14). GRSOs are also viewed as political havens for ethnic outsiders or rival political groups. In 1986, Zimbabwe restricted the community development work of a GRSO in Matabeleland because its programs were benefiting ex-Zapu combatants who had fought against the Zanu-led government.[29]

In other words, "the act of challenging . . . a given policy has sometimes been perceived instead as a challenge to the government's right to govern. This confusion over roles and responsibilities . . . also helps explain why NGOs have yet to play a significant role in policy-making in most of Africa" (Swartzendruber and Njovens 1993, 14). In Zaire, for example:

> NGOs are officially tolerated and even encouraged by the government, but privately officials concede that they find them annoying and disturbing because they have outside funding, refuse to allow the state to examine their books and seem to accord scant attention to the views of the single party. NGOs resent official attempts to control them, the inadequate level of training of government representatives, and the failure to be included in policy dialogue. The Planning Department has proposed setting up NGO technical committees to prepare for a national NGO council, but NGOs, although they are networking with each other in every province, have not formed a national network to influence policy and remain wary of public patronage (Kabarhuza 1990, 34–7).

Ironically, by treating African GRSOs as opposition parties, governments have politicized them, even though NGOs range across the political spectrum from fundamentalist Protestant or Islamic to Catholic liberationist to socialist (Anheier 1987, 10–1).[30] In Kenya, despite the weight of government pressure, organizations such as the National Christian Council and the Law Society have both "figured prominently in opposition to Moi's attempts to alter the country's democratic institutions," and Kenyans, including many in the government, have begun to regard them as an opposition party (Maren 1987, 212).

Despite the suspicious and somewhat dicey relationship between NGOs and governments in some African countries, any generalization about NGO–government relationships in Africa should be met with a degree of skepticism. First, governments sometimes appreciate GRSO advocacy on issues—female genital mutilation, for example—that they oppose privately but fear to deal with publicly. Second, joint government–NGO councils have been created in some countries—Niger and Burkina Faso, for example.[31] Third, privatization policies have led to better treatment of NGOs. In Ghana, for instance, a law issued by the military government during the 1970s forbade the establishment of private voluntary associations unless authorized by a government-appointed commission. As of the late 1980s, communication between government officials and NGOs was sporadic, and many government officials were ignorant of the role of NGOs. By the early 1990s, however, NGOs were operating "more or less without interference," partly because of the influx of funds that accompanied structural adjustment policies promoted by the World Bank (Salamon and Anheier 1994, 93). Ghanian government policy cannot be described as simply "hands off," however. Although GRSOs are given wide discretion, they are encouraged, like GRSOs in Burkina Faso, to work in small communities with few public services (Anang 1994, 103).

Factors Determining Government Policies Toward NGOs

Despite contrasts among government policies toward NGOs in Asia, Africa, Latin America, and the Middle East, the ways in which governments react to NGOs are more likely to be determined by the national political context than by regional geographic location. Political context, whether authoritarian or democratic, stable or unstable, weakly or strongly institutionalized, constrained by political culture or not, probably helps define the initial political boundaries within which governments and NGOs interact.[32]

Yet ongoing interactions between governments and development organizations can begin to reshape or expand those boundaries. And it is what happens *within* the governmental and independent sectors that often initiates this interaction. In Chapters 3, 4 and 5, I explore the direct impact of NGOs on governments. Later in this section, I explore how political context can indirectly influence the growth rate of NGOs, which, in turn, can influence government policies. Then I describe how bureaucratic reforms within governments can affect development policy and relationships with NGOs.

The National Political Context: Direct Influence

The key factors defining the national political context within which policies toward NGOs develop are type of regime, political culture, degree of state capacity to implement policy, and degree of political stability.

TYPE OF REGIME   A democratic political context defined by freedom of expression and freedom of association obviously makes it more likely that a country will avoid repressive policies toward NGOs. Freedom of association and freedom of the press also enhance the visible role of NGOs, which can mitigate potential repression (Commuri 1995, 5). For example, in the Philippines and in many Latin American countries, democratization has enhanced the national roles of GRSO leaders. On a local level as well, democratic governance can strengthen the role of GROs. In Botswana, where the traditional *legotla*, or village assembly, operates as a kind of direct democracy, GROs that focus on development extend and fit in to existing cultural patterns.[33]

Freely operating opposition parties, however, are not inevitably the allies of NGOs. Concertación, a coalition opposition movement that developed at the end of the Pinochet dictatorship in Chile, had little contact with any grassroots movements other than trade unions. In fact, Concertación had trouble understanding the nonmaterial values of GROs. When Concertación organizers explained that community kitchens would no longer be needed once Pinochet was replaced, community organizers replied, "That is up to us to decide" (Schuurman and Heer 1992, 40). In Peru as well, leftist parties never adjusted well to the transition to democracy, perhaps because they, like the rest of society, had been weakened and intimidated by the assassination of grassroots leaders by the Shining Path guerrillas (Diaz-Albertini 1993b, 322).

Nor is there an automatic connection between the form of government and the treatment of GROs and GRSOs, as was noted in the discussion of "schizophrenic" policies (Riker 1995b, 119). Not only do security ministries within generally democratic regimes sometimes harass GRSOs, but authoritarian governments do not always repress them.[34] In Burkina Faso under Presidents Sankara and Compaore, and in Bangladesh under President Zia, nondemocratic governments supported civil society (Uvin and Miller 1994, 8). Authoritarian regimes have, in fact, adopted the entire range of NGO policies, from the most repressive to the most collaborative. Sometimes, as in the case of Marxist states such as Vietnam, positive attitudes toward NGOs may reflect the weakness of the independent sector. Regimes that are not threatened by NGOs may improve their image through ties to NGOs, with little political risk. In other cases, authoritarian regimes may be trying to improve their international image. The Pinochet dictatorship in Chile, in cooperation with international and national NGOs, supported the campaign against the Nestle Company by curbing the aggressive marketing of baby formula and by providing resources to promote breast feeding. By allowing international and Chilean NGOs to take over the state's responsibility for the poor, Pinochet was relieved of political pressures to change his policies.

There can also be islands that are friendly to NGOs within otherwise repressive governments.[35] When the international cocaine dealers were in power in Bolivia during the 1970s, for example, the Ministry of Education was hiring peasants involved in their own "theater for development" to teach peasants in other areas about their techniques (Clark 1991, 66). In fact, with the possible exception of the Guatemalan military regime during the 1980s, there are few, if any, examples of governmentwide repression of the independent sector once GRSOs began to proliferate. It is much easier for repressive governments to keep independent organizations from developing in the first place, as in China or North Korea.[36]

However, GRSOs may fare relatively better under dictatorships than do autonomous GROs. One reason for this is that they have contacts with foreign donors. Another reason for the difference is that GRSOs, "when dominated by urban professionals . . . rarely provoke a perception of overt threat on the part of entrenched political and economic interests," whereas grassroots membership organizations are often seen as potentially destabilizing.[37] In Guatemala during the 1980s, even a local health committee was forced to go underground because its activities were seen as subversive (Fox and Butler 1987, 3).

Yet authoritarian governments pursuing basic-needs development policies have tended to be more positive toward GROs than other dictatorial regimes. Despite political repression at the national level, both Taiwan and South Korea promoted local institutional development in the 1970s and 1980s, although they sometimes tried to control it.[38] Such productive connections between basic-needs policies and tolerance for local institutions were partially explained by a major cross-national study of land reforms that concluded that receptivity rather than control characterized the top-down–bottom-up relationship in eleven of sixteen countries, even though many of the governments were authoritarian (Montgomery, 1972). Montgomery hypothesized that the linkages themselves were associated with higher productivity and that shared goals changed relationships between national governments and local institutions (both GROs and local governments).

Basic-needs policies can promote grassroots empowerment and stimulate local demands, even in authoritarian or semiauthoritarian contexts:

- Local women's organizations in Zimbabwe have used agrarian reform legislation to force the government to focus on the needs of farmers.

- In Mexico, government-sponsored rural development programs have played a key role in weakening local *caciques* and "shaping what eventually became [an] autonomous smallholder movement," with a feedback effect on national development policies (Fox and Hernandez 1992, 177, 180).

- Local agrarian reform administrators in Peru became the targets of peasant demands, which shifted power downward, because peasants seized the opportunity to acquire resources on their own terms (McClintock 1981, 24).

- In Chimborazo, Bolivia, where state agencies promoted agrarian reform and green revolution technologies for some years, a whole generation of young indigenous adults now in leading positions "grew up knowing a state presence in their communities" and continue to demand state services (Bebbington 1993, 283).

To be sure, government ties to GROs may also be used to limit contacts with GRSOs or international NGOs that might strengthen local autonomy. In the Gambia, for example, support for women's GROs has enabled the government to retain almost complete control of a World Bank women's project.[39] The only GRSOs permitted to participate in the project were those that specialized in family planning and health care, with long track records of working with the government. Because it governed such a small country, the Gambian regime was highly concerned that international NGOs might infringe on its autonomy, a concern that presumably extended to GRSOs receiving foreign support (Brautigam 1994, 74).

In summary, positive treatment of NGOs is linked to democracy, but it also occurs within individual bureaucracies in authoritarian regimes, particularly in relation to basic-needs policies. Authoritarian regimes that use GROs to implement basic needs may actually strengthen both GROs and, as I show in Chapter 5, subnational governments. However, authoritarian regimes that have less local implementation capacity or do not even attempt to implement development policies on a local level may be more threatened by autonomous GRO than by GRSOs.

POLITICAL CULTURE   Political culture, defined by Almond and Powell (1966, 50) as the "pattern of individual attitudes and orientations toward politics among members of a political system," is a kind of intricate tapestry, unique to each country on earth, that consistently impacts political behavior, including government policies toward NGOs. For example, human rights NGOs have had less impact in Algeria than in Morocco or Tunisia, because "Algerian political culture offered little by way of support to the practice of democracy" (Waltz 1995, 236).

The uniqueness of each political culture usually has deep historical roots that condition relationships with NGOs. In South Africa, for example, where NGOs have been increasing in numbers for many years, there could be no significant relationships between the state and NGOs as long as apartheid continued (Jeppe, Theron, and Van Baalen 1992, 29; see also Lee 1992, 93).[40] In a completely different political context in West Bengal, the leaders of GRSOs operating under the Marxist government have been frustrated by restrictive corporate and union laws:

> The local political culture does not allow for an empowerment orientation. . . . This culture included infiltration of the Communist Party of

India . . . the party's long history of mobilization of the organized urban poor, [and] stagnation of the local economy because of the party's policies. (Sen 1994, 23–4)

Even paternalism, perhaps the most pervasive and widespread aspect of political culture in the Third World, is translated into unique political behaviors. In Thailand, for example, hierarchy and paternalism lead to extreme overlap and duplication among state bureaucracies. Because so many people need to be involved in any decision, it is difficult for government to implement grassroots development policies in cooperation with GROs, even though GROs such as irrigators associations have functioned for centuries (Rigg 1991, 202). Government behavior may also be a reaction against the predominance of patron-client relationships. In Senegal during the early 1980s, the government began using GRSOs to increase its access to rural areas and to reduce the power of the Marabouts, or Islamic brotherhoods. Ironically, because this also threatened NGO autonomy, a GRSO network led a long and complicated legal fight to forestall government intervention, thus creating an NGO-Marabout alliance (Anheier and Romo 1992, 17).

DEGREE OF STATE CAPACITY   Although the phrases used to describe a low degree of governmental capacity vary from Myrdahl's "soft state" to a contrast drawn between the "rigidity" of governments and the flexibility of NGOs (Ahmed 1994, 171), most observers would agree with Thomas-Slayter (1994, 1484) that "[in Africa] there is not yet a developmental state." Indeed, Diaz-Albertini's (1993b, 321) description of Peru could arguably apply to a majority of, if not to all, Third World governments:

The weakness of the Peruvian state is due to the lack of not only resources, but also institutionalization. This condition implies, among other things, an authority structure with low legitimacy, that the functions of control and supervision are inefficient or corrupt, that obtaining resources is mired in incoherent taxation and enforcement measures, and that the linkages or challenges from government to the rest of society are based on informal, personal, or clientele criteria. Without clear and relatively static rules of the game, dealing with the Peruvian state becomes a very frustrating experience because it does not constitute an effective agent with which to negotiate, bargain and reach agreements.

The main impact of this political condition may be that NGOs can influence policy but not ensure policy implementation. A second impact is that it is difficult for governments to develop consistent, coherent policies toward NGOs. Third, weak institutionalization helps explain why governments are often schizophrenic in their treatment of NGOs. Fourth, the lack of local implementation capability may encourage the growth of GRSOs, as discussed later.

DEGREE OF STABILITY   Under conditions of civil war or ethnic conflict, governments tend to become increasingly suspicious of even the relief activities of NGOs. For example, during the civil war in Ethiopia, the government was hostile to the presence of the Eritrean Relief Association in conflict areas (Fowler 1991, 57). Governmental mistrust accompanies even lesser degrees of instability if GRSOs are organizing people at the grassroots level (Fowler 1991, 59–60).

These pressures are accentuated by the environmental crisis in the Third World. As population growth undermines access to resources through patronage, and NGOs step in with foreign financial support and growing effectiveness, official accusations of impropriety may actually increase. A common charge against NGOs in Africa, for example, is that they misuse duty-free imports (Fowler 1991, 60–5).

A change of regime, however, even if not the result of democratic processes, "can rapidly open the political space necessary for human rights NGOs to press their agenda on a national basis" (Welch 1995, 311).

The Political Context: Indirect Impact on NGO Proliferation

In addition to having an impact on policies toward NGOs, political context affects NGO proliferation, which can, in turn, impact government policies and alter political contexts. There is, for example, considerable evidence linking the GRO and GRSO growth curve to pluralism and "political space," if not to full-fledged democracy. NGOs of all types flourish in democratic countries such as Costa Rica, and also in partially democratic countries such as the Philippines and Senegal. In the Middle East, Kandil (1994, 127) contends that NGOs tend to proliferate more rapidly in countries undergoing democratization, such as Egypt, Lebanon, Jordan, Tunisia, Morocco, and Yemen.[41] Under conservative, authoritarian Arab regimes, most voluntary organizations are traditional charities, not NGOs.

I have argued that authoritarian regimes able to implement basic-needs policies on a local level may indirectly encourage local demand making and grassroots organizing. When local implementation capability is combined with even a degree of pluralism, however, GRO proliferation may be more dramatic. Sheldon Annis argues that GROs tend to be most numerous and important in strong Latin American states such as Costa Rica and Mexico:[42]

Inevitably they emphasize their separateness, their political independence, their *non*-governmental character. Yet in practice, [GROs] tend to be most numerous and most important where the state is strong; and generally, the larger, more democratic, better organized, and more prosperous the public sector, the greater are the incentives for the poor to barter for concessions or to "co-produce" with the state. (1987, 131)

Often, as mentioned earlier in the discussion about basic needs, the connection between governmental reach and the growth of GROs may be unintentional. When the Zimbabwean government prohibited small agricultural plots near riverbanks to prevent soil erosion, women merged their plots and organized themselves into farmer groups. The Harambee movement promoted by the Kenyan government was not designed to bring about the democratic control of development, yet it encouraged a feeling of self-reliance and helped stimulate a vast increase in the number of women's GROs (Wanyande 1987, 95).

GRSO proliferation, in contrast, seems to be inversely related to governmental capacity to implement local development.[43] Dictatorial regimes with a strong ability to deliver services and control rural areas obviously make it hard for GRSOs to emerge at all, much less proliferate. This applies not only to Marxist regimes such as China, Vietnam, and Cuba but also to Taiwan and South Korea during the 1970s and early 1980s (Fisher 1993, 78).[44] Even in less rigidly authoritarian contexts, such as Mexico, "the high degree of state social spending and the omnipresent role of the state is one key factor in explaining the relative political underdevelopment of [GRSOs]" (Fox and Hernandez 1992, 189). Similarly, although the Allende regime in Chile (1970–73) promoted many neighborhood committees, there was little growth in the number of GRSOs during this period (Schuurman and Heer 1992, 47).[45] And in Tanzania, state dominance of a basic-needs approach to development inhibited the development of GRSOs, although women's groups were common at the local level.

Not surprisingly, therefore, GRSOs tend to proliferate under both repressive and less repressive regimes that lack local implementation capability. In moderately repressive contexts, there are always unmet needs, particularly in rural areas. Once the Tanzanian government retreated from its heavy socioeconomic role, GRSOs multiplied rapidly, along with GROs such as rotating credit associations and business groups (Tripp 1994, 122).

In more repressive contexts, GRSOs may provide the only safe political space within which to oppose a regime (Fisher 1993, 77–8; Levy 1996, 135). During the 1970s, GRSOs proliferated rapidly under a traditional dictatorship in Paraguay, a series of military regimes in Bolivia, and a strong dictatorship in Indonesia that was unable to control and implement policy in its far-flung territory.[46] In South Africa, despite the Group Areas Act, the state of emergency, and repressive attempts by the government to co-opt the black majority, there was room for NGOs of all types to grow and flourish (Walters 1993, 3). In Chile, both GROs and GRSOs exploded in numbers during the Pinochet dictatorship (1973–90), because of the devastating economic impact of the regime's policies on the poor (Schuurman and Heer 1992, 49).[47] And Levy (1996, 55) found that the advent of military regimes in Latin America had led to "a massive migration of social researchers from the public sector to the non-profit sector."[48]

Although organizing GRSOs may be one of the few possible political acts available under repressive regimes, GRSO organizing also accelerates with the overthrow of dictators (Levy 1996, 64). In the Philippines, militant students who had gone underground in the 1970s reemerged and began organizing GRSOs after the Marcos regime was overthrown. Returning exiles organized hundreds of GRSOs in Brazil during the 1970s. In Uruguay, half of the ninety-two GRSOs listed in a directory were organized between 1984 and 1986, after the end of the military dictatorship (Fisher 1993, 78). Bolivia's return to democracy in 1982 "helped create a national political and social context that opened opportunities for popular participation by the indigenous rural majority" (Healy 1996, 261). And in Nepal, NGOs proliferated after the new democratic regime lifted the requirement that NGOs submit a police report when they registered (Canadian Centre for International Studies and Cooperation 1992, 32).

In summary, the generally positive relationship between pluralism and the proliferation of NGOs is only part of the story. Indeed, GROs can flourish under authoritarian regimes with the ability to implement basic needs at the local level, as well as under more democratic regimes of all types. GRSO proliferation, however, provides evidence supporting Estelle James's (1987) argument that nonprofit organizations flourish when excess demand is *not* met by government, whether the government is democratic or dictatorial. In other words, GRSOs proliferate *except* under regimes that are both dictatorial and have considerable capacity to reach down and implement policy in local areas. It may be that they also develop more slowly in semiauthoritarian regimes with strong local implementation capability.

Of course, none of this is meant to overshadow the more obvious related factors fueling the rapid proliferation of GRSOs that began in the 1970s: the increased availability of international funding and a high level of unemployment among educated professionals (see Fisher 1993, chap. 4). But the inability of most regimes to raise living standards in local areas and the continued depletion of productive and natural resources by power elites set the political stage for the entrance of increasing numbers of NGOs.

There are also other factors that may be associated with the growth of the independent sector, including country size, general level of development, and religious heterogeneity (James 1987). The strength of the dominant religion, however, may have a widely differing impact. One observer credits religion for the "survival of pluralism" in Nicaragua (Lernoux 1984, 26). A majority of INGO and GRSO employees surveyed in Zaire said that church ties provided protection and enhanced positive government attitudes toward NGOs (Renard 1987, 28). In contrast, the dominance of Islamic culture in the Middle East has tended to inhibit the formation of an autonomous independent sector.

Bureaucratic Reform

Many discussions of bureaucracy in the Third World could have been written about bureaucracies anywhere. For example, Riggs (1964) argued that Third World budgets "reflect substantively not the relative priority of program needs so much as the relative power position of bureaucratic elites." More recently, another observer noted, "Bureaucratic culture teaches officials to resist and overcome autonomous behavior through recourse to professional standards and myths" (Calavan 1984, 215).

What, therefore, distinguishes the typical Third World bureaucracy from its cousin in the First World? First of all, the narrow political monopolies described by Organski still dominate many regimes and often promote the "premature or too rapid expansion of the bureaucracy," even as they inhibit the development of broad-based political representation (Riggs 1964). Without legitimacy or a sense of shared values between state and society, government bureaucracies become employment factories for the middle and upper classes, while perpetuating a lack of accountability to the vast majority of citizens who are poor. As a study of ministries and parastatal agencies in southern Africa concluded some years ago:

> Activities addressed to the external environment, including citizen clients, were not very frequently on the agenda of action, even when essentially managerial features were included in the count, like streamlining services, negotiating for additional resources, or bending rules in order to get something done. . . . [The greatest surprise in the study was the] infrequent appearance of episodes directly involving the public. . . . [The] current hopes that development will take place through the unleashing of citizen energy in Africa will thrive only if managerial behavior changes. (Montgomery 1987, 347, 350, 358)[49]

Sometimes, however, organizational behavior can change. For example, the Brazilian bureaucratic reform, initiated in 1979, surveyed points of contact with citizens and eliminated a great deal of paperwork, based on a presumption of honesty. By 1984, 600 million documents had been eliminated, at an estimated savings of $3 billion a year, or 1.5 percent of the Brazilian gross domestic product (World Bank 1984, 73).

Although international assistance to enhance the planning and implementation capacities of bureaucracies has been available since the early 1970s, a growing international consensus about the need for grassroots participation in development has probably had a stronger impact.[50] Beginning in the 1970s, publications such as the Food and Agriculture Organization's *Ideas and Action*, which strongly espoused this point of view, were widely circulated among individual professionals in Third World governments.[51] Northern NGOs such as Save the Children and a few official donors carried this approach into their own projects. By the early 1980s, UNICEF was encouraging municipal governments in Lima and Rio to provide social services through neighborhood associations. These new attitudes were also promoted by many of the South-South NGO networks.

To be sure, early experiments between governments and GROs were often disappointing. In Zambia, for instance, the Department of Cooperative Societies was provided with ample government resources to assist local cooperatives along with pressure to produce immediate results. The easiest response for the new appointees was to distribute cash rather than services. The political director of the department interpreted field reports detailing the complexities of assisting cooperatives as delaying tactics and staff feedback was belittled. Once cooperative policy lost its unique popularity and political priority, policies improved but earlier errors could not be overcome (Quick 1980, 40–63). Moreover, given the strength of the vested interests within bureaucracies, reforms related to improving development administration usually have little impact on results. Even uniform procedures that enhance predictability may lead to unforeseen side effects. For example, promoting firewood plantations everywhere may mean that grazing land will decline or surrounding forests will be further degraded (Romm 1986).

Paralleling the long roster of administrative changes that did little to alter relationships with the grassroots in the 1970s and early 1980s were a few pioneering efforts that succeeded in linking up with GROs and GRSOs and building on their strengths. By the early 1970s, those arguing that the organizational resources and ingenuity of urban squatters should be utilized by governments began to get a hearing. "Sites and services" projects that depended on the continuing willingness of squatters to build their own housing became more common and were often financed by international lenders such as the World Bank. Although "sites and services" sometimes became a slogan that allowed governments to ignore squatter settlements, many government housing officials had already learned through hard experience that ignoring or uprooting squatters was more politically dangerous than using neighborhood improvement associations to help upgrade neighborhoods (Skinner 1983).

Other pioneering efforts were initiated by GRSOs with particular sectoral agendas. In Thailand, the Community Based Family Planning Service succeeded in getting the Ministry of Health heavily enmeshed in a primary health care project that served more than one-fourth of the national population by 1980 (Coombs 1980a). Another Asian pioneer in linkages with government was the Social Work Research Center (SWRC), founded in Rajasthan in 1972 by a group of young university graduates; by 1980, it had established a network with both governmental and other nongovernmental organizations, resulting in a direct impact on 20,000 people (Kale and Coombs 1980, 291).

Bureaucratic reforms based on support for autonomous GROs have continued to replace top-down development management in some countries since the early 1980s. Although it is not easy to evaluate either the thoroughness or the results of such reforms, a few governments previously noted for excessive centralization have recast large development bureaucracies or even groups of bureaucracies, as in the Philippine governmental reform of 1986 (see Box 2.3). Both the Saemaul Undong village approach in South Korea and the Panamanian Ministry of Health's use of village health committees show that firm ministerial leadership can promote community management (La Forgia 1985). These reforms are often reinforced by incentives to strengthen staff accountability.[52] Although such reforms may still be mainly rhetorical in some countries, they do represent an important challenge to traditional bureaucratic culture. In India, it is now official government policy to encourage GRSOs to organize the poor in order to make bureaucracies more responsive (Qureshi 1988, 3).

These examples also suggest that it is easier to transform rhetoric into reality within smaller agencies or sections of ministries. Such reforms have been actively, if indirectly, promoted by the Asian Institute of Management in the Philippines, the Instituto Centroamericano de Administracion de Empresas (INCAE) in Central America, the Indian Institute of Management at Ahmedabad, the Instituto de Estudios Superiores de Administracion, and the Population and Social Development Center (CIDES) in Caracas. All these organizations train professionals from several countries. INCAE, for example, holds public management and policy seminars for government decision makers from throughout Central America (Korten and Alfonso 1983, 241–3).

Although most of these management institutes began by working with for-profit businesses, their distinctive role in working with development bureaucracies is to emphasize a learning process based on real develop-

---

Box 2.3 Governmentwide Reform in the Philippines

In 1986, the Presidential Commission on Government Reorganization launched a sweeping reform of the Philippine bureaucracy. In addition to removing Marcos loyalists, tens of thousands of other government employees were fired, often indiscriminately. "This reorganization, however, also promoted privatization, decentralization and community self-reliance, and as its powers and functions were whittled away, the bureacracy established new relationships with local government units, the private sector, and the NGO . . . community. . . . In many cases the establishment of NGO desks represented tokenistic commitment to democratization and 'popular empowerment,' but in others, links with NGOs represent an attempt to overcome strategic restraints on state capacity and to promote public policy reform." (*Source:* Clarke 1995, 79–80.)

---

ment experience at the grassroots level. Although their managerial techniques and approaches may differ, management institutes share a common outlook on administrative reform: delivery of services improves with the increasing clout of those who are to receive them. "In short, the professional's role is to *bring about participation*" (Bryant and White 1980, 8).

One major example of this approach in the Philippines was the Asian Institute of Management's work tying the National Irrigation Administration (NIA) to the local irrigators associations in order to prepare farmers to speak independently and assert their needs (Alfonso 1983, 52). As a result, the NIA was able to turn irrigation projects over to local communities. Although the extra initial investment of the participatory approach was $25 per hectare, a conservatively estimated community contribution of $12 dollars per hectare per year meant that the new approach paid for itself in two years (Bagadion and Korten 1985, 79). In contrast, the NIA found that there were many problems with nonparticipatory "control" projects. Whereas NIA officials were invited to village celebrations in pilot areas, relationships were often acrimonious in other regions.

The top-down promotion of bottom-up autonomy was also linked to bureaucratic reform in the Gal Oya irrigation project in Sri Lanka. Based on the NIA model in the Philippines and on the Small Farmer Development Program in Nepal, Cornell University helped link the government's Agrarian Research and Training Institute to water users associations. Unemployed university graduates with farm backgrounds used a problem-solving approach to create a demand for organization rather than organizing the associations themselves or creating a demand for services. Through rehabilitation of existing canals, 1,000 acres left fallow during the dry season were brought under cultivation. The associations started monthly meetings with officials in 1981, ahead of schedule. By 1984, after 2,500 farmers had met with the minister of agriculture, the Sri Lankan government agreed to get legal recognition for the water users associations.

> With farmers meeting more of their own needs, these officials were able to make more effective and equitable use of their limited resources, and this in turn stimulated further farmer initiative. Thus we observed an interactive process between farmers and engineers where a positive change in one group stimulated reciprocating change in the other. (Uphoff 1986a, 213–4; see also Uphoff 1993)

Where no GROs exist in a local area, however, there is a risk that agency organizers "become little more than representatives of the engineers" (F. Korten 1983, 191). One solution to this dilemma would be to work with GRSOs that organize local groups. Another solution, proposed by an Indonesian observer, would be for governments to create local "micro-information environments" to enhance cooperation with villagers using decentralized radio and citizen-band systems (Soedjatmoko 1986). Still another method would be to re-train government employees, whether or not local organizations exist. For example, the Philippine government's earlier "village immersion program" that required civil servants to spend time in villages probably influenced individuals within the NIA (Hernando 1982). What Calavan (1984) calls "generic and a-hierarchical" skills can be cultivated in a wide variety of local settings where government employees are working. These include group processes such as self-analysis, group discussions, and goal and task definition that challenge both trainers and trainees.

Government officials in key positions, with access to computer technology, can also exert considerable leverage against bureaucratic inertia and local power monopolies, even when they are unable to challenge national power elites. As Satyen Gangaram Pitroda, a former technology adviser to Prime Minister Rajiv Gandhi, explained:

> It took us one year to get a list of names of waterless villages from the system. Nobody wants to give you names because information is power, and information also brings about accountability. As soon as you share information you pinpoint accountability. . . . As soon as you computerize you break the power of the village *patwaris*. . . . They write the documents so that no one else can read them. They have power over the village because they own all the documents. One day, our computers will open that whole system. (Crossette 1989, 4)

Another source of internal bureaucratic reform, which may become increasingly common in the future, is the pressure that change-oriented bureaucracies can exert on more traditionally oriented ministries. In

Zimbabwe, for example, the Ministry for Cooperative and Community Development and Women's Affairs serves as the liaison between women's GROs and the other ministries. As a result, the Ministry of Natural Resources sponsored a tree-planting competition among women's groups, and the Ministry of Energy has worked with groups on fuel-efficient cook stoves (Williams 1989b). Still, pressure from below may also be essential. Ruth Bemela-Engo, the former minister of women's affairs in the Cameroon, argues that efforts to work with other ministries and increase awareness of women's problems must be accompanied by organized groups of grassroots women who have become "difficult citizens."[53]

Despite such scattered innovations, the reform of one bureaucracy, "especially when limited to the actions of line ministries, may not truly reflect regime change and may still be open to contradictions by other parts of the regime."[54] Moreover, most bureaucracies are unlikely to undertake internal reform on their own. As Klinmahorm and Ireland (1992, 61) point out, "bureaucrats don't need to act to resist, they just need to continue their usual behavior." A Brazilian NGO explicitly recognizes this in targeting its training and technical assistance toward the few "democratically responsive managers" (Reilly 1989, 18). What *is* more common, as described in Chapters 4 and 5, is for bureaucracies to begin to change in response to repeated contacts with NGOs working on every conceivable issue related to development.

This chapter has focused on the governmental side of the government–NGO relationship. Government policies toward NGOs range from total repression to active collaboration and interactive learning. However, governments are not seamless webs, and they increasingly reflect the complexities of the societies they rule. With democratization, repression is perhaps more likely to be confined to particular ministries that may be in conflict with other ministries actively collaborating with NGOs. Governments are less and less likely to be able to ignore the rapid proliferation of GROs and GRSOs, even though some governments will develop clever strategies for co-opting NGOs rather than being forced to question their own elitist or self-serving behavior.

African GRSOs, originally ignored by governments, have more recently been viewed as threatening to the existing order. One result is that some are assuming an advocacy role similar to that of their counterparts in Latin America. Although Asian governments are more likely to pursue collaborative policies with NGOs, they are also more likely to include suspicious security ministries that are out of sync with mainline ministries focusing on development.

Although the impact of political culture on NGO–government relationships appears to be highly idiosyncratic, and governmental incapacity generally affects implementation rather than policy, political instability generally increases governmental mistrust of NGOs. Democratic regimes are less likely than dictatorships to repress NGOs, yet authoritarian regimes with basic-needs policies may also be permissive, particularly toward GROs, and may encourage GRO proliferation. GRSOs proliferate under democratic regimes but tend to be inhibited under authoritarian regimes with a strong reach in local areas. Both GROs and GRSOs tend to proliferate where governments have little impact on what happens in local areas, be they dictatorial or democratic.

Management reform within Third World governments could accelerate positive changes in policies toward NGOs. Despite considerable promise, however, the inclusion of participatory methodology within government bureaucracies almost certainly requires long-term intensive intervention with a high ratio of costs to benefits.

Collaboration between NGOs and governments, addressed in Chapter 4, may produce some of the same results at lower costs, particularly if it grows out of the comparative advantages of both sides. Third World NGOs may have many comparative advantages over governments, including lower costs, strong grassroots ties, participatory and managerial experience, and technical expertise. Yet although the comparative advantages of Third World governments are not often actualized, it would be difficult for NGOs to implement a tax or land reform or devise intelligent macroeconomic policies, even though these may be crucial to long-term sustainable development. Unfortunately, with the possible exception of Chile, there are few, if any, examples of government initiatives that build strategic development plans around what has worked for NGOs or that try to piece together the comparative advantages of governments and NGOs in local areas.

Yet de facto piecemeal collaboration is becoming more common, as I demonstrate in the next three chapters. Although governments have not yet even taken notice, much less advantage, of this worldwide phenomenon, NGO impact on governments may, in the long run, lead to the scaling up of successful NGO projects or processes. *It is what happens within the independent sector, therefore, that can, at least in the long run, reshape the political contexts that prevent governments from building on and learning from the creative energies of NGOs.* The next chapter focuses on the characteristics of those NGOs that are already having an impact on national governments.

For their part, governments employ small but growing numbers of people who consciously work with NGOs to increase governmental legitimacy and promote sustainable development. They understand that to accomplish these goals, NGOs themselves must become stronger. Even though these individuals are usually in a minority within the public sector, they share similar objectives with the vast majority of those who work in the independent sector. Because both groups understand that empowerment is a win-win game, the slow, sometimes frustrating process of reforming government and government policies has already begun. How NGOs promote that process is the subject of the next three chapters.

Notes

1. El-Baz (1992, 7–8) points out, however, that in contrast to the rest of the Third World, this is generally accepted by Arab NGOs. However, Bennett (1995, 137) points out that after the war in Lebanon was over, there was considerable mutual suspicion between NGOs and the government.
2. In addition, local NGOs making a documentary about urban squatters were firebombed. However, state repression in Kenya has focused mainly on the larger, urban-based NGOs, and smaller organizations working in more remote areas are allowed to remain more autonomous (Hulme and Edwards 1997, 13).
3. See also talk given by Fasle Abed at the Interaction Forum, Danvers, Massachusetts, May 8, 1989. The situation in Bangladesh is still difficult, according to Edwards (1996, 40): "NGOs are deliberately encouraged to take on mainstream (large scale) service-provision and actively discouraged by political elites and large landowning interests from taking on a role in grassroots organisation and advocacy, if necessary by force."
4. For a historical view of NGO governmental relationships in India, see Sen 1996.
5. The Kenyan government exempted church-based NGOs from registration, since they are considered charitable organizations (see Bennett 1995, 108). Nonetheless, those involved in human rights activism may not be treated as well. See also Canadian Centre for International Studies and Cooperation (1992, 33) on Nepal.
6. The Philippine government has labeled some GRSOs as communist fronts while extending favors to others (Constantino-David 1992, 140).
7. In Tanzania, the board of the Youth and Development Foundation is filled by senior government officials (Fowler 1991, 68).
8. In Kenya, governmental promotion of *harambee*, or self-help, has been described by Barkan and Holmquist (1989, 360) as an area of "contested terrain" between co-option and the articulation of peasant interests. Initially designed to shift the burden of service provision to the peasants, *harambee* has resulted in "a greater transference of resources from the center than would have occurred had the movement never grown to its present size" (Barkan and Holmquist, 1989, 374).
9. Brian Smith, talk given at the conference on the voluntary sector overseas, Center for the Study of Philanthropy, City University of New York, April 26, 1989.
10. Included in NAFTA, however, is the Mexico-U.S. tax convention, which

provides for mutual recognition of income tax exemptions across the border. Although U.S. foundations are aware of the remaining 34 percent tax rate, this makes them somewhat more likely to support Mexican NGOs (Stevenson 1994).

11. Among these are Uganda and the Cameroon (Swartzendruber and Njovens 1993, 20).

12. A survey of forty NGO leaders collaborating with governments in five Asian countries on maternal health and family planning concluded that 14.3 million people were being reached at an annual cost of only U.S. $1.30 per person (Allison and Kak 1992, 164).

13. Yet in the case of collaboration through national agricultural research and extension, the "shadow of structural adjustment still constitutes an obstacle to closer relationships between NGOs and the state" (Farrington and Bebbington 1993, 190).

14. According to Arellano-Lopez and Petras (1994, 565), the fund accepts proposals from both NGOs and local governments. After three years of operations, 81 percent of the 551 institutions selected were NGOs, and 19 percent were governmental agencies. However, only 32 percent of the available resources have been channeled through NGOs.

15. Among the other African examples of growing positive collaboration are Mali, where "the government has been making a major effort to understand the work of NGOs" (Montague and Kabouchy Clough 1995, 26).

16. During the elections in the Dominican Republic in 1994 the PRD (Dominican Revolutionary Party) promised that if it was elected it would incorporate representatives of "civil organizations" in a "shared government" (Levitt 1996, 10).

17. Brautigam (1994, 65) points out that most NGOs favor coordinating offices over having to coordinate integrated development projects with more than one ministry.

18. Johnson (1966) called these diverse groups the "middle sectors."

19. The quoted phrase is from Diaz-Albertini 1993b.

20. See note 14.

21. Some GRSOs in Brazil have close ties to the Worker's Party, and there are some partisan GRSOs in Peru.

22. Although GRSOs are nonpartisan, they are not apolitical about the policies needed to combat poverty. Indeed, Latin American intellectuals affiliated with GRSOs have assumed a strong advocacy role. For example, Federico Velarde (1989, 66), a Peruvian GRSO leader, argues that talk about international dependency and its impact on prices is insufficient: "It is also necessary to respond to the concrete conditions in the cotton market, to the state policies relating to them and to the specifics in such a way that the *campesino* can alter his production."

23. In the past, Bangladeshi NGOs had to undergo a second registration after they registered to receive foreign funds, a third to use the funds for development projects, a fourth to release funds once a project was approved, and a fifth in subsequent years in the case of multiyear projects.

24. In Malaysia, not included in the survey, registration is still used as a repressive tool (Serrano 1994, 278).

25. This was described in *Asia Week*'s November 20, 1987, issue. Harrison

Ngau, another environmental activist arrested in 1987, was called "even more dangerous than the communists" by Sarawak's chief minister Abdul Taib Mahmud. In October 1990, however, Ngau was elected to the federal parliament (Rush 1991). And Clarke (1996, 14) points out that Malaysia's NGOs have fought back by organizing SUARAM, the country's major human rights NGO, and by achieving broad support among the middle class and the media. By the mid-1990s, government ministries were collaborating with NGOs.

26. See also Walters (1993, 6–7) for an almost identical classification.

27. This has been true in Mali and the Cameroon, for example.

28. Letter from Mike Savage, founder of an educational NGO in Kenya, to my parents, David and Frances Hawkins, October 10, 1993.

29. In Kenya, NGOs "have come to be dominated by central province (essentially Kikuyu) elites and intelligentsia. To the KANU government, these organizations . . . represent entrenched ethnic interests" (Ndegwa 1996, 116).

30. Advocacy is more often focused on development than on political reform, however, as I show in Chapter 4. Kenyan GRSOs produced a position paper on national policies needed to support their work (Fowler 1990). Ethiopian GRSOs (with international NGO support) were the first to report on the food crisis in the Sahel in 1983, when the Ethiopian government refused to admit the problem.

31. The Burkinabe government created the Bureau for Following NGOs (BSONG) to influence the geographic placement of NGOs, gain support for the government's development priorities, and collect funding data (see Schneider 1985; Sawadogo 1990, 61). Of course, new tensions inevitably developed. BSONG has been more effective in resolving conflicts with INGOs than with GRSOs. Burkinabe GRSOs, whose strong ties to local communities were forged during the droughts of 1973 and 1985, maintain that government sponsorship and planning have weakened BSONG's networking role.

32. Krasner (1985) describes this in terms of a distinction between "relational" politics and "metapolitics."

33. This is also true in Indonesia, where local governments are traditionally more democratic than national regimes.

34. See, for example, Levy's (1996) book on private research centers in Latin America, which were less threatening to military regimes than large universities, sometimes had church protection, benefited from divisions in government, and sometimes provided policy advice.

35. Clarke (1995, 90), writing about the Philippines, calls these "pockets of efficiency."

36. Human rights NGOs usually have a more difficult time. Welch (1995, 27) points out that in Nigeria, human rights NGOs can raise issues, but the military government does not respond.

37. In Chile, the Centro de Estudios Técnicos was allowed to work on natural fertilizers for squatter settlement vegetable gardens, even though the GRSO had been organized by Socialist Party members (see note 9).

38. See also Farrington and Bebbington (1993, 54–5), for a more detailed discussion of government attitudes toward the rural poor, government

presence in rural areas, and government attitudes toward NGOs.

39. For three decades, beginning with independence in 1965, the Gambia was a democracy. Yet in July 1994, a group of young military officers seized power, and the Gambia has become one of the most repressive regimes in Africa (Freedom House 1995–96, 235).

40. Welfare and charity organizations, however, have been dependent on the South African government for many years, despite apartheid, and with the end of apartheid, NGOs are moving toward closer collaboration.

41. Kandil also added Algeria, prior to the clampdown on Islamists, to this list.

42. Bratton (1983, 17) provides evidence that this may not be true in Africa, however. Grassroots farmer organizations in relatively pluralist Zimbabwe are more numerous and make stronger contributions to agricultural production in areas where the government presence is weak.

43. This may be less true at the beginning of basic-needs implementation. The Nepalese government policy of the late 1970s requiring university students to spend a year in a rural village was revoked because the students were becoming too politicized and critical of the government. Many of these graduates joined existing GRSOs or founded new ones; others entered the Nepalese government and began to change its policies in small but subtle ways.

44. This may be changing in Vietnam. According to Clarke (1996, 6), Vietnamese NGOs were legalized in 1991 and must adhere to the Communist Party program. However, NGOs are proliferating and "increasing their autonomy from state-controlled mass organisations to which they are loosely affiliated, emboldened by state policy of *Doi Moi* (Renovation)."

45. Under President Eduardo Frei (1964–70), a few NGOs with international contacts had developed.

46. Indonesian NGOs often provide political cover, even though many of them nominally support the officially sanctioned image of the self-sufficient village (see Holloway 1989c, 155). Despite the political caution of Indonesian NGOs, Holloway points out that government officials tend to believe that NGOs split off the people from the government, encourage religious extremism, and expose government mistakes.

47. Research institutes with grassroots support capabilities were also organized by academics who had been removed from the universities by the regime.

48. Levy's (1996) book deals with private research centers, which often deal with humanitarian or development issues and sometimes have grassroots support capabilities.

49. The study was undertaken by the nine countries that are members of SADACC, the Southern Africa Development Coordinating Conference (Angola, Botswana, Lesotho, Malawi, Mozambique, Swaziland, Tanzania, Zambia, and Zimbabwe). As a way of identifying skills needed in the region, the study gathered reports of 1,868 separate management events that displayed either effective or ineffective administrative behavior.

50. One early participatory development experience that influenced international opinion was the Etawah project in Uttar Pradesh initiated by Albert Mayer during the early 1950s. It was based on village workers trained in technical agricultural skills and democratic decision making. It was also

designed to loosen bureaucratic structures, which Mayer termed "up-down watertight compartments," by including government workers in project implementation. Unfortunately, the Etawah model, like so many pilot projects, did not survive wider replication into a statewide program (Alliband 1983, 39).

51. *Ideas and Action* is, unfortunately, no longer published, because of funding constraints.

52. See Korten 1986a on "community management." See also Uphoff 1986b, 230.

53. Speech at the Association for Women in Development, Washington, D.C., April 1987. The ministry is encouraging and promoting GROs such as rotating credit societies.

54. I am indebted to the anonymous first reader of this chapter for this quote.

3

The Impact of NGOs on Governments: The Role of NGO Autonomy

■ In dealing with government, it is . . . important to make sure that you participate on your own terms. This means you do not access money from government, nor do you sit down in meetings, just to be co-opted. . . . You must be able to enter as an NGO into relationships where you can participate in the conceptualization and onward to the implementation of every project.

—Philippine NGO leader

■ We do not define our projects in terms of services the government offers, but rather in relation to the processes that must be encouraged.

—Centro de Estudios Para el Desarrollo
y la Participacion (CEDEP), Peru

■ The single most important advantage of Christian Church [NGOs] in Africa today is their independence from local and regional politics . . . [although they] have superb government contacts.

—Karen Jenkins (1994, 91, 93)

SUSTAINABLE DEVELOPMENT ACHIEVED through grassroots participation is a remarkably widespread NGO goal, promoted more or less successfully on the local level by hundreds of thousands of grassroots organizations (GROs) and tens of thousands of grassroots support organizations (GRSOs). One of the conclusions of *The Road from Rio* was that nongovernmental organizations (NGOs) are also beginning to "scale out" through networking at both the GRO and GRSO levels. Yet in attempting to also "scale up" politically through advocacy and/or collaboration with governments on issues as diverse as deforestation, collaborative support for family planning clinics, or tax relief for contributors, NGOs face formidable political barriers. African GRSOs, for example, are often able to extract resources from government programs but are not yet able to have a voice in government policy, much less to become empowered on a national level (Bratton 1989, 13).[1] In repressive contexts, even "claim making" may be difficult.

Given the complexity of their agenda, it is remarkable that NGOs are able to achieve anything at all. In most countries, as noted in Chapter 2, NGOs confront the "soft" or "weakly institutionalized" state (Myrdahl 1970; Diaz-Albertini 1993b, 317). Even though weak states allow fledgling NGOs to create political space, established GRSOs must simultaneously "strengthen civil society via grassroots empowerment and . . . ensure the viability for the state as an apparatus capable of processing political demands and claims in a more or less democratic fashion" (Diaz-Albertini 1993b, 317).[2] It takes great ingenuity to avoid some of the trade-offs involved in maintaining grassroots ties, strengthening ties to the state, and building up NGO advocacy functions. A survey of ninety-five Kenyan, Ugandan, and Tanzanian GRSOs, for example, revealed that many of them were drafting politicians to serve on their boards, both to gain access to government information and to provide protection from government repression (Gariyo 1996, 163).

Nonetheless, NGO success in influencing government policy, although not the norm, is increasingly common. And the key factor associated with the political clout of NGOs appears to be organizational autonomy. Despite the varying political contexts faced by GROs and GRSOs and their networks, organizations that strengthen their own identities and autonomy *before* seeking to influence policy makers are likely to have greater latitude in initiating their own political strategies or in responding to government policies within a wide range of political contexts.[3]

Autonomous NGOs are also better able than less autonomous organizations to *further* strengthen both autonomy and policy impact once interactions with governments have been initiated. Since policy change may be ephemeral or merely rhetorical, this is a crucial long-term role, albeit more difficult than advocacy on an immediate issue. For example, an environmental NGO in Lima organized a lawyers network to define an ecological belt around the city; yet soon after the code was enacted, the executive annulled parts of it and failed to inform local law-enforcement officials about the surviving provisions of the law (Diaz-Albertini 1993b, 326).

Precisely because some organizations are far more autonomous than others, overall characterizations of independent–public sector relationships should be treated with caution, even within one country. Some observers, for example, have characterized relationships between Indian GRSOs and the government as dependent; yet as long ago as 1983, a field study found all degrees of dependence and independence in twenty organizations surveyed in the field.[4] African family planning organizations tend to be dependent on government policies and attitudes, yet the Association for Family Welfare of Guinea, which is partially self-supporting through the sale of contraceptives, has been invited to assist in the implementation of the government health program because of its innovative approaches.

This chapter first focuses on the relationship of autonomy to accountability and then on the attributes and activities of NGOs that are likely to strengthen autonomy.

Autonomy and Accountability

The term *accountability* has many meanings. There is a difference, for example, between accountability to grassroots constituents, accountability to donors for resource use, and "strategic accountability" for outcomes that NGOs have on the wider environment (Edwards and Hulme 1996b, 8; see also Najam 1996a). It might appear, therefore, that the more successful NGOs are in achieving multiple accountability, the less autonomous they become. Yet more areas of accountability may also provide them with greater room to maneuver (Biggs and Neame 1996, 48–9). This is particularly true if GRSOs and GROs rank downward accountability to the grassroots ahead of other forms of accountability. Although "most NGOs may be neither advocates of grassroots justice, nor, if failing on that standard, opportunistic pretenders," there is "clearly a level at which the absence of accountability [to the grassroots] begins to make the likelihood of ineffective or illegitimate actions by an organization much more probable" (Meyer 1995, 1287; Edwards and Hulme 1996b, 8).

Fortunately, in Asia and Latin America, there are thousands of GRSOs that have grown out of ties that young dissidents had established with GROs. And even in Africa, where GRSOs emerged more recently in response to the availability of foreign funding, grassroots accountability and a base of support are "within reach" (Swartzendruber and Njovens 1993, 16).

Organizational autonomy, defined as "the freedom to make decisions with the optimal degree of discretion," has an interesting twist in the Third World context related to accountability (Kramer 1981, 288). GROs need to be accountable to, rather than autonomous from, their members, even as they develop autonomous relationships with GRSOs that permit technical and financial support to continue. By the same token, a GRSO's autonomy from GROs would mean that the GRSO was not accountable, and therefore not doing its job. Networks also need to be accountable to their member organizations while preserving their autonomy from donors and governments. The meaning of autonomy, therefore, should be confined to what might be called upward relationships. GROs and GRO networks should be autonomous from GRSOs, donors, and governments; GRSOs and their networks should be autonomous from governments and donors.

Seven Keys to Autonomy

What factors are tied to organizational autonomy? First is a clear, self-conscious organizational commmitment to autonomy. A second key to automomy is diversified financial support that enables NGOs to be independent of any single donor, including the government. A third, even more important factor is strong grassroots ties. Although financial diversification and grassroots ties may be more difficult to achieve in a repressive political context than under a democratic system, they may enable an NGO to survive until a more responsive government emerges.[5]

GRSO autonomy is also enhanced by three related kinds of knowledge —technical expertise, managerial excellence, and strategic knowledge about development, which is needed for a successful demonstration project. These capacities are most likely to emerge in less repressive contexts, where collaboration is viewed as a positive opportunity for influencing government policy. Finally, the seventh key to autonomy is staff experience in training government professionals, which enhances the self-confidence and autonomy of GRSOs while propelling them toward continuing active contacts with governments.[6]

Organizational Commitment

First and foremost, NGOs need a clear, self-conscious organizational commitment to autonomy.[7] Somewhat surprisingly, this commitment often increases as contacts with governments become more common. According to Sanyal (1991, 1375), Bangladeshi NGOs take advantage of being different from local and national government, yet "do not usually miss any opportunities to work with the government." In Brazil, NGO contacts with the state have been multiplying, and "in this context the NGOs have raised the banner of autonomy more visibly" (Landim 1988b, 45). In Mexico, post-1968 grassroots movements have been far less willing than previous popular movements to accept incorporation into official structures, even though interactions with the state are frequent; according to Rubin (1990, 262), "What is different is the priority placed on continuing autonomy." In Peru as well, NGOs collaborating with the government have, according to most observers, maintained their values (Diaz-Albertini 1993b, 335).

Consciously dealing with the issue of autonomy may also have an impact on NGO relationships with political parties. In discussing whether North African human rights NGOs should or should not develop partisan linkages, Waltz (1995, 166) concludes that "no single path is optimal. What does seem clear is that the stronger groups have wrestled with these issues, and it is the failure to address them rather than a particular resolution that most threatens a group."

Financial Diversification

The most difficult task in strengthening autonomy may be to diversify financial support. Although raising private money domestically probably has the strongest positive impact on autonomy, in most Third World countries, philanthropic traditions are weak, domestic fund-raising is still in its infancy, and there have been few attempts by GRSOs and their networks to lobby for changes in tax policy that would favor individual donations (Fisher 1993, 175). A Philippine observer argues that although 10 to 15 percent of the population are potential contributors who would support broader goals such as agrarian reform, "the NGO community is still moving within the circle of the converted" (Liamzon 1990, 1–2).[8]

To be sure, traditional charitable institutions that are supportive of domestic philanthropy are reaching out to NGOs in some countries. For example, the Jordan General Union of Voluntary Societies represents 630 GRSOs and other charitable organizations, runs the national lottery, and raises up to $30 million a year (Tandon 1989a, 17). However, some umbrella funders are themselves vulnerable to political manipulation. This occurred in Chile, where the Fondo de Solidaridad e Inversion Social (FOSIS), organized with money from the Copper Fund, was emptied prematurely by the Pinochet regime to pay off the country's foreign debt; it now has to be financed through taxes or foreign money.[9]

Financial support from foreign donors initially enhances autonomy in relation to governments, allows GRSOs to exert political pressure, and helps them retain independence when governments want to hire them as subcontractors. Yet foreign ties, particularly to a single donor, can also lead to dependent rather than influential relationships with governments. In Kenya, for example, Voluntary Agencies Development Assistance (VADA) was too closely tied to both the U.S. Agency for International Development (USAID) and the Kenyan government. As a consortium, VADA undercut its own organizing ability by accepting USAID's goals rather than defining its own. The National Farmer's Association of Zimbabwe

(NFAZ) has had more influence on government than VADA did, because it had financial support from a mass base and technical assistance from the University of Zimbabwe (Bratton 1989, 23, 32).

International debt swaps, in contrast, are more likely than direct foreign assistance to empower GRSOs in relation to both governments and donors. Although some support for debt swaps comes from official donors, Northern NGOs, particularly environmental organizations, are the principal promoters of these arrangements. For example, as part of a debt swap, the Nature Conservancy helped promote the Bolivia National Environmental Trust Fund, which has both government and GRSO representatives on its board.

Federated GRO networks that charge dues or regional GRO networks that support for-profit enterprises and barter among villages have built-in sources of financing that enhance autonomy, even if these activities cover only a portion of expenses.[10] Although GRSOs that promote GRO networks from above do not have this particular advantage, a mass base of any type tends to have an independent impact on GRSO autonomy.

A Mass Base

Two types of NGO networks have mass bases—horizontal GRO networks, sometimes called "social movements," and vertical linkages between GRSOs and GROs or other mass membership organizations, such as unions or even political parties. In contrast, GRSO membership in a consortium or umbrella organization without direct grassroots ties may have little impact on autonomy.[11]

NETWORKS AND SOCIAL MOVEMENTS   Grassroots or social movements have influenced policy in the past, usually over many decades. An organized peasant movement against the feudal system in Kerala, India, for example, initiated in the mid-nineteenth century, led to decades of conflict with landlords. In 1927, reform legislation that left out the poorer peasants only reactivated peasant protest. Government response was agonizingly slow, but by 1966, almost all tenants had secured fixed tenure over their leases, thanks to the efforts of an articulate, organized labor force.[12]

Today, regional grassroots movements and networks are having a far more rapid political impact than they did in Kerala, even without the mediating role of GRSOs. Nowhere has GRO autonomy been more dramatically and effectively asserted than in the explosion of new and reorganized GROs emerging after the Mexico City earthquake in 1985 (Eckstein 1990, 287).[13] Six days after the quake, more than 100 GROs, encompassing both victims and support groups, formed a self-help network (Esteva 1986, 74). International organizations, with government backing, initially proposed that subsidized packaged food be sold in the damaged neigh-borhoods. The newly organized GRO network responded that this would severely weaken the local economy, since one-third of the low-income residents sell food. The network's counterproposal to use part of the available money to organize a direct link between peasant GROs and neighborhood food sellers was adopted with government support.

These post-earthquake organizations in Mexico City not only high-lighted the need for self-help but also exposed political favoritism and corruption. When corruption was publicized by GROs and their allies, the government began to back away from passing decrees that would have assisted mainly middle-class areas affected by the earthquake. Tenants unions were organized or revived in response to official efforts to evict tenants and replace low-income housing. Mass marches pushing for expropriation of tenements succeeded, and tenant organization plans for reconstruction were adopted when rebuilding began (Qureshi 1988, 7; Brown 1990, 17). Within one year, 48,000 new houses based on tenant plans had been constructed, with tenants charged only the monthly cost of building.

Enrique Krauze, a Mexican intellectual, declared that the disillusion-ment that stemmed from the earthquake went beyond anything in mod-ern Mexican history. Unlike previous popular reactions to unpopular policies, post-earthquake protest was not susceptible to the typical Mexican pattern of co-optation. One result of the protest was the creation of the National Forum for Effective Suffrage, composed of twenty-six organizations, including GRSOs and political parties, which agreed to push for honest voting in the 1988 elections (Levy 1987, 132–3). Although most observers would argue that they did not succeed in this purpose, it has since become increasingly difficult for the dominant PRI party to con-tinue to co-opt all challengers. Some kind of sea change in Mexican poli-tics had begun, based in part on the networking and autonomy of GROs in rural as well as urban areas.

Grassroots movements are often willing to use confrontational tactics to achieve their purposes. Land invasions, a common tactic in Latin America, have been particularly well orchestrated in Honduras. In 1987, the Honduran peasant movement demanded the replacement of the direc-tor of the National Agrarian Institute, the release of imprisoned members of their organization, and a rapid resumption of agrarian reform. Although the immediate crisis was "resolved" by the creation of a study com-mission, land invasions soon resumed to push for further steps (Millet 1987, 410).

In India as well, peasant protest is a highly refined political technol-ogy. *Pradarshan* demonstrations sometimes progress into *dharna* or sit-down strikes, and then into *gherao*, where the key figure is surrounded by protesters and heckled until he or she agrees to their demands. Among the other techniques used are the *rasta roko* (road blockade). Protesters, borrowing a page from the independence movement, may also resort to filling the jails or mass fasting (Gadgil and Guha 1994, 121).

A mass base may emerge out of the political activities of one or more isolated GROs. For example, a national fishermen's network was formed in Malaysia as a result of successful protests against a highway in one fishing area (Peng 1983, 30–2). Similarly, although migrant associations in the Sudan are uncoordinated and irregular in their political demands, they were able to replace a large irrigation scheme in Port Sudan with a project that met their needs more directly (Bratton and Baldo 1989, 148).

Individual GROs can also have a collective impact by simultaneously engaging in individual problem solving and political protest.[14] In Bogotá, for example, promoters of co-ops and housing associations were so active in 1985 that the municipality had to register them, and within sixty days the national Congress gave them official title to the land they occupied (Williams and Riofrio 1987, 179). During the Pinochet dictatorship in Chile, women in many city neighborhoods organized community kitchens to feed their families under extraordinarily acute conditions of economic hardship. But these also functioned as a spontaneous form of protest.

Grassroots networks or "social movements" that are not formally organized may also impact policy. Uncoordinated but multiple urban squatter invasions have helped shape a kind of de facto government policy in Latin America for many years.[15] In the past, some governments reacted violently and tried to displace squatters. But this reaction has gradually been replaced by an acceptance of the invasion process as a safety valve on popular discontent.[16] Squatter neighborhood improvement associations have been carrying out a wide range of demand-making activities since the 1960s. These include neighborhood petitioning, contacting individual acquaintances in government bureaucracies, building ties to opposition parties, and holding local demonstrations, such as a symbolic "funeral" for an unpopular highway in Bogotá in 1973. During the 1970s, most such political activities were competitive; in other words, squatters lobbied for improvements in their own settlements but not for changes that would benefit squatters in general. Since that time, squatter neighborhood federations have gradually become more effective at aggregating the demands of their member federations and at becoming national political players on urban issues (Fisher 1984).

More formally organized GRO networks greatly enhance the possibilities for individual GROs to become major political players. In Brazil, for example, sixty representatives of six indigenous tribes, coordinated by the Union of Indigenous Nations (UNI), lobbied for protection of their land against developers during the writing of the new constitution in

1987. As a result, indigenous land rights were written into the constitution. The votes in the constitutional convention showed that the tribes had built a great deal of support among their fellow citizens, even though the convention did not fully safeguard their land against mining interests and the repressive policies of FUNAI, the official "protector" of native Brazilians (Graham 1987; Mayberry-Lewis 1989, 4).

Even officially sponsored networks can sometimes develop autonomy and clout. The district and provincial federations of the Panamanian health committees established by the government in 1969 met twice yearly during the 1970s with the Ministry of Health and reviewed their problems before an audience including health officials. Tentative solutions were agreed upon, and informal meetings were held until all requests were dealt with. Similar problems were not addressed where there were no federations of health committees (Uphoff 1986b, 85, 300).[17] In Lima, Peru, a large squatter settlement, Villa El Salvador, received favored treatment in the 1970s under the populist military regime of Velasco Alvarado. Through its horizontally linked block organizations, it has since become prosperous, providing considerable social services to its population.[18]

Whatever its origins, grassroots organizing to influence governments is growing on a global scale and frequently focuses on a mix of environmental and resource issues.[19] In Mindanao, for example, unproductive state lands have been taken back by dispossessed tribal people (Colchester 1994, 88). Massive environmental movements in India, Malaysia, the Philippines, Kenya, Brazil, Ecuador, and several Central American countries are based on lower-class constituencies or indigenous peoples.[20]

- Having lost much of their forests, Himalayan peasants also faced the loss of their water. The Narmada dam proposal led to huge protests over many years that garnered international support. In 1993 the World Bank pulled out of the project. As of 1994, plans for the Vishnuprayag Dam had been indefinitely shelved because of pressure from the Chipko movement (Gadgil and Guha 1994, 111).

- Mass protests against limestone quarrying in India's Doon Valley were joined by hotel owners who were worried about the detrimental impact of quarrying on tourism. In 1989, a landmark Supreme Court decision recommended closure of all but six limestone mines. In Kumaun, where women have been particularly active against unregulated mining, several mines have been forced to close, and villagers are working on reclamation through reforestation (Gadgil and Guha 1994, 115–6).

- In the Philippines, opposition to the Chico dams and the Cellophil Corporation in the Cordillera has been organized over a wide area through the revival of the *bodong*, or peace pact. Hundreds of local GROs have joined a coalition that also focuses on land use, education, economic development, health, and women's rights (Colchester 1994, 85).

■ The Confederación de Nacionalidades Indígenas del Ecuador (CONAIE) represents all the native people, from the Shuar of the Amazon rain forest to the highland Quichua. In 1992, CONAIE organized a march of thousands to Quito to protest deforestation. Well-versed in law, some activists negotiated with the government while others camped in public parks. A month later, then President Rodrigo Borja granted 148 indigenous communities legal title to three million acres in the Pastaza, "the last intact parcel of the Oriente and one of the world's richest zones of biodiversity."[21]

■ Indigenous peoples in Central America are lobbying for land. In Honduras, Tawahka Sumu, which works with other tribal federations and a GRSO called MOPOWI, has been granted a biosphere reserve by presidential decree along the Patuca River. The indigenous peoples of El Salvador have also been campaigning, with some success, for communal lands through the national agrarian reform program. In Nicaragua, MIKUPIA is pushing for an indigenous-managed reserve for the entire Miskito Cays area. The Kekchi and Mopan Maya of Belize are campaigning for a homeland of 200,000 acres in their traditional territory. And in Panama, the Embera, Kuna, and Wounaan have had partial success in negotiating with the government to establish semiautonomous homelands (Chapin 1992, 8).

■ The Association of Peasants in Central America (ASOCORE), comprising seven national farmers organizations with memberships between 15,000 and 50,000, is working hard to influence the regional strategic planning process of governments (Uvin and Miller 1994).

To be sure, not all social movements or grassroots federations are environmentally benign. In Bihar, India, the Ho people have mobilized against official forestry policy and developed their own forest-cutting movement as a way of reasserting their rights, despite their own ancient traditions of using sacred groves for religious ceremonies (Colchester 1994, 83).

And achieving a powerful voice is undoubtedly easier when opponents are foreigners or when powerful domestic interests are not mobilized against grassroots movements. The All Indonesia Fishermen's Association influenced the government's decision to ban commercial trawlers in 1983, after trawlers engaged in violent conflict with small fishermen. Since the commercial trawlers were wealthy Chinese, however, the decision was easy for the government to make (Bailey 1986).

VERTICAL NETWORKS: GROs AND GRSOs Networks combining vertical and horizontal ties among GROs and GRSOs are among the most effective organizational relationships for achieving sustainable development (Fisher 1993, chap. 8). Similarly, there is evidence that GRSOs with their own mass base or strong ties to GROs have greater autonomy and policy influence than either GROs or GRSOs working alone. The National Farmer's Association of Zimbabwe (NFAZ), with over 200,000 members, persuaded the government to exempt agricultural inputs from the sales tax in 1976 and in 1978 helped repeal taxes on crop and livestock sales by small farmers (Bratton 1989). The National Farmers Association in St. Lucia was successful in getting the government to reduce duties on farm equipment and to exempt a portion of agricultural income from taxes (La Gra, Leighton, and Oechsle 1989, 115).

Yet, in a more profound sense, GRSOs with strong grassroots ties become what Ritchie-Vance (1991, 71) calls "links between people and policies." In his study of twenty-five NGOs, Uvin (1995, 936) found that "leaders that were politically well connected before they began working within community-based organizations often constitute cases of enlightened charity, while those people who, through their successful work with the poor, became a political force to be reckoned with, are rather cases of 'people's power.'" For example, women lawyers working for the Colombian Association for the Study of Population discovered a dormant provision in the law that led, after an eight-year struggle, to domestic workers being included in the social security law, with medical and dental care (Inter-American Foundation 1993). In Kenya, concessions gained from a repressive government by the NGO movement since 1990 have been facilitated by grassroots organizing.[22]

To be sure, GRSOs often face difficult potential trade-offs between increasing professionalization and grassroots ties. Diaz-Albertini (1993a, iv) found that as Peruvian GRSOs construct more complex and varied ties to other middle-class and professional groups, their grassroots strategies are increasingly challenged by competing demands, which "[limits] their potential as agents of profound social change" (339). He suggests that this trade-off can be avoided when advocacy is buttressed by an upsurge in grassroots participation, so that professionals become "organic" (355–6). This occurs, for example, when GRSOs are created from the bottom up by federations of GROs that hire their own professionals (Fisher 1993, 203–5).

By the same token, GROs and their networks benefit from ties with professional advocates that can build autonomous linkages with governments.

Indeed, it is difficult for GROs to achieve political change without allies such as GRSOs (Covey 1996, 199). Bratton (1989) has shown how an extensive, successful GRO network in Zimbabwe, the Savings and Development Movement, was actually too "bottom heavy." Over 5,000 women's savings groups had only a few professionals to represent them at the national level. Not only did they fail to influence government, but the failure to develop political support led to the virtual demise of the movement (Bratton 1989; De Graaf 1987, 293). Federated membership organizations such as the NFAZ, however, have both a popular base and "a channel for articulation of demands to the policy center." This channel includes intermediate district and provincial committees and a national organization that functions like a GRSO (Bratton 1989, 29).

GRSOs can also help GROs build ties with governments that were initially intent on creating their own local organizations. For example, in 1972, the Colombian government began to establish fishing cooperatives, ignoring the indigenous organizations of people living along the coasts and rivers. At that time, fishing communities were dependent on middlemen and were suffering from water pollution and unlawful appropriation of swamps. After a group of university students and professors founded a GRSO to sponsor regional seminars with the fishermen and help them dramatize their plight on videotape, the government finally responded. By 1980, the Ministry of Agriculture had set up the National Fisheries Commission to advise the government, with representation from fishermen. Through the Association of Colombian Artisanal Fishermen (ANPAC), regional centers were established to provide training and to organize grassroots exchanges (Rivera Franco 1986, 3–7).

Moreover, when GRSOs link GROs to international donors, both types of NGOs are better able to influence governments, as well as the donors themselves (see Box 3.1). The World Bank uses Mexican GRSOs to administer programs that were once run exclusively by the government. Because they are part of the World Bank planning process, GRSOs can take plans directly to GROs and exert immediate pressure on the government if funding is not being used properly (Marklein 1991, 13). Likewise, political pressure from international donors in Kenya has strengthened NGO and political party protests against government repression (Ndegwa 1996, 8).[23]

Although GRO–GRSO–government connections are a potentially powerful vehicle for grassroots empowerment, some of the contextual factors outlined in the previous chapter may override any positive influence on government policies. For example, in Colombia—in contrast to most other Latin American countries—GRSOs tend to adapt to a political culture in which major political parties rarely assume roles that challenge the existing distribution of power and resources. In assessing a sample of thirty-six GRSOs in Colombia, Brian Smith (1990, 248) found that they

---

Box 3.1   Saving the Rain Forest

Building a mass base can have an international political impact as well. Brazilian GRSOs working with the Catholic Church in the 1970s raised money, initiated a massive popular education process in the Amazon, collected information from the government and other sources, and shared it with GROs and the environmental movement in Europe and the United States. GRSO and GRO representatives came to the United States to get more information about Brazilian government plans and pressured the European Community and the World Bank to stop supporting them. In 1987, the World Bank stopped providing money for the government's Amazon project. By 1993, the Brazilian Forum on Environment and Development included 1,000 NGOs that successfully transmitted rubber-tapper demands and led to the official establishment of fourteen extractive reserves covering 3 million hectares—about 1 percent of the Amazon. Although the Amazon continues to burn—at an accelerating rate, according to recent newspaper accounts—awareness of its role as the commons for the planet may also be increasing. (*Sources:* Presentation by Maria Alegretti, Symposium on Shaping the Policy Debate: The Role of Non-Governmental Organizations in International Development, John F. Kennedy School of Government, Harvard University, April 22, 1993; presentation by Gabriel Camara at the Interaction Forum, Danvers, Massachusetts, May 1989.)

---

generally shunned the use of mobilized networks of the poor to challenge or even to deal with political and economic power structures, even though they were tied to GRO networks. European and Canadian donor organizations working in Colombia, in contrast, were more willing to challenge the structures of power.[24]

Despite such varied patterns, Brian Smith's (1990) prediction that the long-run impact of a mass base need not be precluded by short-term constraints is being partially fulfilled in Colombia. In 1990, a tribal network in the Amazon, with help from GRSOs, successfully lobbied the government to cede half of the remaining rain forest to the people who inhabit it.[25]

The potential long-term impact of the grassroots is also illustrated by the success of the women's movement in Brazil. In the 1970s, Brazilian feminists began building linkages to women's GROs. At first, they downplayed feminist issues in favor of such projects as small-business development. By 1980, however, the GROs themselves, including mothers clubs created by the church, were demanding attention to the issue of domestic violence, family planning information, and sex education. Sectors of the military government supported family planning, and by 1982, because of popular pressure, the Ministry of Health was outlining a new women's health program that included activist participation in planning. Among the innovations in the plan were educational practices developed by the women's movement, such as refresher courses for health professionals (Barroso 1987). Since then, what has become the National Council on Women has successfully promoted legislation on labor rights for domestic servants, paid maternity leave, and domestic violence.

GRSO NETWORKS   In contrast to GRO networks and GRSO–GRO linkages, consortia usually lack a mass base. Ties between GRSO networks and GROs are often indirect, through member organizations. This can make GRSO networks less politically influential than GRO networks or even some individual GRSOs. Although such networks sometimes mold policies that affect them directly, such as registration procedures, they do not often challenge government policies. The Nicaraguan Federation of NGOs, for example, is a forum for policy discussions but lobbies only on issues relating to the role and status of nonprofit organizations.[26]

Some GRSO networks are dominated or even organized by governments, and others spend so much time as government subcontractors that building autonomy through strengthening member cooperation is neglected. According to Stremlau (1987, 216), it is far more common for them to serve as a "forum or point of contact for a ministry than it is for them to function effectively as an advocate for NGO views on policy." Fowler (1990) observes that in Kenya, Zimbabwe, and Zambia, formal consortia are either closely identified with the government or avoid political advocacy.

Moreover, GRSO networks may actually be weakened, rather than strengthened, by their institutional ties to large donors, particularly in the absence of other factors promoting autonomy.[27] In Senegal, CONGAD worked with the United Nations Development Program (UNDP) for two years to convince the government to set up a Partners in Development Fund managed by its member NGOs. After a ministerial reshuffle, the new head of the Department of Social Development reversed the decision.

Yet the lack of GRSO networking in the Middle East is a "major handicap in the face of the strength of political elites in the Arab World," according to Marzouk (1997, 198). In contrast, by the late 1980s, some GRSO consortia in other regions were using the experience of their members in grassroots organizing as a tool to enhance autonomy and influence. By being willing to let government share the credit, they were also having an increased policy impact (Edwards and Hulme 1992a, 18).

■ In February 1988, ADAB, the GRSO consortia in Bangladesh, held a meeting of eleven major organizations that had been highly successful in organizing landless peasants. This led to the creation of forty-five regional ADAB chapters to see who was doing what in each district. ADAB pays travel expenses so that district representatives can attend monthly meetings. According to an ADAB leader, the government "wants to use us, because it is literally incapable of extending services such as livestock vaccine to these areas."[28]

- The Voluntary Health Association of India has had an influence on government policy through its sophisticated use of the media and its strong ties with grassroots health workers all over the country. Its strong policy role is "anchored in real experience" (Edwards and Hulme 1992a, 23).

Joint governmental-nongovernmental commissions on the environment, set up in some countries after the Rio Conference in 1992, also build on the grassroots connections of GRSOs. In Lesotho, the National Environmental Council, which was organized to make policy and coordinate activities of the ministries at the central and local levels, includes local development associations, as well as GRSOs such as the Lesotho Planned Parenthood Association. In Rwanda, a national environmental strategy coordinating council—organized with support from the World Bank, USAID, and UNDP—included GROs as well as GRSOs (*Brundtland Bulletin* 1990, 33). In Guatemala, a coalition of government organizations and Guatemalan NGOs called the Consejo Nacional de Areas Protegidas (CONEP) developed a new law defining forty-four conservation areas within the rain forest that CONEP now oversees.[29]

Moreover, a recent survey of nineteen NGO consortia in sixteen African countries concluded that having a coordinating body has helped create an enabling environment for NGOs in those countries where NGO–goverment relationships are unfriendly. And in countries where relationships are friendlier, African consortia are having a policy impact. The recently organized Association of NGOs of Zanzibar (ANGOZA) is being consulted by the government on issues of women, poverty, and the environment. In Swaziland, CANGO (Coordinating Agency of NGOs) was asked by the government to organize NGOs during a recent drought and has helped formulate new government policies on health and women (Montague and Kabouchy Clough 1995, 10).

Other GRSO networks may make up for the lack of a mass base by developing strong technical expertise, as shown in the next section.

Technical Expertise

Knowledge acquired by GRSOs is quite deliberately both scientific or technical, on the one hand, and policy related on the other. How can technical expertise be enhanced? Usually, technical expertise emerges from field research. In Bangladesh, for example, BRAC's field-tested knowledge of poultry production had, by 1990, been replicated in 7,400 villages by both the government and other GRSOs (Farrington and Bebbington 1993, 86).[30]

Sometimes field research is funded by national, state, or provincial governments. In Rajasthan, for example, a GRSO learned to construct irrigation/percolation tanks by perforating the rock bed below a drilling rig so that the water could seep into the ground. The method was then evaluated and endorsed by the Rajasthan Ground Water Department, which had funded the research (Kale and Coombs 1980, 306). Yet collaborative research between governments and GRSOs is still uncommon (Bebbington and Farrington 1993, 210). In São Paulo, Brazil, where both the public and the nonprofit sectors are involved in environmental research, neither side has done much to coordinate their efforts (Thompson 1990, 37).

Where collaborative research does occur, it is often sponsored by specialized GRSO networks. Indeed, specialized networks may compensate for weak grassroots ties by using member organizations to develop a broad technological expertise. Unlike governments, which tend to compartmentalize research, GRSOs that share their expertise with one another or with GROs strengthen both their autonomy and their political influence (Bebbington 1991, 22–3). A network of Kenyan NGOs called KENGO, for example, worked with the Kenyatta University's Appropriate Technology Center and the Ministry of Energy to improve cookstoves (United Nations 1988, 26–7).[31] A group of well-established GRSOs in Bangladesh designed and implemented a $4 million component of a World Bank–sponsored government project to intensify family planning and maternal and child health (Population Institute 1987a, 1).

GRSO networks in Latin America have also helped speed up the dissemination of sustainable technologies and methodologies to government agencies (Reilly 1990, 43). A Bolivian network called UNITAS strengthened its own ties with the Instituto Boliviano de Tecnologia Agropecuario (IBTA) so that its member organizations could transfer technologies to the government, set the research agenda, and collaborate in research trials.[32] In Brazil, the Instituto Brasileiro de Analises Sociais e Economicas (IBASE) compiles and synthesizes a monthly analysis of government policies written by twenty to thirty people representing its GRSO members. The report is organized around government positions on major issues; societal demands and government responses; and analyses of other sectors such as labor, agrarian reform, environment, and health. This critical evaluation is distributed to 3,000 institutions, including many in government (Theunis 1992, 217).[33]

Collaborative research with underpaid government field agents often requires social as well as technical skills. SOPRODER, working with the Mapuche tribe in Chile, found that plowed-under wheat seedlings reemerged with more vigor than weeds. But because the government agent was providing free herbicides, SOPRODER suggested that half of each field be treated with the old method and half with the new one, to avoid offending him until the positive results of the organic method became obvious (Wali 1990, 18).

Whether based on scientific knowledge acquired in the laboratory or in the field, technical research is sometimes used for direct policy advocacy, instead of being filtered through grassroots development projects. In Bangladesh, Savar Gonoshasthaya Kendra conducted detailed medical research on internationally marketed pharmaceuticals to determine which were useless or harmful. It then established its own drug company to break the power of the international drug cartel in Bangladesh and help the government write a new policy on pharmaceuticals (Korten 1990, 121). GRSOs in Sri Lanka wrote their own economic and environmental appraisal of a proposed coal power plant in Trincomalee before revealing that the government team that had drawn up the proposal had not even visited the area (Clark 1991, 97).

Sometimes, specialized knowledge is combined with well-planned, ongoing advocacy. The Sri Lankan Environmental Congress of 170 NGOs successfully pressured the government to drop an environmentally destructive plan and to become more receptive to environmental appraisal in the future (Clark 1991, 117). In Mexico, the mission of the Autonomous Institute for Environmental Research is to educate government and the media on environmental issues, including the need to reorganize the environment ministry. The institute is participating in the negotiations aimed at creating the Federal District's first hazardous-waste treatment facility.[34]

Social and Managerial Knowledge

GRSOs and GRSO networks sometimes pressure governments to fund the social research needed to change government policy. In Latin America, private research centers that undertake social as well as scientific research are increasingly funded by governments (Levy 1992).[35] In India, the Self-Employed Women's Association pushed the government into creating a commission on the self-employed. With strong GRSO participation, the commission traveled to eighteen states over twelve months and sent out a million questionnaires to GRSOs and other voluntary organizations to collect information on women's work and other family issues. Many of its specific policy recommendations to protect the self-employed and raise their standard of living have been adopted (Bhatt 1989, 1064).

More often, however, as with technical knowledge, it is field experience that reinforces social or managerial understanding to strengthen advocacy. An organization that documents and evaluates its work over time "has an enormous potential to build a highly reliable data source" that can strongly influence government projects and policies (Dichter 1986a, 6). In Colombia, the Centro de Cooperacion al Indigena (CENCOIN) has ties to seventy communities that provide it with a unique flow of reliable data on local resources, problems, and solutions that have informed both governmental and nongovernmental assistance (Ritchie-Vance 1991, 71). In India, the Center for Science and Environment, Myrada, AVARD, and Lokayan have worked together to develop expertise in involuntary relocation that has been utilized by the government (Cernea 1988, 34).[36] Such policy changes differ from government acquiescence to special interests, since governments often act logically in the national self-interest once pertinent information is made available to them (Dichter 1986a).

Social or organizational innovations developed through grassroots experience have a potentially broad impact. The Chilean government, for instance, is adopting the small-farmer grain-marketing practices developed by Agraria, a GRSO (Bebbington and Farrington 1993, 206; Farrington and Bebbington 1994, 6). The participatory methods of the Comprehensive Rural Health Care Project at Jamkhed, India, strongly influenced the government's rural health care reforms (Sethi 1983, 22). And in Indonesia, the government has established a village cooperative unit for transmigration projects based on the methods developed by Bina Swadaya, a GRSO that emerged out of GRO networking. Since Bina Swadaya began cooperating with the government to expand this approach, thousands of GROs have gained access to government family planning and agricultural programs (Prijono 1992, 622).

Field experience also provides GRSOs with a measuring rod against which to evaluate new insights. When GRSOs are continually challenged from below, they are more likely to develop flexible, responsive managerial strategies that offer alternative approaches to service provision; this makes them attractive to governments, despite their being difficult to co-opt. Demonstrations accompanied by participatory evaluations based on grassroots input can also lessen potential government risk (Garilao 1987, 117).

New managerial approaches that emerge from specific circumstances are not necessarily easy to scale up, however (Holloway 1989c, 159). For example, Human Settlements of Zambia (HUZA) works with squatters and has convinced the government that women involved in their own development can be trained as auxiliary staff. HUZA has also advised government on the role of local communities in natural resource conservation and helped prepare the national conservation strategy. With a staff of only eighteen, however, HUZA cannot easily increase the scale of its operations or train the government to deliver services to half a million squatters in Lusaka (Rakodi 1990, 16).

Moreover, participatory innovations are more difficult than technical expertise to communicate to policy makers (Farrington and Bebbington 1993, 187). NGOs may find it difficult to become what Ritchey-Vance (1991, 71) calls "incubator[s] for new ideas," even if they are collaborating with governments. One reason for this is that governments are often impatient with social organizing. Within Agraria in Chile, this has led to tensions between staff members working under government contract, who have little time for social promotion, and those working under foreign donors committed to the participatory approach (Bebbington and Farrington 1993, 207).

Social or managerial innovations developed by NGOs are most likely to influence policies on redistributive social issues such as agrarian reform when governments are already committed to major change. In Peru, for example, which passed agrarian reform legislation in 1969, Proterra used its experience in land titling in the Lurin Valley to influence legislative changes in land distribution policies (Livernash 1992, 19; Reilly 1993, 28). And Technoserve-Peru persuaded the Banco Agrario that it should provide credit to individual farmers through its service cooperatives, thus strengthening these organizations.[37] In India, it was only after the government set up a commission on bonded labor that a GRSO called DISHA became an influential member, able to share its expertise (John Clark, unpublished memo).

While enhancing their own understanding of participatory management at the grassroots level, GRSOs also have to manage themselves, thus providing governments with demonstrations of effective service provision.[38] BRAC in Bangladesh, for example, with a "reputation for effective development work, professional management and careful control of money," has had a number of significant impacts on official development policies (Lovell 1992, 160). Conversely, "internal weakness—lack of procedures and financial controls—fuel [government] harassment [of NGOs]," according to Tandon (1988, 12), an observer of the Indian scene.

Given government's need to reach larger and larger populations, even a well-managed GRSO or GRSO network may have less policy impact than GRO networks. The ability of some GRO networks to scale out is impressive and immediately visible:

■ In Bihar, India, where 8,000 women are members of women's dairy cooperatives, government decision makers became convinced that the women's cooperatives were more productive and less vulnerable to corruption than other cooperatives.[39]

■ A national peasant federation in Mexico has dealt with a wide range of agricultural financing issues. "Because of the number of peasants the organization represents, the amount of land they control and the organization's own gradual expansion and continued credibility, UNCORA was able to attract the attention of the [official and private] banking system and bring about reforms" (M. Morgan 1990).

■ The "model" Peruvian squatter community of Villa El Salvador, based on hundreds of block organizations that collaborate with one another, has attracted the attention of both government and foreign donors. As one observer put it, "Villa El Salvador is a social movement fixed in one place" (Annis and Franks 1989, 19).

Strategic Knowledge

General principles such as the need for participation and bottom-up management, although often widely accepted, must be reinvented in practice each time they are used. This reinvention depends on the availability of skilled trainers, who may be in short supply in specific fields such as accounting, marketing, or health education. Reinvention also depends on organizational or technical expertise gained through field experience that may be highly specific to particular cultures, regions, climates, soil conditions, or resources.

Somewhere between general principles and technically specific knowledge are strategic "lessons learned," which have the potential to inform development efforts everywhere, including those of governments. In contrast to geographic expansion of an existing development project, "strategic knowledge" can be copied or replicated more easily in diverse settings. Whereas "traditional replication" attempts to copy demonstration or pilot projects, nontraditional replication uses knowledge gained at the local level to influence wider decision making (Dichter 1989, 7).

Sometimes these lessons have near universal applicability. Among the good examples are the following:

■ Beneficiaries must be encouraged to "buy in" to projects in some way.

■ Excellent performance has been obtained around the world from revolving loan funds that focus on women.

- It is best to concentrate on one agricultural sector, from production to distribution to marketing (Dichter 1989, 7).

- Combining women's education with the provision of family planning has a more consistent and dramatic impact on fertility than projects that include either component in isolation.

Although the potential of this acquired knowledge base is beginning to be realized, many such lessons are not diffused and continue to be wastefully reinvented elsewhere. Other lessons are increasingly recognized as useful but are not fully understood as being central to the entire process. A good example is the training of GROs in data collection and in monitoring their own progress.

Some new approaches, such as microcredit, are easier to copy, with measurable and rapid results. The conviction that the poor, particularly women, are good financial risks and can be provided with credit on a mass scale is probably the most common policy change being inspired by GRSO example in the Third World. Peruvian government programs, modeled on the enterprise development activities of GRSOs, granted over 100,000 loans to microentrepreneurs that contributed to a 15 percent increase in the gross domestic product between 1985 and 1987 (Annis and Franks 1989, 14).[40] The Grameen Bank has inspired not only the government of Bangladesh but also the governments of other countries, such as Mali and Nigeria (Zeuli 1991, 64).

The spread of credit to the poor and its influence on government policies have been promoted by Northern NGOs and their nationally staffed counterparts or partners that focus on micro and middle-sized enterprise development. For example, with help from Accion International, the business sector in the Dominican Republic created ADEMI to vastly increase lending programs for the poor. By 1987, the Dominican government had contributed $275,000 in grants and loans to the program, even though policy change had not been ADEMI's initial goal; in fact, it "backed into the policy arena" (Accion International 1987). Both Accion International and Opportunity International have helped create counterpart but now largely independent GRSOs working on credit and small-business development in a number of Latin American countries. And in Africa, Technoserve-Kenya and the Kenya Union of Savings and Credit Societies developed a model for a nationwide loan policy that was later adopted by the government. They also convinced the government not to tax income produced from mutual trading among cooperative members (Dichter 1986a).

Educational reform strategies based on carefully planned, small-scale excellence can also scale up well, with the potential to impact policy. In

India, the Educational Resource Centre of Calcutta seeks out schools and teachers who want to get beyond rote learning, links them, and provides materials. Its pre-primary kit, used in sixty-nine centers, has been approved and promoted by the Indian Ministry of Education (Ashoka 1990).[41] The Centro de Cultura Luis Freire in Brazil has developed an alternative educational approach for slum dwellers; as the key force behind national GRSO networking on this issue, the center succeeded in having federal funding for alternative schools built into the new Brazilian constitution (M. Morgan 1990).

Experience in Training Government Workers

NGO–government partnerships in project implementation may lead to either increased autonomy or increased dependency. Autonomy is most likely to be strengthened when GRSOs train government personnel:

- In Bangladesh, the Women's Health Coalition, which serves 75,000 women and children annually at low cost, places a strong emphasis on training others, especially government health and family planning workers (Germaine and Ordway 1989, 13). Traditional birth attendants and government doctors are also being trained by BRAC, which then links them to one another (Lovell 1987).

- The Indonesian Foundation for the Advancement of the Environment, the Lembaga Studi Pembanguan Institute for Development Studies, and the University of Bandung jointly train the government's rural bank personnel and government extension workers (Terrant and Poerbo 1986).

- In Barbados, the Caribbean Conservation Association is training "environmental economists" to advise both governments and industries throughout the Caribbean.[42]

Governments sometimes ask GRSOs to provide training. The Colombian government provided the Granja Taller de Asistencia Colombiana with a farm and an endowment to train interns for agricultural policy-making positions (Ritchie-Vance 1991, 71). Officials in the Philippine Health Ministry are "trying to learn from NGO experience and develop partnerships with community health services" (Qureshi 1988, 3). In India, the Ministry of Agriculture's watershed management program coordinates NGOs that train government and other NGO staff in evaluating social impacts and diagnosing organizational problems (Farrington and Bebbington 1993, 159). In other countries, management institutes have facilitated these contacts. In Mussorie, India, for example, the Lal Bahadur Shastri Academy of Administration sends trainees out to see NGO programs (Society for Participatory Research in Asia 1991, 87).

Government initiatives may also be the result of earlier contacts with GRSOs or with international donors. During the 1970s, a group of social scientists working in Bangkok at the Asian Development Institute (sponsored by the UNDP) undertook studies of grassroots movements and established close ties to PROSHIKA, a Bangladesh GRSO, and to the government-sponsored Rural Action Project (RAP) in India. This international network persuaded the Sri Lankan government's Ministry of Rural Development to initiate training and action research in participatory rural development. Development workers trained government officials to train village-level change agents. This "effectively demonstrated the feasibility of 'training' government officials to play the role of catalytic agents in participatory development" (Dasgupta, Tilakaratna, and Wignaraja 1984; Saouma 1985, 20).

When NGOs develop a strong internal commitment to autonomy, diversify their funding, and cultivate strong grassroots ties, they are likely to enhance both their own autonomy and their influence on government. The knowledge that they acquire and share with government determines how and to what degree they can impact policy. Despite the problems inherent in communicating what works internationally—or even within one country—technical, managerial, and strategic knowledge gained through grassroots experience is beginning to influence governments worldwide:

■ In Argentina, public housing policies now incorporate criteria developed by GRSOs that specialize in housing.

■ GRSO and government respondents in a Thai survey mentioned many policy approaches adapted from GRSOs, including basic-needs indicators, the use of schools as centers for village development, the concept of beneficiary participation, and the linking of secondary-school curriculum to rural development (Tongsawate and Tipps 1985).

■ Indian government policies on the rehabilitation of the disabled were pioneered by the Mahvir Relief Society in Jaipur. Other Indian GRSOs assisted the government in planning the National Adult Education Program (Sethi 1983, 22).

■ The Savings and Development Movement in Zimbabwe, despite its small staff, attracted the attention of the Ministry of Community Development and Women's Affairs; as a result, savings training became standard extension practice in four of eight provinces (Bratton 1989, 17).

Clearly, this growing influence depends on a strong commitment to research as well as field demonstration in many countries. As Velarde (1988, 17) writes about Peru:

> The vast majority of the intellectual production of the country is pro-vided by the *Centros* [GRSOs], their experience and personnel. Research themes, seminars, and debates . . . are in the center of the national debate . . . [and] many themes and alternatives launched from the "cen-ters" appear . . . in the rhetoric of the government. (See also Levy 1996.)

However, in writing about Colombia, Arbab (1988, 45) throws out a potential warning to GRSOs: "Much of the effort is usually carried out in an atmosphere of frantic action with little analysis of the underlying assumptions . . . especially when NGOs also become the salesmen of their own ideas, further burdening over-extended institutions."

Another potential pitfall is that NGO success will allow governments to back off from their responsibility for service provision and thus free governments from the social pressures needed for change. The dilemma is described clearly by a leader of a Bolivian GRSO, the Instituto de Educa-cion para el Desarrollo Rural (INEDER):

> In INEDER, we consciously take on this ambiguous role, in the interest of achieving social change. We constantly evaluate the effect of our role as state substitute. Wherever [the] organizational bases for meeting the needs of the population have been developed, responsibility for these . . . programs is transferred to the public sector (Theunis 1992, 241).

Yet another pitfall is that government policies can undermine even the scaled-up, successful efforts of NGOs. For example, when the V. P. Singh regime in India waived outstanding dues for farmers with good repayment records, many borrowers withheld repayments, "with the result that the banks are now wary about lending to the poor" (Robinson 1992, 412–3).

Most important, all NGOs are not created equal; indeed, they range from highly effective and committed to poorly organized and dependent. Some are dishonestly capitalizing on flows of foreign funding—charac-terized by one Philippine wag as "Come NGOes."[43] However, those NGOs that are autonomous and highly effective tend to use their ties to govern-ments to do more than adapt to political constraints. They are likely to help redefine policies shaped by the political contexts explored in Chapter 2 and to create new political spaces and opportunities through government contacts.

Even though the more capable and knowledgeable NGOs are likely to be autonomous and politically influential, the shift to government implementation on a wider scale will be slow and "more difficult than imagined" (Bhatt 1995, 88). For one thing, the evidence presented in Chapter 2 suggests that governments can be capricious and inconsistent, with one ministry undoing what another has supported. For another thing, managerial reforms within Third World governments remain scattered at best. Indeed, Bhatt (1995) argues that Asian governments are becoming less capable and more corrupt. Finally, NGOs may be trapped into becoming state substitutes, as governments retire from their social responsibilities (Wils 1996).

Both national and international policies should therefore focus not just on building partnerships with the most capable NGOs but also on learning from, building on, and supporting the strengths of existing indigenous NGOs. Given the immensely complex task of balancing grassroots empowerment and accountability with organizational autonomy and government ties, it is inconceivable that any Northern donor or international NGO could begin to match the diversity of experience and knowledge already extant within the Third World.[44] Rather, foreign donors need to support strategic networking that strengthens the autonomy of NGOs, particularly in their relationships with governments. Chapter 6, which includes recommendations for donors, provides more details on how they might do this. If individual professionals within Third World governments also come to view autonomous NGOs not as threatening but as empowering the government to do more and with greater efficacy, they too may significantly advance the processes of democratization and sustainable development.

Notes

1. An African theorist (Mulyungi 1990, 57) postulates a scale of 1 to 4: (1) fatalistic acceptance; (2) development from within, enabling the poor to enter the lower middle class; (3) radical change not only of the poor themselves but also of the institutions that maintain them in poverty; and (4) radical change of the entire system. He concludes that African NGOs are not equipped for goal 4 but should be able to accomplish a combination of goals 2 and 3.
2. See also Fisher 1993, 10–18. On Tanzania, where NGOs have only recently begun to proliferate, see Tripp 1994, 126.
3. After tentatively isolating this variable, I participated with Habte Woldemarian on a panel at the Independent Sector's Spring Research Forum in Boston. His paper (1992) helped me crystallize my own thinking on this point.

4. See, for example, Kothari 1986. For the Indian study, see Alliband 1983, 12.

5. NGOs that emerged under dictatorships, however, may also tend to be more circumspect about contacts with more democratic successor states (see Farrington and Bebbington 1993, 45).

6. These seven factors emerged clearly from an extensive survey of the literature cited in this chapter. After completing this research, I found that Bratton (1994b, 55), without focusing on autonomy as an intervening variable, identified four similar characteristics tied to policy impact: federated representation of and accountability to homogeneous subgroups of the poor; domestic financial contributions, especially from members; policy issues of limited scope in which staff can acquire technical expertise; and leadership that cultivates formal and informal political ties, particularly with senior government officials.

7. Woldemarian (1992, 271) calls this "self-identity and independence."

8. AIM, a Malaysian GRSO, is beginning to fund-raise by emphasizing the obligation of the rich.

9. Although it is a regionally decentralized funding organization that targets poverty-related projects, the Fondo's structure also makes it difficult for GROs or GRO networks to bypass GRSOs (Schuurman and Heer 1992, 56–7).

10. NFAZ, according to Bratton (1989), has 40,000 dues-paying members.

11. See Fisher 1993, chap. 6. See also Levy's (1996, 160–73) discussion of private research centers (PRCs), on the other hand, in Latin America, many of which do not have grassroots ties. Welch (1995, 305–6), argues that African NGOs that rely primarily on an elite membership and action through the courts are more likely to be sucessful on human rights issues than organizations with grassroots ties: "A single triumph in court, at least in a common law system, can set a precedent from which many can benefit. Hence, although small membership limits financial and advocacy resources, it does not preclude effectiveness . . . *assuming that the requisite court system and independent judiciary exist.*"

12. Gadgil and Guha (1994, 104) point out that resistance to state forestry policies was widespread in India during the colonial period.

13. Eckstein also points out, however, that tenant groups had already gained experience during the 1970s.

14. Diaz-Albertini (1989) points out that this raises some questions about the academic debate over individualistic "rational choice" versus collective motives in voluntary group behavior.

15. Albert Hirschman (1963, 259) made this point long before GROs had become so widespread in the Third World. He noted that "a final characteristic of the violence we have met in our studies is that it is not only protest and pressure on problem solving authorities, but also *direct problem solving activity.* The Colombian peasant satisfies his craving for a piece of land when he squats and the Northeastern drought refugee solves his immediate problem of hunger when he loots food stores in the coastal cities as does the Chilean worker when he wins higher wages through strikes. Hence, these individual decentralized actions not only signal a

problem to the central decision makers, but they reduce the size of the problem that remains to be solved by the authorities."

16. In Lima alone there were 282 invasions of public and private land during 1983. Although eight out of ten houses built in Lima between 1977 and 1987 were in the informal sector, Peru's Liberty and Democracy Institute has shown that 247 separate administrative operations would have been necessary to secure the transfer of land from public to private domain. Despite this paralysis within the national government, the Municipal Council led squatters to a new site, and the central government was providing services to the new settlements (Fisher 1977, 1984; Williams and Riofrio 1987).

17. Although health committees are still active in some areas, their national role declined with political change at the top.

18. During the early 1990s, much of this progress was threatened by local terrorists representing the Shining Path. However, once Anibal Guzman was arrested in 1992, community organizations began to reassert their previous role.

19. Among the many sources, see Colchester 1994, 85.

20. In addition to the examples listed in the text, see Gadgil and Guha (1994).

21. However, although there is a serious pollution problem from petroleum extraction in the Oriente, the agreement did not include mineral rights. As of 1995, CONAIE was working out a system with government and the companies to protect the Pastaza from petroleum spills during exploration and extraction (Weber 1995, 41).

22. In fact, Ndegwa (1996, 16) argues that Kenyan GRSOs that have not done this "democratize only their own space."

23. Fowler (1991), however, says that this also depends on donor support for what he calls the "internal democratization" of NGOs.

24. Brian Smith (1990) suggests that this caution is related to the use of isolated tactics such as civic strikes to achieve particular goals, as well as to the direct benefits to neighborhood local development associations provided by the government.

25. The agreement to alternate power between the dominant Liberal and Conservative parties was a long-run result of the civil war of 1948. Traditionally, neither party has represented a real challenge to the Colombian oligarchy. In most other Latin American countries, the process of scaling up to affect policy had begun by 1985, at least in terms of thinking, according to Arruda (1985). See also Landim 1987.

26. Valerie Miller, presentation at the symposium Shaping the Policy Debate: The Role of Non-Governmental Organizations in International Development, John F. Kennedy School of Government, Harvard University, April 22, 1993.

27. ASINDES in Guatemala, for example, has strong USAID backing yet has been able to become politically influential (Checci and Co. 1989).

28. Presentation by Khawja Huda, Interaction Forum, Danvers, Massachusetts, May 1989.

29. Alternatively, ALIRAN in Malaysia has spearheaded dialogues among NGOs, professional associations, religious organizations, cultural organizations, unions, and political parties (see Riker 1995b, 113).

30. The new methods influenced 10 percent of poultry production and included 33,000 key rearers operating commercially and almost 5,500 poultry workers trained.
31. Montague and Kabouchy Clough (1995, 23) found that some formal consortia in Africa have specialized subgroupings. The AIDS subcommittee within CANGO in Swaziland, for example, "enables members within that sector to share experiences . . . with government."
32. Remarks by Jose Pinelo in Toranzo Roca 1992, 122. See also Kaimowitz 1993, 1148; Bebbington and Farrington 1993, 210.
33. Although specialized networks seem to be more effective than formal multisectoral umbrella organizations in providing technical assistance and other services to their members, patterns of cooperation are developing that lead to multisectoral approaches to sustainable development. The population issue still lags, but networks may prove to be the most powerful force to spread knowledge about population and family planning among GRSOs (see Fisher 1993, 128–35; 1994b).
34. The institute was founded by an Ashoka fellow, Luis Manuel Guerra (see Ashoka 1988, 43–4).
35. The private research centers also receive considerable support from U.S. foundations such as Ford and Rockefeller.
36. Technical knowledge also provides the politically easiest way for international NGOs to impact development policy. Technoserve's Salvadoran counterpart found that assistance to henequen cooperatives was undermined by government policies encouraging imports of synthetic fibers. Armed with knowledge of production and with marketing and financial data, Technoserve and a group of henequen co-ops helped change this policy (see Dichter 1986a). Technoserve is an international NGO whose Salvadoran field office has gradually been evolving into a Salvadoran GRSO.
37. Based on my own field research. This is part of an unpublished evaluation done for Technoserve in 1989 and 1993.
38. Many Christian churches in Africa are acquiring "grassroots support functions" (Fisher 1993, 6). Jenkins (1994, 91) points out that African churches established school systems during the colonial era and have a long-accepted practice of collecting financial donations from their members.
39. Presentation by Karen McGuiness of the Ford Foundation, Association for Women in Development, Washington, D.C., November 1989. In spite of this increased awareness, however, the women's co-ops still did not have access to artificial insemination services provided by the government.
40. Unfortunately, the effect was later undercut by fiscal policies leading to spiraling inflation.
41. The center's materials and approach have also been adopted in Maryland, Indiana, and Virginia.
42. The course is being offered at the University of the West Indies, in collaboration with the World Resources Institute (*Brundtland Bulletin* 1990, 49).
43. Yet as Meyer (1995, 1280) points out, "Entrepreneurship should not be confused with opportunism. While much of the NGO literature has defined 'opportunism' as activity motivated by financial gain, opportuni-

ties for financial gain can stimulate beneficial entrepreneurial activity."
True opportunism, defined as "self-interest seeking with guile," conceals
the truth.

44. Fowler (1996, 179), for example, argues that GRSOs must have the "ability
to do, that is to achieve stakeholder satisfaction, [and] the ability to relate,
that is, to manage external interactions while maintaining autonomy."

4

Promoting Democratization and Sustainable Development

■ Acknowledging the systemic nature of things means seeing and acting within the big picture. And while the big picture may not mean that our actions must be big, inevitably it does mean that we must integrate our actions at higher levels and at larger aggregations than the individual, the micro level all by itself.

—Thomas W. Dichter (1986b)

■ This is not the story of good NGOs confronting evil governments. . . . This is the story of humanity assuming responsibility for its own future, through increasingly representative forms of political organization and through a fully engaged civil society.

—Martha L. Schweitz (1995, 3)

Patterns of Interaction

ONE WAY TO UNDERSTAND NGO–government interaction is to observe the entire relationship. Najam (1996b), for example, characterizes NGO–government relationships as confrontational, complimentary, or collaborative, a clear and useful way to grapple with the entire universe of NGOs—Northern, Southern, and international—in relation to governments.[1] This discussion, however, because of its Southern focus, has dealt first with Third World government policies toward NGOs and then with the relationship between NGO autonomy and political impact. In this chapter, I focus on three Southern NGO strategies toward governments. One strategy is for NGOs to isolate themselves almost completely from the state. A second strategy is to engage the state through advocacy, which may or may not be confrontational. A third strategy is for NGOs to cooperate with the state through parallel or collaborative field projects.[2] Finally, I revisit the discussion in Chapter 1 of how NGOs scale out their own impact through NGO–government interactions and explore the possibilities for NGOs to achieve a "critical mass" for change.

The analysis of NGO autonomy in Chapter 3 implies that any NGO political strategy may be proactive, reactive, or somewhere in between. Autonomy tends to push NGOs toward proactivity, allowing them to strategize while simultaneously responding to the political context that confronts them. Some NGOs, such as many of those described in Chapter 3, do so with confidence, sophistication, and flexibility.

There are many other NGOs, however, less certain of their own identity and autonomy, that tend to reflect rather than redefine political culture and context. In Nigeria, for example, a GRSO network called NADA mirrored the costly resource fights characteristic of Nigeria's fragmented elite. In other cases, NGOs may "produce public goods skewed toward international tastes or government objectives" (Meyer 1995, 1286). A network in Togo (TADA), for example, has become financially dependent on the state and tends to reproduce its policies (Anheier 1994, 158–64). GRSOs may also reflect the historical context of their origins. In Bolivia, the leaders of older GRSOs founded under the dictatorships of the 1970s tend to be more suspicious of the government than are younger leaders (Toranzo Roca 1992, 95).

Sometimes, NGOs are simply not ready or able to focus on relationships with government. A study of 250 Asian GRSOs concluded that mixed rationales and worldviews within NGOs have caused conflict and confusion in relation to policies toward governments (Society for Participatory Research in Asia 1991, 20). In Africa, many NGOs are not yet active in policy analysis and advocacy (Chitiga-Machingauta 1995b, 15).

The proactive–reactive continuum may also help determine whether the overall relationship becomes catalytic and empowers both sides or whether it leads to co-optation (Najam 1996b, 12–3):

> Being catalysts for change is . . . not a "role" for NGOs but the goal of all NGO activity in the policy stream. . . . Similarly, cooptation is also not a "relationship" per se but a goal of all players in the policy stream, and is in many regards the other face of the catalytic influence. . . . [Governments and NGOs will] take strategic institutional decisions to use the resources they command to attempt to—catalytically or co-optively—influence the other to conform to their preferred decision path. It is in the resulting relationship between them that the direction of change, one way or the other, will be determined. (Najam 1996b, 16–7)

Although NGOs are more likely to act as catalysts and governments are more likely to try to co-opt, the strength of the direction of change depends on the capacities of the particular players as they relate to the overall political context. Just as autonomous NGOs are likely to be more effective advocates, democratization or bureaucratic reform may mean that governments are more likely to value, support, learn from, and build on the autonomy of NGOs, rather than seeking to co-opt them.

Although being "catalysts for change" is indeed "the goal of all NGO activity," it is also true that NGOs focus on two less instrumental goals, which Berg (1987, 38) calls "the twin challenges of empowerment and development." Just as empowerment and development depend on each other at the local level, the more autonomous, proactive NGOs (the focus of this chapter) promote both democratization and sustainable development at the national level in their relationships with governments.[3]

Although the ability to promote sustainable development policies is likely to be tied to technical expertise, strategic knowledge, or the training of government workers, successful advocacy on behalf of democratization is likely to be tied to a mass base. In Chapter 1 I argued that NGOs are the vanguard of a civil society that, in turn, interacts with government to promote political development. Yet one of the vanguard roles of NGOs is the deliberate promotion of democratization as part of the broader process that includes them.

Empowerment achieved within GROs has the potential to democratize community power structures and challenge GRSOs to continually live up to their rhetoric. To the degree that GRSOs strengthen grassroots ties and become more internally democratic, they enhance not only their own autonomy and ability to influence governments but also their ability to promote two types of democratization:

1. *Bottom-up democratization:* As I argued in Chapter 1, grassroots empowerment promoted by GROs and GRSOs can strengthen the autonomy of civil society and, therefore, tends to have an indirect, long-term impact on enlarging political space and enhancing the accountability of the political system. There are also, however, some bottom-up protest initiatives focusing on the rights of women, tribal peoples, or the landless, that have forced governments to enlarge the concept of citizenship very quickly.

2. *Top-down democratization:* NGOs (usually GRSOs and their networks) can also, as explained in Chapter 1, promote political reforms that advance what O'Donnell and Schmitter (1986, 8) call the "progressive extension of citizenship." Even though they do it from below, NGOs promote top-down reforms by serving as election observers, by protesting human rights abuses, and by challenging government repression in court. Top-down reforms are also, of course, promoted by human rights organizations without grassroots ties (see Fisher 1993, 98–100, 104–5).

NGO Strategies

This section explores three strategies—isolation, advocacy, and cooperation—that GROs, GRSOs, and their networks use to achieve these "twin challenges" through their contacts with governments. Although such strategies are not limited to the more autonomous NGOs, their leaders are more likely than their more passive colleagues to calculate and plan such strategies.

Political Isolation

Both GROs and GRSOs may consciously decide to steer clear of the state for some time, build a mass base, strengthen independent-sector networks, and develop alternative approaches to development that can influence policy over the long run. Isolation is particularly suited to repressive contexts. In South Africa, NGOs used isolation to ensure their own survival. Once apartheid began to crumble, GRSOs began to establish government contacts (Theunis 1992, 70). Isolation is also used to avoid co-optation. In Tanzania, a long history of state domination and extraction of local resources led GRSOs to resist official registration (Tripp 1994). Despite the apparent efficacy of isolation under repression or co-optation, however, if NGOs have not cultivated international support, a low profile can also leave them vulnerable to attack.

In some cases, the motive for isolation from the state is unrelated to official repression. In Peru, according to Diaz-Albertini (1993a, 98), GRSO isolation from government is linked either to doubts about their own limited resources or to their need to nourish grassroots ties by avoiding political connections based on hierarchy and bureaucracy. Since ties to a mass base are a crucial component of autonomy, a strategy that postpones political connections until a later date may be a politically rational choice.

Grassroots economic networks that have created their own GRSOs or depend on barter among villages are particularly adept at implementing this approach. This allows them not only to survive short-run isolation but also, in the long run, to have the potential for providing less repressive successor governments with a powerful self-replicating model for sustainable development. This may mean that development has to take a backseat to self-defense. In Atitlán, Guatemala, beginning in the late 1980s, security patrols of young men carrying whistles and white flags conducted nightly rounds. They were drafted and directed by the Committee for Security and Development, representing all the cantons, churches, and cooperatives in the towns of the region. After the army massacred fourteen people in 1990, the committee successfully called on both the army and the guerrillas to leave the area. It then rejected the offer by a local contingent of the national police to supply the townspeople with arms and achieved police withdrawal through negotiation (Louckey and Carlsen 1991, 68).[4]

Although a strategy of isolation and self-preservation can have little impact on either official sustainable development policies or top-down democratization, it may have a long-term impact if it leads to alternative approaches to sustainable development and strengthens the autonomy of civil society. Moreover, through their work with GROs, GRSOs can promote political participation and democratization at the local level.

Advocacy

A second political strategy, political advocacy, is also based on a refusal to be co-opted or controlled but involves direct communication with government about policy. Because advocacy may involve everything from quiet negotiations on limited organizational objectives to mass protests on major issues, it is hard to generalize about its suitability to different political contexts, but it is not usually relevant to repressive contexts, unless the issue of security has first been confronted directly, as in Atitlán. In some Middle Eastern countries, for example, "advocacy organizations are totally nonexistent" (Kandil 1994, 127). Even though NGOs concentrating on human rights and the environment began to emerge in the Middle East during the early 1990s, most Middle Eastern organizations tend to appoint leaders who are on good terms with the government (Kandil 1994, 133–4).

NGO advocates use many different advocacy techniques, sometimes simultaneously, including friendly persuasion, "acupuncture" (defined below), legal and lobbying efforts, electoral politics, networking, and mass advocacy. The Zambian Association for Research and Development, for example, trains grassroots activists in advocacy, publishes position papers on women's issues, and communicates continually with policy makers.[5] This strategic diversity may be the result of confusion or mixed worldviews within the same NGO, or it may represent a carefully thought out, multifaceted strategy that responds to a range of governmental actors. Sometimes GRSOs with different advocacy styles collaborate with one another.

FRIENDLY PERSUASION   At the quiet end of the scale are efforts by NGOs to reduce government suspicion and initiate a more positive relationship with policy makers. Peruvian GRSOs, faced with a suspicious regime in the early 1980s, invited government officials to visit their headquarters and projects, opened their books, and were rewarded with a shift in government attitudes (Toranzo Roca 1992, 92). In Kenya, the Undugu Society invited officials to visit 1,200 shelter-workshops while simultaneously encouraging international donors to ask tough questions about the treatment of NGOs.[6] This led to better treatment of NGOs, improved community development policies, and more advanced discussions on land tenure. Such efforts also enhance personal relationships with individuals in government. One of the more innovative examples of this approach is the "convening" or "bridging" function of the Fundación Esquel Ecuador (FEE), which brings NGOs together with representatives from the private and governmental sectors in order to develop "a national consensus on key development issues and identify alternative policies and programs" (Brown and Winder 1996, 14, 16).[7]

ACUPUNCTURE   The willingness of NGOs to take on the state, while becoming permanently involved in the process of change through the state, has been described by a leader of WALHI, an NGO network in Indonesia, as "acupuncture," or "placing a needle into the sensitive points of a sick system."[8] WALHI initiated an environmental lawsuit against five government agencies but did not have to take the case to court, because the government admitted its mistake. WALHI then persuaded the government to undertake a joint lawsuit on deforestation against the Scott Paper Company. As a result, environmental impact assessments have become a legal requirement in Indonesia. Among other examples of acupuncture are the following:

■ In Zimbabwe, the Women's Action Group (WAG) writes letters to female members of parliament and organizes meetings with them as a way of pressuring the government.

■ CEMUJER in El Salvador is promoting a nonsexist penal code by arranging meetings with top officials, including judges and legislators. CEMUJER has also cultivated strong ties with female reporters and has held workshops to sensitize government employees to women's issues.

An interesting twist on acupuncture was provided by Thai NGOs, which "gleefully appropriated" Prime Minster Mahatir Mohamed's description of them as a "thorn in the flesh" (Clarke 1996, 14). A Brazilian activist justifies the use of acupuncture in another way: "To the degree that one doesn't think of the state as a thing, as something impermeable to changes in the correlation of forces in society, work with the state becomes possible." NGOs do not, she argues, try to "occupy the state," but rather function as "multimediators or micromediators of power, of civil society, permanently, through the forum of the state" (Landim 1988b, 46–7).

LEGAL AND LOBBYING EFFORTS   Legal efforts to influence government policies are costly and are not usually successful. Although professional associations of journalists or lawyers in Africa increasingly use the courts to challenge governments on human rights issues or environmental policies, such advocacy is often based more on the need to educate the public than on any expectation of victory (Fowler 1991, 73). Even in Asia, where NGOs have prevailed against governments, legal action is uncertain. For example, the Consumers Association of Penang, Malaysia, goes to court only as a last resort and wins only 30 to 40 percent of its cases (Theunis 1992, 43).

Nonetheless, legal efforts sometimes lead to partial victories. WALHI, the environmental network in Indonesia, lost its suit against five government agencies and a pulp and rayon factory but acquired legal standing as an environmental advocate (Schweitz 1993, 148). NGOs that battle against the most egregious wrongs are sometimes willing to take major risks to achieve modest advances. In India, the Bandhua Mukti Morcha (bonded labor liberation front) was able to get the Supreme Court of India to rule against bonded labor, although, as of 1992, the court's decisions had not been implemented (Theunis 1992, 43).[9] Under South African rule in Namibia, the Legal Assistance Center used the court system to make gains against apartheid and to push Namibia closer to independence (Welch 1995, 27).[10]

In contrast to legal actions, attempts to reform legislation may offer stronger long-run possibilities for promoting sustainable development and top-down democratization. Some legislative proposals may be relatively easy for governments to accept. A Nigerian law prohibiting rural women from selling in the markets was altered as a result of lobbying by the Country Women's Association (COWAN) (Zeuli 1991, 72). Other legal reforms may require careful groundwork. In Niger, the Programme Solidarite Canada Sahel and Development Innovations and Networks (IRED) sponsored a national seminar on land laws in June 1995. Among the forty-five attendees were GRSOs, GROs, jurists, government representatives, financial backers, Rural Code Committees, and other experts. The purpose of the seminar was to promote research on solutions to Niger's many land problems and to build partnerships among those attending (Doulaye Maiga 1995, 19).

Another legislative approach—alliances between NGOs and the legislative branches of governments—is uncommon but seems to be increasing.[11] The National Farmer's Association of Zimbabwe (NFAZ) invites parliamentary officials as well as ministers to speak at its field days (Bratton 1989, 37). The Permanent Ecological Assembly in Argentina, created in 1989 to prepare for the Rio Conference in 1992, is composed of members of parliament and leaders of well-known GRSOs. And in Brazil, contacts with NGOs have helped empower the national Congress itself.[12] Ties with legislatures may also have less than positive results. In the Philippines, the Congress's Countryside Development Fund, channeled to local NGOs, "represents 'pork barrel' politics in its purest form and enables politicians to reward NGOs (GRSOs) and POs (people's organizations or GROs) that provide electoral and other forms of support" (Clarke 1995, 78).

ELECTORAL POLITICS   Although most NGOs are not involved in electoral politics, some have personal contacts with opposition parties.[13] When the executive branch of a government ignores or refuses to deal with NGOs without necessarily repressing them, it may be a viable strategy for NGOs to work through the opposition and force governments to take notice. In Nepal, for example, an environmental organization called LEADERS used opposition parties to get environmental issues on the agenda for public discussion of a new constitution.[14] In India, extensive grassroots organizing by the Self-Employed Women's Association (SEWA) has attracted the support of opposition parties. However, Indian activists fear that GRSOs *organized* by political parties are likely to be dominated by self-interested politicians (Society for Participatory Research in Asia 1991, 92).

A few GRSO leaders have entered politics more directly. In the Philippines, GRSOs are fielding political candidates and campaigning on issues such as agrarian reform (Liamzon 1990). In the Dominican Republic, the president of ADEMI, a counterpart GRSO affiliated with Accion International, was elected to congress from Santo Domingo by arguing that the poor and hungry can feed themselves if they have access to credit insured by public policy (Accion International 1987). More often, however, GRSOs combine political (but nonpartisan) activity with networking.

ADVOCACY NETWORKS   Networking has been flagged by many observers as the key to NGO success, both outside and inside the policy arena (Fisher 1993; Biggs and Neame 1996, 41). Networking to influence sustainable development policy is probably more common than networking for democratization in most countries. Some sustainable development networks are not limited to GROs and GRSOs.

■ In São Paulo, Brazil, the Fundacao S.O.S. Mata Atlántica organized an NGO forum to draw up an environmental platform addressed to presidential candidates to seek their public endorsements. The candidates' opinions were published in newspapers (Thompson 1990, 33).

■ In India, the Voluntary Health Association, with 3,000 organizational members in seventeen states, has played a key role in influencing drug policies.[15] The National Campaign for Housing Rights, created by a "vast number" of Indian GRSOs, GROs, political parties, unions, academics, and other professionals, negotiates with the government over housing policy (Society for Participatory Research in Asia 1991, 83).

The tendency of GRSOs with different advocacy styles to cooperate with one another temporarily on national advocacy campaigns is particularly important to environmental and sustainable development issues.

▪ The Malayan Nature Society, one of the oldest environmental organizations in Asia, produces scientific studies and generally avoids publicity until people in the government have a chance to read them. Yet it also works closely with more confrontational environmental groups while stressing that advocacy needs to convince government.

▪ In India, the Chipko movement used mass marches to dramatize the perils of deforestation, and the issue was included in political party platforms as early as 1980. The next step, however, was to cooperate with the lobbying efforts of the 6,000-member Indian Science Congress. This alliance resulted in the passage of the Conservation of Forests Act, including a moratorium on felling green trees in the Himalayas.

▪ A Thai coalition protesting deforestation—the Project for Ecological Recovery (PER)—included, by 1985, representatives of government, business, GRSOs, and thirty-eight environmental GROs that often led reporters to newsworthy stories. In response to a national advocacy campaign jointly sponsored by PER and Wildlife Fund Thailand, the government banned all timber cutting on public lands, including forest reserves, national parks, and wildlife sanctuaries. Rush (1991, 54) argues that although the ban is "widely violated," this was nonetheless a "monumental victory."

In Latin America and in the Philippines, NGO networks are also becoming strong advocates for top-down democratization.

▪ In Colombia, local politicians, GRSOs, and thirteen local networks of GROs organized the Movimiento Democratico Colombia Unida to challenge the electoral dominance of the Liberal and Conservative parties (Fals Borda 1990, 120–2). According to Fals

Borda (1990, 122), this coalition's "emphasis on pluralism and tolerance is the biggest lesson learned by social movements in the last twenty years."

■ In Mexico, the Convergence of Civic Organizations was organized in response to a government proposal to tax NGOs and cooperatives at the same level as large corporations. With 120 organizational members, Convergencia later joined the Mexican Human Rights Academy and the San Luis Potosi Human Rights Center as poll watchers for the 1991 gubernatorial elections (Fox and Hernandez 1992, 185–6).

■ In the Philippines, the National Citizens Movement for Free Elections (NAMFREL), the citizen arm of the Commission on Elections, "played a major role in observing the elections, conducting a parallel 'quick count' and helping to unmask the widespread fraud that occurred" (Jason 1992, 1805). A Mindanao NGO network entered politics more directly by organizing voter education, promoting alternative policies, and assuming an electoral watchdog role in relation to potential fraud and violence. According to Ledesma and Decena (1992, 10–3), such political activity is a natural outgrowth of the dramatic expansion of NGOs under Corazon Aquino. This activity has expanded the "political space" of NGOs and has led to their representation at various levels in government development councils and coordinating bodies. Even more important, it has increased NGO access to information and resources relating to the pervasive conditions of inequality and corruption that perpetuate poverty and environmental degradation.

Yet networking may have less influence on human rights violations than on elections. Even as a group, Indian NGOs have been unable to stop the killings of low caste and tribal groups. Nor have Indonesian human rights lawyers been able to acquit a single person accused of subversion by the government (Riker 1995c, 202).

MASS ADVOCACY   Mass advocacy strategies on more fundamentally contentious issues are, like networking, often viewed as risky. The move in Bangladesh to create a national political organization of the landless has been opposed by some GRSOs whose strategy is to organize small local groups to make demands of government (Sanyal 1991).

However, mass protests on sustainable development issues are growing in number and importance. When combined with media campaigns and alliances with foreign donors, mass protests allow NGOs to become strong policy advocates, particularly on issues in which they have expertise.[16] In Durango, Mexico, the local Committee for the Defense of the

Environment, which was protesting river pollution, began working through peasants and factory workers in the late 1970s. By 1989, the group had met with the president of the country and had become so powerful and knowledgeable about pollution that the committee was made accountable for the dispersal of federal funds for river cleanup.[17] In Brazil, demonstrations by thousands of rubber-tappers and years of pressure from environmental groups led the government to slowly shift away from subsidizing the deforestation of the Amazon and to create fourteen extractive reserves that benefit 9,000 families and cover almost 7.5 million acres (Garrison 1991, 43; see also Box 3.1).

Mass demonstrations are often tailored to a particular sustainable development message. In Karnataka, India, in 1987, a lumber company organized by the state government leased out 70,000 acres of forestland for eucalyptus trees, thereby depriving 500,000 villagers of fodder, fuel, fruits, and small timber. In response, a group of GRSOs organized "pluck and plant" marches, with thousands of villagers pulling up eucalyptus seedlings and planting a wide range of native trees.[18]

Despite the risks, mass protests involving human rights or the expansion of citizenship are also becoming more prevalent. Demonstrations organized by NGOs in Thailand in 1992 led to the collapse of the National Peace-Keeping Council (Clarke 1996, 16). Indeed, one observer argues that "there is no sector in Thai society . . . more closely identified with and committed to political democracy and economic development for all than the private voluntary organizations" (Gohlert 1992, cited in Clarke 1996, 16). In Brazil, a national street children's movement involves street children in its decision making and has invited hundreds of them to its conventions and marches on Congress. Its activities have resulted in two new child protection articles being added to the Brazilian constitution and a congressional statute codifying children's rights (Moreira 1993, 39). Protest may also focus on pervasive national injustices backed by special-interest groups. An Ashoka fellow in Maharashtra formed a mass-based organization to protest debt slavery among tribal people. Despite a violent reaction from landowners, the state government collaborated by forming vigilance committees, and the Indian Supreme Court appointed a commission on the rehabilitation of freed debt slaves (Ashoka n.d.).

People don't have to march in the streets to be part of a mass protest. NGOs with large national memberships often use their members or other citizens to build a database or to write letters.

■ The Alliance of Costa Rican Women uses its 15,000 members to work with women's groups, negotiate with health officials, and represent women on policy-making commissions.

■ The Brazilian Institute of Political Ecology sponsors a "24-hour green phone" for the public to report environmental problems; these are registered in a data bank, and the information is then transferred to the appropriate public agencies (Thompson 1990, 24).

■ In Bangladesh, BRAC decided to take on the issue of official corruption in the distribution of relief supplies. To do this, it drew on the detailed knowledge of hundreds of members of the landless organizations it works with at the village level. Yet, according to an activist who had interviewed "the power elites," they also "supplied us with considerable information about themselves and each other. Later, we obtained help from a government official, who gave up substantial time to clarify various points for us" (Bangladesh Rural Advancement Committee 1986, 136). Armed with these data and supplementary information, the staff of BRAC was able to create a complete, up-to-date map of local corruption patterns and connections. Finally, it was able to identify and publicize key power brokers, whose networks extended across villages and into different levels of government.

These examples demonstrate that when protest is coupled with careful research and planning, it can enhance organizational autonomy and overcome enormous political obstacles. In Ecuador, for example, the Centro Ecuatoriano para la Promocion y Accion de la Mujer (CEPAM) sponsored a mass protest campaign to keep open government-run safe houses for victims of domestic violence. Although CEPAM used demonstrations and the media, it was its carefully researched presentation to the Congress that swayed legislative opinion.[19]

Whatever form it takes, knowledgeable advocacy allows NGOs to confront a wide range of government policies, including indifference. It makes co-optation more difficult and may lead to closer forms of collaboration that do not detract from the autonomy of NGOs. Whether advocacy can be viewed, overall, as more or less effective than collaboration, it has probably had more impact on service delivery than on service redistribution, more impact on local environmental crises than on national policy, and more impact on strengthening civil society than on instituting top-down democratic reforms. For example, Kenyan NGOs are not prepared, according to Ndegwa (1996, 111), to act as a group against the dictatorship until their existence is threatened. "Civil society does not cause political liberalization, . . . the democratic movement is a larger force engulfing the whole of society to which civil society actors respond."[20]

Yet, as Ndegwa (1996, 1) also argues, the right leadership may allow GRSOs to contribute to top-down democratization. He contends that organization, resources, alliances, and political opportunity are necessary but not sufficient conditions "to advance democracy." Just as I have argued that some NGOs play a vanguard role in lobbying for democratization, Ndegwa shows that GRSOs such as the Greenbelt Movement, which openly advocates political pluralism and top-down democratization, influence the political system. In contrast, the leadership of the Undugu Society remains "politically obtuse" and "aloof to political reform, even though the grassroots empowerment of Undugu members may contribute to bottom-up democratization" (Ndegwa 1996, 117, 4). Because of such differences in leadership, "the organizational contributions of civil society to political reform are much more nuanced than many studies of activist organizations would have us believe" (Ndegwa 1996, 115).

Cooperation with Government

Chapter 2 examined a few systemwide policies of cooperation between NGOs and governments. Cooperation at the project level is far more common, whether initiated by NGOs or by governments. Cooperative project strategies include everything from parallel cooperation to full field collaboration.

Cooperative strategies often coexist with advocacy within any given NGO (see Box 4.1). A Malaysian environmental network, for example, plays the role of critical outsider, yet has good relationships with people in key national ministries (Rush 1991). Sometimes NGOs pursue mixed strategies in order to tailor their tactics to particular issues and relevant official bureaucracies. Under Pinochet, Chilean GRSOs made a distinction between the public sector, which implemented government policies and with which they collaborated, and the dictatorial regime, which they viewed as temporary. This meant that Chilean GROs could raise money for neighborhood first-aid rooms used by government health workers, and their efforts were encouraged by GRSOs, which understood that "there is a collective memory in the health service of a long tradition of good relations with the community" (Infante 1989, 64).

Although some GRSOs oriented toward advocacy shun cooperation with government, other GRSOs point out that if organizations with strong grassroots ties are reluctant to cooperate with governments, less scrupulous organizations attracted to official funding are likely to evolve (Clark 1991, 79). In fact, Alyosis Fernandez, the director of a large Indian GRSO called Myrada, argues that "it is the poor who suffer as the result of our ideological pride" (Leach 1988, 90–1). Myrada has made deliberate shifts

---

Box 4.1 Cooperation and Advocacy

In Dharwad, India, in 1985, a scientific team from Samaj Parivartana Samudaya (SPS) accepted financial support from the Karnataka State Pollution Control Board for a yearlong study of water and soil pollution, even as SPS was organizing mass protest marches and filing suits about the pollution of the Tungabhadra River. As of 1991, the board had improved its performance with NGO representation, the Tungabhadra was less polluted, fishermen had obtained legal aid as compensation for fish kills, and far more people were willing to complain to the government about environmental problems. (*Source:* Hiremath 1991.)

---

toward meeting the Indian government's "People Sector" challenge by channeling funds made available under government programs to the poor instead of relying on foreign funds.[21]

Such deliberate NGO initiation may have other benefits as well. In their study of thirteen field collaborations in Asia and Africa, Brown and Ashman (1995, 19) found that "the catalyst organizations associated with the clear successes are indigenous NGOs or grassroots networks. The catalysts for the three questionable cases, in contrast, are a government Ministry, an international donor agency, and a collection of competing agencies of different sorts."

Despite the complexity of their political strategies, some GRSOs concentrate on one ministry or autonomous agency (see Box 4.2). For example, the Grameen Bank works almost exclusively with the Bangladesh Central Bank. The Asociación Colombiana de Promoción Artesanal (ACPA) has played a major role in helping the Ministry of Education develop a hands-on curriculum for the Escuelas Nuevas, now in half of Colombia's 26,000 rural schools (Goff 1994, 134).[22] Other connections with single bureaucracies are more surprising. Widjanarka, an antipesticide campaigner in Indonesia, persuaded several of the leading rural GRSOs to participate in a test of organic farming on thirty-five acres of prime Jakarta land owned by the Indonesian Air Force (Ashoka 1985).

Although cooperation between NGOs and governments may be less likely than advocacy to lead to top-down democratization, habits of give-and-take with NGOs may increase tolerance for the autonomy of civil society. In Sri Lanka, formal conferences between government and NGOs have been held at the national and provincial levels to assess official plans and search for new areas of cooperation (Fernandez 1987). The 1985–90 national plan in India included the incorporation of NGOs into eighteen sectors of activity (Berg 1987, 29).

Box 4.2 Cooperation between NGOs and Autonomous Agencies

It may be easier for GRSOs to cooperate with autonomous governmental agencies than with line ministries. Autonomous agencies tend to be less dependent on top-down approval, have similar technical or programmatic interests, and are more recently established. The Instituto Boliviano de Tecnologia Apropriada (IBTA), for example, is a semiautonomous government institution that provides technical assistance and training for GRSOs and their field technicians, who are, in turn, responsible for field extension. Participating GRSOs are represented on the national technical directorate of IBTA and also on its regional councils.

Implementation research carried out in the United States flags the importance of selecting new agencies for reform strategies. Where this is not possible, as with compensatory education in the United States, reform is far more difficult. (*Sources:* Bebbington 1991, 25; Sabatier 1986, 27.)

Cooperation may also, of course, lead to co-optation, particularly when NGOs fit themselves into government plans. Co-optation depends as much on tacit acceptance by NGOs as on heavy-handed official bureaucracies. It may also be that some capable bureaucrats who initially want to listen to and learn from NGOs are later overcome by political pressures related to major redistributive issues. For example, in the Philippines, extensive field collaborations between NGOs and a number of different governmental departments have produced widely varying results—from a dramatic increase in reforestation, where redistributive issues were not involved, to the siphoning off of 70 percent of agrarian reform funds for landlord compensation.[23] Fear of co-optation may lead some NGOs to cooperate only with subnational governments (as illustrated in the next chapter), remain isolated, or opt for parallel cooperation.

PARALLEL COOPERATION   Some NGOs prefer mutually supportive but parallel field relationships with government rather than joint field collaborations. In addition to fears of co-optation, NGOs with strong ties to GRO networks and independent foreign financial support may see little advantage in collaborative implementation. They may also view parallel cooperation as a positive short-term strategy to avoid duplication.[24] On a somewhat more active level, the health unit of Seva Mandir in India has secured government recognition of its credentials, so that it can refer patients to government health centers when necessary. And in Zimbabwe, when the government forbade the planting of individual gardens less than thirty meters from a riverbank, Environnement et Developpement Action-Tiers Monde (ENDA) reached an informal agreement with the government, allowing it to help groups of farmers plant group vegetable gardens (Thomas-Slayter 1992, 139–40).[25]

Parallel cooperation may also be a precursor to full field collaboration. A GRSO organized by an Ashoka fellow in Guerrero, Mexico, uses a deliberately nonconfrontational approach with the government that promotes horizontal economic networks of farmers that parallel failing government programs; this increases the chances for cooperation, which may even evolve into collaboration (Ashoka 1988, 4).

For their part, governments may see parallel cooperation as a simple way of stretching limited resources, thus handing funding as well as implementation responsibility to an NGO (Robinson 1997, 71). The Ghanian government, for example, confines its provision of basic services to larger communities and allows GRSOs to organize on their own in other areas (Anang 1994, 103). In many other cases of apparent parallel cooperation, however, it is more likely that governments are simply unaware of NGO efforts (Holloway 1989c, 151–2).

FIELD COLLABORATION   Field collaborations between governments and NGOs involve joint planning and implementation and are more diverse than parallel relationships. Despite the common perception of NGOs as subcontractors for service provision, Farrington and Bebbington's (1993, 186) intensive look at NGO–government collaboration in agriculture in Asia, Africa, and Latin America provides a different perspective:

> *structural linkage mechanisms* in which one organization . . . [usually a government] has an influence over resource allocation and programming decisions in the other organizations . . . [usually NGOs] are not nearly as common as *operational linkage mechanisms* in which organizations collaborate around more specific project objectives.

This is probably because so many NGOs initiate linkages.[26] Although some NGOs function as government service providers, autonomous organizations are well aware that they are more likely "to retain an institutional identity that in some sense resembles their past, if they pursue a link with government in which they develop innovations for presentation to government, rather than one in which they implement public programmes" (Farrington and Bebbington 1993, 48). Even strong, autonomous organizations can become weaker and more vulnerable, however, if they accept government financial support.

Fortunately, NGOs subcontracted by the government also fill new roles not previously carried out by the government and can institutionalize and disseminate innovation. In Costa Rica, INBIO was created as a unique nonprofit organization designed to develop an inventory of the country's biodiversity, in collaboration with the Ministry of Natural Resources,

Energy, and Mines. Yet INBIO also helps attract and channel both domestic and international funding for national parks and, like other Costa Rican NGOs, is free to collect samples or proceed with any research, as long as it communicates the results to the National Park Service (Meyer 1995, 9–10).

Diversity is also related to the importance of individual contacts.[27] In their worldwide survey of NGO–government ties in agriculture, Farrington and Bebbington (1993, 46, 189) point out that the quality of individual relationships may have "more influence on any decision regarding inter-institutional coordination than generalized institutional relationships and images" and that "personal networks cutting across institutional boundaries [are] one of the most important prerequisites for successful collaborations." They argue strongly for support for staff secondments and working groups to lay the bases for such ties.[28]

Sometimes personal ties can have a major impact on policy.[29] Thai Forestry Department scientists who were in contact with NGOs broke with the bureaucracy during the controversy over the proposed Nam Choan Campgiang Dam, and the project was defeated (Rush 1991, 54). In other cases, the impact of a personal contact may be visible only in retrospect:

> Yayasan Indonesia Sejahtera (YIS) is an Indonesian public health and family planning GRSO that organizes GROs and has close relationships with the Departments of Health, Social Affairs and the National Family Planning Board. This represents a big change from the 1970's, when the government was trying to impose goals from the top down. The policy shift began when the provincial governor of Central Java, a strong NGO advocate, became the national Minister for Home Affairs. As YIS was one of a relatively small number of groups pioneering such participatory approaches . . . at that time, it can reasonably be inferred that YIS had some significant impact on his thinking. (Eldridge 1988, 13)

Sometimes, however, personal ties between GRSOs and governments may "undermine attempts to weaken the patrimonial character of bureaucratic decision-making."[30] And the long-term impact of the "revolving door" phenomenon between governments and NGOs is still unclear (see Box 4.3).

Grassroots organizations also develop personal contacts within bureaucracies. Squatter neighborhood associations in Latin America are particularly adept at petitioning bureaucracies for urban services through personal contacts and have sometimes even used the wives of presidents (Fisher 1984). Ironically, GROs that depend on government financial support do not always maintain these ties. Rural local development associations in Colombia lost government support for an excellent program of road building that lowered costs through volunteer labor because project organizers failed to build support among high government officials (Uphoff 1986b, 283).

Box 4.3 The Revolving Door

In addition to building up personal contacts within governments, GRSO "graduates" have been moving into government positions. As the founders of the Dominican Development Foundation were joining the government in 1989 and some politicians were creating their own GRSOs, Enrique Fernandez, the Dominican head of Solidarios, a Latin American GRSO consortium, noted that "the Third Sector is gaining political space in Latin America." In Namibia, there has been a brain drain from NGOs to the new government since independence.

Such appointments can also foster systemwide cooperation. In the Philippines, some GRSO leaders joined Aquino's government in both traditional departments and new commissions, including the Commission on the Urban Poor and programs for rural employment generation. The Department of Environment and Natural Resources, headed by an environmentalist and former human rights lawyer, has granted no new timber licenses and closed hundreds of illegal sawmills and wood-processing plants.

In fact, the flow of personnel between the independent and the government sectors now moves in both directions, and some governments are "aggrieved by NGOs headhunting." The Haribon Foundation in the Philippines was founded by Celso Roque, a physicist who had been Marcos's minister of natural resources. Haribon launched a white-paper series linking environmental degradation to poverty and garnered a million signatures to ban international trade in logs and wildlife. In 1987, Roque again joined the new government of Corazon Aquino. (*Sources:* Fruhling 1985, 66; Viola 1987, 23; interview with Enrique Fernandez at the Interaction Forum, Danvers, Massachusetts, May 8, 1989; Levy 1996, 146–9; Sandberg and Martin 1994, 172; Garilao 1987; Rush 1991, 79, 82; Farrington and Bebbington 1994, 11; Allison and Macinko 1993, 45.)

FIELD COLLABORATION AND SCALING OUT DEVELOPMENT EFFORTS

NGOs increasingly use contacts with government to extend the reach of local development efforts. Although scaling out through GRO networks without government collaboration is common in some countries—Peru and Bolivia, for example—and GRSOs have developed extraordinary management innovations to extend their reach in others—such as Bangladesh and Colombia—in many other countries, collaboration with government may offer the best hope for NGOs to enlarge their impact beyond the micro level.

A particularly hopeful means of scaling out can be built on direct government collaboration with GRO networks, even without GRSOs (see Box 5.4 in the next chapter). In Bangladesh, for example, where the admittedly vast numbers of people reached by GRSOs constitute only 20 percent of the total population, horizontal networking among GROs is the only possible vehicle for scaling out either government or GRSO efforts. Although GROs and their networks also develop contacts with governments in other Asian countries and in Latin America, they are less likely to do so in Africa, because of the weakness of governments (Farrington and Bebbington 1993, 192). In many cases, of course, GRO–government collaborations are facilitated by GRSOs. In Bombay, for example, SPARC (Society for the Promotion of Area Resource Centers) has facilitated government negotiations with a GRO network of pavement dwellers (Clark 1991, 115).[31]

The combined efforts of governments and NGOs may, in fact, be more effective than solo interventions by either sector. An evaluation in southern India showed that a combination of subsidized credit from official banks through the government's Integrated Rural Development Program (IRDP) and NGOs has reached the poorest of the poor, increased savings and land sales to smaller farmers, and led to a higher standard of living. A previous evaluation showed not only that the IRDP's solo operation had failed to benefit the poor but that "the evidence strongly indicated that NGO involvement improved the effectiveness and impact of IRDP investments" (Robinson 1992, 398, 399, 406, 416).

For their part, NGOs are likely to become more effective when the government provides infrastructure and "removes economic distortions against the rural sector and human capital formation" (Farrington and Bebbington 1994, 9).[32] Although Mexican GROs and GRSOs were instrumental in pressuring the government to sponsor self-built low-income housing after the 1985 earthquake, NGO financial resources were meager. Government contractors built or repaired more than 44,000 units in record time, compared with only a few thousand built by NGOs (Fox and Hernandez 1992). De Coninck (1992, 114) argues that in Uganda, NGOs are "better placed to strengthen governmental institutions weakened by civil war than to set up their own delivery systems."

If collaboration provides governments with lowered costs and NGOs with an increased ability to scale out, why isn't everybody doing it? The first answer to this question is that we don't know that they are not. Collaboration is widespread and growing, but there is no systematic cross-national, cross-sectoral research on how common it really is. The second answer is that even successful development is full of trade-offs. For example, lowered costs are dependent on popular participation. Yet GRSOs that find it easy to establish government linkages may find it hard to maintain grassroot ties and strengthen government accountability once they become collaborators with governments. Concentration on the provision of services may also erode political advocacy, as GRSOs become identified in the public mind with a particular regime (Fowler 1988,

22–4). For their part, governments may find that they have bitten off more than they can chew in terms of popular challenges to established bureaucratic power and vested interests. Alternatively, collaboration may dilute the government's need to listen to beneficiaries.

Scaling out also provides formidable management challenges for both sides, particularly in service provision. Some argue that although NGO pilot projects may be useful demonstrations, innovations in service provision are more difficult to administer when initiated by NGOs and should be operated within the government (Klinmahorm and Ireland 1992, 67). Others claim that NGO pilots can lessen government suspicion of NGOs and make wider replication more likely (Farrington and Bebbington 1993, 162–3). What is not in contention is that jumping from pilot to wider replication is difficult even within one NGO. Adding government to the equation further complicates implementation.

Perhaps some of the complexities and difficulties of collaboration might be avoided if NGOs and governments could strengthen mutual learning processes. Unfortunately, built-in learning processes are not always viewed as important. Farrington and Bebbington (1993, 165) found that joint government–NGO evaluations in agricultural research were common only in Asia.[33] Nor does collaboration negotiated in the capital city necessarily translate into field learning. In Colombia, where GRSOs provide services in the remote regions of southern Santander and the southwest Pacific coast, Brian Smith (1990, 260) found that government responsiveness to conditions of poverty in these regions had not increased. In fact, collaboration may have a weaker impact on government policies than that achieved by less intense but longer-run forms of influence, such as training government officials (see Chapter 3).

Collaboration can, however, lead to informal learning on both sides.[34] Collaborative experience provides GRSOs with the continuing ability to refine their political as well as technical skills. And governments rely heavily on the technical knowledge and experience that GRSOs can offer them. Small specialized GRSO networks may offer even more educational advantages to governments. In Bolivia, the Programa Campesino Alternativo de Desarrollo (PROCADE) of the network UNITAS included twelve GRSOs working in 322 communities by the end of 1990. With a combined field staff of ninety agronomists and educators, PROCADE has a research plan that assigns topics and channels funds to reorient the Instituto Boliviano de Tecnologia Agropecuario (IBTA) (Bebbington 1991, 28).

A common assumption in much of the NGO literature is that NGOs that engage in advocacy tend to be more independent of government and to have more impact on government policy than those that collaborate with governments. The evidence presented here suggests that advocacy, like collaboration, may have more impact on the delivery of services than on redistributive policies, more impact on local environmental crises than on national policy, and more impact on strengthening civil society than on engendering top-down democratic reforms. Yet collaborative strategies are not inconsistent with maintaining NGO autonomy and are not always limited to service delivery.

With the possible exception of a strategy of isolation under extremely repressive contexts, there appears to be little relationship between NGO political strategies, which are often proactive and flexible, and political context (see Najam 1996b, 15). Advocacy can be tailored to a wide range of contexts, and collaboration may be possible even under repressive conditions, if it is limited to autonomous or technically oriented government agencies. Moreover, collaboration and advocacy often coexist within one NGO or within an NGO network.

Despite the promise of scaled-out grassroots organizing, the political obstacles to both advocacy and innovative collaboration remain formidable, even where a measure of pluralism prevails. In Colombia in 1987, for example, peasants not tied to any political party took over many haciendas. Although most of the takeovers were in areas where armed guerrillas were not active, President Betancur chose to negotiate a modest agrarian reform proposal with the guerrillas rather than with the peasant organizations. In addition, NGOs have only begun to forge partnerships with other political players who could help strengthen civil society.[35] In Chile, NGOs face the challenge of building ties to a strong multiparty political system that had been suppressed by the Pinochet regime and has now reemerged.

Will NGOs achieve a critical mass and be able to help reform the inequities and injustices that plague the Third World? One way of tackling this question—by assessing the collective weight of many small interactions between NGOs and governments—is particularly daunting. On the plus side, the sheer growth in numbers of GROs, GRSOs, and their networks is bound to make contacts with governments more likely in those countries—now probably a majority—where NGOs are not perceived as a general threat by national governments.[36] Once governments understand the value of reaching more people through collaboration with autonomous organizations, they may provide NGOs with increased resources that make scaling out more possible. The government of India, for example, has been gradually ceding rights to local users of forestland, in response to NGO pressures (Colchester 1994, 90). On the minus side, the likelihood that this collective accumulation will eventually reach a critical mass that successfully challenges entrenched interests is problematic at best. Reforms that threaten power monopolies are notoriously difficult to convert into political action. In Bangladesh, for example,

ADAB's remarkable national success in organizing the landless will be difficult to convert into government support for agrarian reform.

The key unknown—which will probably vary dramatically, depending on the country—is the potential strength of grassroots networking. If organizational autonomy and capabilities are expanded into larger networks at the grassroots or national level, then the widening collective impact of NGOs can affect not only sustainable development and government policy but also democratization.[37] By the mid-1990s, it was increasingly evident that the vitality and spread of horizontal grassroots organizing in some Asian and Latin American countries had strengthened NGO autonomy and also offered promise that bottom-up democratization might eventually translate into top-down political change.[38] The environmental movement in Asia is increasingly dependent on mass mobilization linking the structural causes of poverty to environmental degradation (see Rush 1991). In Brazil, the active political role of the Catholic base communities in the 1980s laid the foundation for a massive movement against hunger and poverty (described later) (Mainwaring and Viola 1984, 19). Perhaps most impressive was the ability of the grassroots tribal movement in Latin America, supported by GRSOs, INGOs, and international networking among Latin American GRSOs, to successfully challenge the very heart of inequitable land tenure based on violent encroachment:

> The Andauja tribe living in Xingu national park in Brazil responded to the violent encroachment of ranchers by rebuilding their burned village and asking the government to survey the land and affirm their lawful occupancy. When the government did nothing, the tribe got help from the Rainforest Foundation and surveyed it themselves. They are also cooperating with the Nucleus for Indigenous Rights in Brazilia to expand the park boundaries, and create a major precedent [for advancing indigenous rights]. (Ireland 1991, 56–7)

Similarly, in Bolivia, over 1,200 indigenous people from the Amazon region marched 750 kilometers to La Paz under conditions of heat and humidity to challenge timber and mining concessions. After the march became a national media story, President Jaime Paz Zamora and his ministers rushed to greet the group as it arrived in the capital and issued three decrees ending the concessions and establishing a million hectares of permanently protected or indigenously managed zones in the Chimanes forest (Arena De-Rosa 1991, 6–7).[39] In Argentina as well, tribal organizations have successfully pressured the government about tribal land rights and gained representation on local government bodies (Sabanes 1988, 88).

A second way to answer the critical mass question is exemplified by Peter Uvin's (1995, 927–39) use of NGO data from the files of the World Hunger Program at Brown University to see how the organizations fall into David Korten's "four generations" of NGO strategies. First-generation strategies, according to Korten, are those concentrating on relief and direct delivery of services. Second-generation strategies focus on local self-reliance. Third-generation strategies look beyond the local level to seek policy change. And fourth-generation strategies look beyond changes in specific policies "to energize a critical mass of independent, decentralized initiative in support of a social vision" (Korten 1990, 114–28).

Uvin's research shows no linkage between third-generation strategies and either the type of NGO (GRO or GRSO) or the national political context. Even though only six of the twenty-five GROs and GRSOs studied were carrying out third-generation strategies, four of these had moved from first- or second-generation strategies. And of the four organizations that began at the first-generation level, only two had remained there. Although the evidence presented in *The Road from Rio* supports Uvin's conclusion that the vast majority of Third World NGOs are at the second-generation stage, the evidence presented in this volume suggests that third-generation and even fourth-generation strategies are becoming increasingly prevalent, regardless of political context, even though sequential routes vary.

Moreover, even one fourth-generation network may impact tens or even hundreds of thousands of people. Wherever fourth-generation strategies are being pursued, they can strengthen advocacy efforts quite dramatically, as exemplified by the international networks of indigenous peoples described in the previous and present chapters. Fourth-generation strategies are also used to unite a much wider variety of people in urban areas.

In Brazil, a Citizens Campaign focusing on absolute poverty has been organized by Herbert Beinho de Souza, a hemophiliac with AIDS, who is the Executive Secretary of IBASE (Brazilian Institute of Social and Economic Analysis). As of 1995, it included 4700 citizens groups in all 27 states, loosely coordinated at the national level, and funded by Brazilian universities, the Inter-American Foundation and other international donors. The campaign functions as a clearinghouse, represents the movement in contacts with the government, and briefs the press on a wide variety of local activities carried out through GRSOs, churches, universities, unions, business groups, GROs and schools. Member organizations survey the level of need for food and jobs, identify local producers and service providers and draw up plans of action that are most likely to reach the poor.

Interestingly, this massive effort is increasingly drawing in employees of state-run corporations and public agencies. Petrobras converted its dry oil wells in the Northeast into water sources for poor families. EMBRATEL, the government communication agency, is using its satellites to beam television programs to health promoters throughout the country. Furnas Central Elétricas, a regional utility, used nine dams as fish farms to feed the hungry and ceded large tracts of lake-side land to small-scale farmers (Garrison and Landim 1995, 40).[40]

In other words, fourth-generation strategies may not be limited to pressuring the government from the outside and may increasingly include individual government employees, if not portions of governments.

In India, the Integrated Child Development Service (ICDS) has "chapters" within the following: the government of India, every state government, local government departments, academic institutions, consulting companies, major bilateral donors, UN agencies, international NGOs, GRSOs, and GROs (Gibbons 1994, 2–3). The network is based on local community volunteers plus "emergent self-organization" at other levels (6). "Remarkably, the centers around the country essentially operate in much the same manner to provide a consistent level of health referrals, parent education, nutrition and education for children, with only periodic supervision. . . . [ICDS is a] decentralized network of empowered local service providers, who know and can do enough, are supported and also trusted enough to operate in their communities independent of the vicissitudes of any of the larger systems of which they are a part" (8). Each governmental and nongovernmental institution in the network offers only a small fraction of what is needed, but together they have a much greater impact.[41]

Do these fourth-generation examples from Brazil and India imply that governments can become more responsive, more aware of the needs of their people, more willing to learn from people outside the government? Not necessarily. But these examples do suggest that despite the elitist, self-serving, and often corrupt reputations of many Third World governments, individual government employees can behave "out of character," given innovative networking models, which could be further promoted by international NGOs and donors.

Even repressive governments are increasingly having to contend with NGOs. For example, the Kenyan government's attempts to repress the independent sector were ultimately defeated by NGOs, which first sought coexistence, then used protests, and finally employed sanctions against the state (Ndegwa 1996).

Moreover, although bureaucratic reforms such as those described in Chapter 2 are uncommon, a kind of slow nongovernmental "subversion" of traditional bureaucratic behavior does seem to be occurring in some countries. Most government employees and policy makers are as smart and opportunistic, if not as reflective, committed, and well educated, as many who lead GRSOs. GRSOs not only fill gaps in government services, particularly in remote regions, but also help mold policies that reflect positively on policy makers. Collaboration will also mean that governments that depend on NGOs for implementation will lose bargaining strength with NGOs and "will not be able to set the agenda independently" (Farrington and Bebbington 1993, 194).

Still a third way of answering the critical mass question, related to the generational lens on NGO evolution, is to take a long-term view. Research on political reforms in the United States indicates that policy changes should be observed over at least a decade (Sabatier 1986, 29). And since Third World NGOs often begin their work in an institutional or political vacuum, it is even more important than it would be in the United States to evaluate their impact over time. In Indonesia, a small group of physicians and social workers founded an affiliate of the International Planned Parenthood Association in 1957. By 1964, it had established fifty-nine clinics; by 1970, the government had established its own program; by the late 1980s, thirty years after the NGO was founded, the Indonesian government was operating one of the most extensive family planning programs in the Third World (Danoewidjojo 1980, 635–98). In Bangladesh, it took many years for the government to take notice of BRAC's nonformal primary schools, which achieve low dropout rates by adjusting hours of operation to a subsistence agricultural economy (Lovell 1987).

Failure along the way can become an essential component of this long-run learning process. The community development movement in India gained attention in the 1950s with the nongovernmental Etawah project. Government attempts to replicate Etawah more widely failed, but that failure contributed to much of the thinking that is now prevalent among GRSOs, which has, in turn, influenced newer government programs (see Box 4.4). In other cases, of course, relationships between NGOs and governments can lead to a dead end. In Tanzania, the Ruvuma Development Association (RDA), active in many villages in the early 1960s, became the model for the national Ujamaa village development program adopted in 1967. When the government dissolved the RDA and incorporated its villages into the government program, it lost the advantages of collaboration and cross-fertilization with an already established model (Hyden 1983, 122).

Although autonomy is crucial if NGOs are to have an impact on government, it is clear that they do not follow a neat, sequential, long-term path by first strengthening autonomy as completely as possible and then influencing policy. Indeed, an autonomous self-definition and strong grassroots ties may be sufficient to allow an NGO to develop the other attributes of autonomy (for example, research capacity) while it interacts

---

Box 4.4   Grassroots Support within a University

Sometimes, the twists and turns in long-term relationships with government are remarkably complex. The Brazilian GRSO called UNIJUI, established within the University of Ijui in Rio Grande do Sul, has been promoting education for development among small farmers for over thirty years. In 1960, UNIJUI organized hundreds of small farmer groups that became a model for other cooperatives and rural workers unions in the state. UNIJUI provided effective rural extension and a major employment training program while government programs faltered. UNIJUI was strong because it was not tied to state patronage, but then the local affiliate of ARENA, the military government's party, claimed control and the project ceased, interrupting UNIJUI's organizational advance to a third-generation approach. By the mid-1980s, however, UNIJUI had been approached for help by other regions of Brazil and by the federal government, including the National Institute for Agrarian Reform. Frantz (1987) considers that this policy impact became possible because of democratic change in the overall political context.

---

with government as advocate or collaborator. Autonomy can be enhanced, even in repressive political contexts. And some advocacy strategies may be less threatening to governments than others.

What moves an organization along a line toward or away from autonomy, empowerment, and policy impact depends not only on political context and internal characteristics but also on the influence of other NGOs and NGO networking. Despite the caution of the more established Colombian GRSOs, environmental organizations in Colombia strongly influenced the government's 1990 decision to legally cede more than half of the remaining rain forests to the tribes that inhabit them. GROs can also push GRSOs into more overtly political roles over time, as evidenced by the urban self-help organizations in the Philippines that helped topple Marcos (Durning 1989, 80).

There is no direct way to estimate how many long-term relationships between governments and NGOs have positive results, although relationships that continue undoubtedly have certain advantages for both sides. GRSOs that do not reject government connections out of hand have the opportunity to reach far more people as they develop more effective ways of attacking poverty and protecting the environment. And governments have the potential to enhance their legitimacy by building bridges to local communities. Perhaps the real question is the degree to which NGOs can maintain their commitment to sustainable development and grassroots empowerment in the face of the inevitable temptations of political power and individual advancement. There is some evidence that the so-called iron law of oligarchy may not inevitably set in as NGOs become more prominent, precisely because many NGO leaders are self-consciously determined to avoid it.[42]

Obviously, long-run change may be accelerated or halted by other variables in political context, such as congruence in development goals. Edwards and Hulme (1996b, 11) argue that positive results usually occur because a "whole series of forces and actors came together," and Bratton (1989) found that congruence has given GRSOs more political influence in Zimbabwe than in Kenya. If governments continue to collaborate successfully with the independent sector over a longer period of time, however, such congruence will not depend so exclusively on the initial ideology or orientation of government policy makers but will be a natural result of the process. A Thai survey done in 1984, for example, showed that although collaboration was still relatively new, it was widely practiced and accepted, and half of both the government and NGO respondents agreed that innovations initiated by development organizations had an impact on government selection of development methodologies (Tongsawate and Tipps 1985, 60).

Is the independent sector becoming more politically sophisticated, more able to work with and through government to reach larger numbers of people? The evidence indicates that reciprocal learning is occurring in many countries. Still in doubt is how extensive it is and whether it will continue at its current accelerating pace.

These first four chapters, which deal with the NGO relationship at the national level, have explored a number of factors that seem to enhance the autonomy of NGOs and therefore the likelihood that they will selectively and consciously use advocacy and/or collaboration to impact government policy. Despite differences among countries and areas of the Third World, the political tactics and approaches of development organizations are remarkably similar. Yet the obstacles to successful mass mobilizations remain formidable. The long-run impact of NGOs will, therefore, also depend on the wider processes of democratization and political development examined in Chapters 1 and 6 and on the NGO–subnational government interactions I examined in the next chapter. NGO relationships with local governments, regional governments, and even local administrators of national regimes often develop independently from relationships at the national level and can reinforce or undermine NGO –government relationships at the national level.

Notes

1. By "complimentary," Najam (1996b) means that NGOs coordinate or at least take account of one another's field activities. See also Farrington and Bebbington's (1993, 127–8) discussion.
2. Clark (1995, 597) describes another pattern characterized by NGOs becoming "dependent clients" of the state, as in Tanzania during the 1980s or China today. This could be added as a subcategory of cooperation. Riker (1995a, 23) adds another category—competition between NGOs and governments. However, he gives no examples of this, and I have been unable to find any in the literature.
3. When multiple goals are pursued, one is sometimes achieved at the expense of the other. Jane Covey (1996, 205) notes that the cancellation of the Sierra Madre forest project by Mexico and the World Bank had "no civil society impact" because the NGO problem definition and tactics were suited to achieving policy change with institutions that themselves have low levels of public accountability, such as the World Bank. A logging ban pushed by environmental NGOs in the Philippines did succeed in building a grassroots environmental constituency, however.
4. I recently visited Lake Atitlan as part of an evaluation for Trickle Up. Although the area still suffers from violence, it is now less likely to be politically motivated than it was in 1990.
5. Beatrice Chileshe, presentation at the Association for Women in Development, Washington, D.C., 1987.
6. Presentation by Ezra Mgani at the symposium Shaping the Policy Debate: The Role of Non-Governmental Organizations in International Development, John F. Kennedy School, Harvard University, April 22, 1993. Sometimes, NGOs play a more aggressive international role. In 1988–89, the Sudan Council of Churches was actively involved in peacemaking between the government and the Southern Peoples Liberation Army. The council sent a delegation to Europe, North America, and other African countries to encourage them to help. Through its ties with Church World Service, it asked the U.S. government to put pressure on the Sudanese government to reach a settlement (see Korten 1990, 188–9).
7. Ironically, FEE has been helped by the absence of a national NGO association.
8. Agus Purnomo at an Asia Society conference entitled Beyond Boundaries: Issues in Asian and American Environmental Activism, April 24–26, 1991.
9. See also Society for Participatory Research in Asia 1991.
10. See also Welch's (1995, 198) discussion of South Africa's Legal Resources Center, which employed forty-two lawyers as of 1992, processing 3,000 new cases in that year alone.
11. For example, the Indian Council of NGOs is a consultative organ of the Parliament (Gueneau 1988).
12. Interview with Connecticut State Representative Irving Stolberg, after his visit to Brazil in 1988.
13. According to Edwards and Hulme (1996a, 5), there are still few examples of NGOs entering the formal political process.

14. Case study done by LEADERS for the conference Beyond Boundaries: Issues in Asian and American Environmental Activism, Asia Society, New York, April 24–26, 1991.

15. The association also has an advocacy unit. Its public education campaign includes medical professionals, NGOs, and people's science movements (Society for Participatory Research in Asia 1991).

16. According to Van der Heijden (1987), this role resembles that of European nonprofit organizations during the nineteenth century.

17. Presentation by Gabriel Camara, consultant to the Inter-American Foundation, Interaction Forum, Danvers, Massachusetts, May 1989.

18. Conversation with S. R. Hiremath at the conference Beyond Boundaries: Issues in Asian and American Environmental Activism, Asia Society, New York, April 24–26, 1991.

19. Like many other politically active GRSOs, CEPAM is also heavily involved in promoting participation and empowering women at the grassroots level. Grassroots enterprises such as lunchrooms are used as meeting places (author's visit to CEPAM and interview with Susana Vasconez, April 1996).

20. Ndegwa excludes political parties from "civil society."

21. Myrada also lets people know about loans provided by DWCRA (Development of Women and Children in Rural Areas).

22. The Escuelas Nuevas have been visited by education officials from forty-six other countries.

23. For an excellent review of the complexity of NGO–government collaboration in the Philippines, see Clarke 1995.

24. A survey of forty Asian NGOs concluded that avoiding duplication was a major factor motivating ties with governments (Allison and Kak 1992). In Peru, the Centro de Estudios Para el Desarrollo y la Participacion (CEDEP) merely seeks to avoid overlap with government programs in deciding where to work (Theunis 1992, 97).

25. ENDA is an international African NGO network, founded by the UNDP.

26. Farrington and Bebbington (1993, 160), for example, found that the great majority of linkages between NGOs and national agricultural research services were initiated by NGOs. Robinson (1997, 75–6) points out that, "for the most part, indigenous NGOs are working with public agencies in a partnership mode with the funds being provided by aid donors and governments. Examples of NGOs acting as PSCs [public service contractors] are few and far between . . . the major exceptions being NGOs with specialist skills."

27. In India, for example, PRADAN collaborates with thirty-six governmental agencies at the district, state, and central levels and all these relationships are "person specific" (PRADAN 1988, 15). The Indonesian NGOs surveyed by Allison and Kak (1992, 164–5) collaborated with a total of twenty government offices and ministries. The NGOs in India, Bangladesh, and the Philippines were, on average, connected to fifteen government entities, whereas the Pakistani NGOs were connected to only eight (Allison and Kak 1992, 163–4). Almost all Thai NGOs in another survey had contacts or more formal collaborations with the government, although only 40 percent attempted to follow government policy when formulating projects (Narkwiboonwong and Tipps 1989, 211).

28. Personal contacts are particularly important in Latin America, where they are often based on school ties (Farrington and Bebbington 1993, 141).
29. In Peru, according to Diaz-Albertini (1993b, 325), accomplishment in NGO–government partnership depends on individuals within government ministries.
30. See Clarke (1995, 90) on the Philippines. He also emphasizes the importance of such ties for effective collaboration.
31. Similarly, an Indonesian GRSO (LP3ES) collaborates with the Ministry of Public Works to strengthen water users associations (Brown and Korten 1989, 31).
32. Paradoxically, NGOs may be less likely to arise in the first place under such circumstances. See Chapter 2.
33. Similarly, Allison and Kak (1992, 165) found that 70 percent of their sample of Asian NGOs involved in family planning had been evaluated by governments. However, only a few respondents provided feedback on government-sponsored programs.
34. For example, Anang (1994, 117) argues that in Ghana, a joint learning process is constantly going on between NGOs and government.
35. Peasant movements in both Mexico and Brazil have ties to GRSOs but still lack strong ties to political parties or labor unions (Grzybowski 1990; Pare 1990). In Mexico, wariness about political parties grows out of the long history of co-optation by the official party.
36. Sabatier (1986, 29) concludes that in the United States, those reforms that are ambitious enough to arouse intense commitment from proponents, but limited in their effect on the entire system, stand the best chance of succeeding in the long run.
37. Some of the GRSOs discussed in *The Road from Rio* are already having an economic impact on large numbers of people. Because of the growth of GRO and GRSO networks, however, the potential to scale out need not depend solely on the extraordinary managerial capability of some GRSOs, such as BRAC in Bangladesh. One of the conclusions of *The Road from Rio* was that GRO networks can offer GRSOs, especially those that have evolved from below, a mechanism for learning and replication and an alternative system of economic exchange.
38. On the democratization question, Charles Curry-Smithson (unpublished memo, 1995) argues that NGOs are more likely to be effective in influencing policy over the short run, yet their longer-term influence is on democratization.
39. This group has received assistance from the Center for Research and Documentation of Beni, funded by Oxfam.
40. See also Korten (1995, 298–9) and Valarelli (1996, 73–84), who estimates that 3 million people belong to committees tied to the movement and 70 percent of the population has heard of the movement.
41. Gibbons builds on the work of Alter and Hage (1993).
42. First advanced by Robert Michels ([1915] 1959), the relevance of the "iron law" is discussed in Fisher 1994a.

5

Subnational Governments and NGOs

■ One of the interesting things about officials and representatives [of Egyptian] municipal councils . . . is their egalitarian attitude and keen awareness of the need to ameliorate the conditions of the village poor.
—Iliya Harik (1984, 81)

■ The national state [in Latin America] is too preoccupied with managing the debt situation, battling inflation and promoting a few superinvestments with international agencies to attend closely to the details of daily life in the thousands of *barrios* throughout the country. I believe this is the main reason for renewed interest in local government.
—John Friedmann (1989, 14)

■ All the cases deepen my conviction that the major issues of governance and citizenship will be resolved in the coming years at the municipal level. . . . I would argue that collaboration between local governments and NGOs has contributed substantially to expanding citizenship for the excluded.
—Charles Reilly (1995c, 247, 266–7)

■ There are certain things I would not do if I were to start again. One of them is the abolition of local government and the other is the disbanding of local cooperatives. We were impatient and ignorant.
—Julius Nyerere

THE THEORETICAL FOCUS of this discussion on subnational governments and NGOs is decentralization, explored from both the governmental and the nongovernmental perspectives. Although most scholars who discuss decentralization are genuinely interested in enhancing responsiveness and accountability to the local level and are not necessarily sympathetic to existing regimes, their discussions assume, almost exclusively, a governmental point of view (see, for example, Rondinelli and Nellis 1986). The underlying assumption in most of these discussions is that decentralization is, by definition, pushed down from national governments. These discussions need to be juxtaposed with discussions of decentralization from the perspective of NGOs, because there is evidence that the interaction of subnational governments with GROs and GRSOs, as well as with other nonprofit organizations, is creating new forms of power at the local level. Interaction with the independent sector, in effect, allows subnational governments to assume new roles that are not being performed by national authorities. Looking at both perspectives clarifies the interactive process of power creation and dispersion indicative of political development. It also opens up discussion of a process that may be planned or unplanned, active or reactive, with either government or the independent sector taking the initiative.

It is worth noting at the outset that there are cases in which subnational governments may be hostile to NGOs. In Rwanda, before the 1995 massacres, a successful agricultural credit program was deliberately sabotaged because it was competing with the economic activities of local authorities (Durning 1989, 79). Philippine NGOs have found it easier to back national political candidates than those running in some local areas (McBeth 1991, 22). And in India, the central government has been more responsive than the state government to environmental opponents of the Narmada Dam (Commuri 1995, 8).

This discussion, however, is based on the plausible assumption that subnational governments, particularly those at the local level, are more susceptible to independent-sector influence than national regimes, which have more complex lobbying pressures from all sides. On the whole, the evidence supports this assumption.[1] Negotiating at the local level provides NGOs and governments with "immediate resources to fill the needs of both parties" and also liberates them from "some of the political and institutional tensions encountered when simple efforts are made centrally" (Bebbington and Farrington 1993, 214).

As used here, the term *subnational government* includes all but national or federal governments. It may be that relationships between NGOs and large state governments in India or Brazil more closely resemble relationships with national regimes,[2] but such distinctions must await the results of more intensive field research.

Another unresolved issue is the distinction between local development associations (LDAs) and village or town government. As one of several types of GROs, LDAs have been considered part of the independent sector. Only rarely are they recognized as the local authority by national, provincial, or even district governments. However, LDAs may have evolved from the original governmental sector, and they seem to flourish

Figure 5.1 Centralization and Decentralization Alternatives

Decision Makers Accountable	Decision Makers Located	
	Centrally	Decentrally
Centrally	Centralization	Deconcentration
Decentrally	Democratization	Devolution

when they assume quasi-governmental powers.[3] Until further research is done on LDAs, it probably makes sense to place them on the conceptual border between the independent and the governmental sectors, but to treat them as part of the independent sector for the purposes of this discussion, since they interact with "official" local governments in many localities.[4]

Decentralization is defined by Rondinelli and Nellis (1986, 5) as the "transfer of responsibility for planning, management, and the raising and allocation of resources from the central government and its agencies to field units of central government ministries or agencies, subordinate units or levels of government, semi-autonomous public authorities or corporations, area-wide, regional or functional authorities, or *non-governmental private or voluntary organizations*" (emphasis added).[5] As a way of distinguishing between two major types of decentralization, Uphoff (1986b, 222) uses the matrix shown in Figure 5.1.

Centralization describes repressive or dictatorial regimes that concentrate decision making and are only minimally accountable to their people. Under top-down democratization, discussed in Chapter 4, decision makers are centrally located but are accountable locally. This chapter focuses on both deconcentration and devolution. Deconcentration is a form of decentralization, even though local administrators are centrally accountable. Devolution, in contrast, decentralizes accountability as well as the location of decision makers and is, therefore, related to bottom-up democratization.[6]

Deconcentration

Does relocating central government staff to the provinces or municipalities (deconcentration) have any impact at all? There are no simple answers, even to such a general question, nor are there generalizable geographic differences among Asia, Africa, and Latin America. Yet in a national survey conducted in Thailand, both government and NGO respondents ranked decentralization as the number-one priority for effective coordination (Narkwiboonwong and Tipps 1989). In Dharampur, India, a high turnover rate and poor morale ultimately led to effective deconcentration through service modules, and similar modules in the barrios of Caracas streamlined the delivery of government services (Gupta 1983; Gomez and Myers 1983). Deconcentration has increased local community access to central resources in Morocco and, to some degree, in Algeria, Libya, and Tunisia (Rondinelli and Nellis 1986). With deconcentration, Tanzanian bureaucrats became more physically accessible to villagers, and it became harder for them to avoid responding to questions in meetings (Maeda 1983, 149).

In contrast, one Tunisian development project excluded local participation, because local residents were supposedly represented by party leaders and government administrators (Skinner 1983, 146). And in Bangladesh, according to Holloway (1989a, 212), local administrators (of the national government) are nearly always corrupted by local governments.

Nor is it clear whether deconcentration precludes devolution or makes it more likely. In Botswana, deconcentration of official local authorities displaced traditional cattle-keeping societies, which had prevented deep inequalities by offering loaned cattle to the poor and herders to the rich.[7] Deconcentration also weakened local government in Tanzania, according to Samoff (1989). And in India, according to Satia (1983), there is a "remarkably consistent view" that the job of the district-level administrators is to operate established facilities and procedures, not to survey local resources, including local institutions.

Yet deconcentration can provide increased space and more access points for NGOs (Reilly 1993, 30) (see Box 5.1). With the return to democracy in Chile, for example, the central government established decentralized corporations to funnel loans and resources to indigenous communities. The system is headed by an anthropologist with NGO experience who has been given a mandate to work closely with GRSOs at the local level (Wali 1990, 28). Similarly, Ugandan NGOs are "well placed to exercise the . . . countervailing power" needed to avoid the risk that deconcentration may lead to stronger central control over local populations (De Coninck 1992, 114). In fact, because of the "energetic decentralization program" initiated by the Museveni government, the interplay between local administrators and "resistance councils" (which grew out of the national resistance movement) has improved government accountability (Swartzendruber and Njovens 1993, 29).

Because the evidence is scattered, however, international comparisons or even countrywide generalizations about the relationship between local administrative units of national governments and NGOs are as difficult as generalizations about the national level. This research gap is perpetuated

---

Box 5.1   Involving All Players in Decentralization

In Zimbabwe, in June 1995, the Ministry of Local Government and Rural and Urban Development opened a workshop on the role of people's organizations in local government, attended by representatives of rural district councils and NGOs. In its conclusions, the workshop acknowledged the "sterling role of NGOs," emphasized the need to "demystify public policy formation," and recommended a study of proposed village and ward assemblies, joint development programming, and reductions in the power of the ministries through legislative amendments. (*Source:* Chitiga-Machingauta 1995a, 11).

---

by the tendency of those writing about development projects or processes to use the term *government* without clearly designating what level is involved. Given the complicated reationships among local government; regional government at the state, provincial, departmental, and district levels; local administration; GROs; and GRSOs, increased descriptive clarity would be useful. Some GRSOs, for example, interact with both bureaucracies at the national level and administrators of these same agencies at the local level. These interactions may have different results. In remote areas, GROs or GRSOs may have more influence on local administrators than do their governmental superiors in the capital.

Devolution

Devolution appears to be more powerful than deconcentration in terms of its impact on governmental accountability and bottom-up democratization. Whereas deconcentration is usually organized by sector or function, devolution is usually territorial, so that people are pushed into intersectoral collaboration (Toranzo Roca 1992, 75). In the Chuquisaca department in Bolivia, the deconcentration of government departments was compelled by a previous devolution of authority to the Departmental Council on Social and Agricultural Development, which included the mayor, NGOs, and foreign donors (Toranzo Roca 1992, 68).

A second, more dramatic contrast is that whereas deconcentration must be pushed down from above, devolution of power and responsibility may be either pushed down from higher levels of government or pulled down by the assumption of new powers by subnational governments, NGOs, or both.

Push-Down Devolution

Devolution initiated by national governments can be directed toward private enterprise (privatization), subnational governments, or the independent sector. Privatization is not dealt with here; rather, this discussion of push-down governmental devolution focuses first on devolution to subnational governments and then on devolution to NGOs.[8]

What kinds of regimes initiate devolutionary policies? Although authoritarian or dictatorial regimes are probably less likely to launch devolutionary policies in the first place, unless they are strongly focused on basic needs, there is little evidence linking the character of national regimes to the outcomes of official devolutionary policies.[9] A study of land reforms in sixteen countries found that the devolution of government responsibility to local organizations (governmental and nongovernmental) did not lead to the capture of benefits by local elites (Montgomery 1972). In fact, the study concluded that the degree of benefits, measured in farmer income, participation, and tenure security, depended more on the active involvement of local organizations than on the ideology of the national regime or degree of local inequality.

GOVERNMENT-TO-GOVERNMENT DEVOLUTION Devolution from national to local governments, like deconcentration, may strengthen local elites and lessen the potential impact of GROs or GRSOs on local policies. In Sudan, provincial councils and commissioners have been given responsibility for nearly all public functions except national security, mail, and foreign affairs. Since the councils grew out of those traditional rural chiefs whose status was left intact by the British, however, devolution has done little to open the political system to new players (Rondinelli and Nellis 1986; Huntington 1988, 90). Observers of rural development have also noted the tendency for coalitions to develop between richer peasants active in local government and national government administrators. In India, local governments (*panchayats*) were elected and given community development functions by the central government in the 1960s, yet devolution was not accompanied by any changes in the social and economic power structure. In fact, *panchayat* elections became contests among individual members of the local elite (Tinker 1968, 224).

In contrast, Adams's (1986) study of rural Egypt concludes that the lack of central government resources can make official ties to local elites much less important. In Bangladesh as well, the Forest Department, realizing that it needed local people to help protect stumps so that the sal forest could regenerate, pushed local governments into appointing forest protection groups not representing local elites (Khan 1991).[10] And

Montgomery (1972, 70) concluded that in the ten countries where devolution of authority to local governments occurred as a result of land reforms, both the income and the political power of small farmers increased, regardless of whether the landlords were weakened before the reform took place.

Push-down devolution may also be a force for democratization (Fiszbein and Crawford 1996, 6). Perhaps because local elites are not always as powerful as they appear, a number of studies have shown that turning over responsibility to local governments can increase local accountability as well as project efficiency (Hadden 1980). Despite the support of the U.S. Agency for International Development (USAID), it was feared that the Egyptian government's Basic Village Service Project (BVSP) would move slowly because the planned road, sewage, and water projects were to be built by 480 local governments. Yet because the size of the tasks was kept manageable in each locality, BVSP was one of the few projects in Egypt to exceed USAID's implementation schedule. It built facilities worth over $200 million and trained 5,000 project managers who acquired long-term practical experience (Uphoff 1986b, 223). And evidence from Niger indicates that involving local governments from the beginning reduces the risk of national government control of both GRSO and INGO projects.

Even if such policies initially strengthen local elites, the long-term results of devolution are neither consistent nor predictable. In Colombia, devolution of housing policy to city councils varied from complete failure—marked by local elites using their new power to undermine a progressive mayor—to a major success—in a city where local elites were civic-minded and worked together successfully (Rothenberg 1980). In Thailand, official devolution of authority to the Tambon (subdistrict) governments in the mid-1970s led to many accusations of corruption. Nonetheless, the $25,000 government grants also generated many projects, such as the digging of wells and the building of roads that villagers can still identify. More important, the national government's Department of Community Development gained competence as a result of this initiative (Calavan 1984, 236). By 1982, the department was supporting both Tambon governments and GROs that were building libraries, roads, playgrounds, and medicine banks. It was also helping local groups make contacts with district and provincial officials.

Even if devolution can avoid capture by elites, however, the results of revenue sharing are probably unpredictable. In Brazil, local and regional governments reduced their own spending when they were given extra money by the federal government; as a result, only 118 community health councils were created, out of a proposed 4,000.[11] Yet in Guatemala, the results of revenue sharing were much more promising. Beginning in 1985, the military government, in an attempt to improve its image, began turning 8 percent of its revenue over to municipal governments, based on population and need. Some extremely poor municipalities received about U.S.$100,000 for development projects, an amount almost ten times that previously available. Communities were required to donate labor and hire local rather than outside technicians. Even though materials such as cement were controlled by monopolies, revenue sharing promoted an increased level of demand and accountability. Charges of corruption led irate citizens to replace unpopular mayors in three highland townships. In this instance, devolution not only led to "virtually unprecedented" political changes but also resulted in "the best managed and most efficient projects ever promulgated in Guatemala" (Smith 1996, 48).

Delegation of taxing power probably has a more consistently powerful impact (see Box 5.2). However, central governments are generally less willing to share the authority to tax than to share tax revenues.[12]

The results of devolution pushed down to subnational governments also depend on relationships between local politicians and NGOs. Some official devolution plans acknowledge this dependence by including both local governments and NGOs from the beginning. In Nepal, legislation drafted in the early 1980s established advisory groups for each municipal and village development committee with NGOs represented (Farrington and Bebbington 1993, 54). In El Salvador, increased funding for municipalities has allowed community education associations to contract teachers directly, manage school properties, and significantly reduce per-pupil costs. Sollis (1995, 526) contends that tying the necessary conditions for grassroots democracy to lower costs presents El Salvador's urban elites with an opportunity that also challenges their traditional privileges.[13]

Devolution is, in other words, propelled by financial necessity. Indeed, Reilly (1995b, 22) believes that the fiscal crisis of Latin American cities "has stimulated the rediscovery of sub-national politics." In Colombia, the lack of local resources and the need for policy guidance would have encouraged collaboration with local NGOs, even if collaboration had not been officially encouraged by the decentralization reforms. For example, the departmental government of Tolima accepted a proposal from the Asociacion Colombiana de Promocion Artesanal (ACPA) to provide gas-burning kilns in the ceramics community of La Chamba, where deforestation is rampant (Goff 1994, 131–2). Partly because of devolution, a GRSO network called the Foro Nacional por Colombia has been able to establish a revolving loan fund for town councils, enabling them to implement regional programs linking municipal management to social movements and GROs (Theunis 1992, 176).

DEVOLUTION TO NGOs   Not surprisingly, devolution pushed directly and often exclusively down to NGOs can also build effectively on local

---

Box 5.2 Devolution and Tax Reform in Colombia

In 1983, tax reform in Colombia led to increases in revenue and revenue sharing with local communities. The municipal share rose from 25.8 percent in
1986 to 45.3 percent in 1992. Colombian municipalities were also provided
with new powers and responsibilities, such as direct mayoral elections,
increased local budget authority, local referenda, legal mechanisms for
broadening participation, and representation of NGOs and other organizations on municipal public enterprises and citizen advisory boards. The main
results of these reforms were stronger municipal finances and expanded
administrative competence. A successful solid-waste collaboration with NGOs
in Bucaramanga (population 500,000) was extended to Manizales (population 400,000), although results were not clearly documented through a data
bank or disseminated to the rest of the country. (*Source:* Santana Rodriguez
1995, 168–71.)

---

resources, without necessarily requiring a major financial commitment by
central governments.

■ In Nepal, local bridge construction committees set up by local
   development associations built sixty-two bridges in four years
   with materials contributed by the national government. It is estimated that the total expenditure was one-fourth of what it would
   have cost the central government to do the job on its own (Uphoff
   1986b, 283–4).

■ In Kwara State, Nigeria, local self-help groups were able to raise
   90 percent of the funds needed for local health, education, and
   infrastructure projects, with only the balance coming from central and state governments (Rondinelli and Nellis 1986, 13).

■ GROs enlisted by the Indonesian government in Jakarta extended
   financial support to other communities through a land tax once
   they had secured their own basic services. This spontaneous
   scaling out occurred even though the government never planned
   for cost recovery or assumed that it would be possible. Between
   1969 and 1984, 537 communities received basic services, an
   astonishing record of replicability as well as sustainability.[14]

Yet some central governments are providing financial support for local
NGO projects. In Tunisia and Pakistan, LDAs have been given a percentage of official taxes and have tended to perform better than local governments. In North Yemen, the Ministry of Health gives grants to LDAs for

constructing primary health care units, with the community contributing the balance of the funds. In Oman, the village community development committees discuss possible projects with national government staff, who then hand over responsibility and funding to subcommittees of interested villagers. By the mid-1980s, 142 villages had participated, and facilities constructed included wells, meeting halls, canals, and latrines (Uphoff 1986b, 56, 249, 293). And in the Philippines, agricultural research responsibility has been allocated to area-based consortia covering the entire country, which link GRSOs to universities and government research stations.

State, provincial, and even district governments can also initiate devolution of their powers to local NGOs as well as to lower levels of government. In Karnataka State, India, government authorities are buying saplings for reforestation from peasant cooperatives (Khan 1991). They have also established the State Watershed Development Cell, which consults with local people through NGOs and creates interdepartmental umbrellas at the district, division, and state levels to coordinate planning and implementation (Farrington and Bebbington 1993, 159).[15] State and municipal governments in Brazil have entered into a number of contracts with BENFAM, the largest Brazilian GRSO concentrating on population and family planning. The state of São Paulo is itself promoting devolution to small and medium-sized city governments in the state by supporting an NGO called CEPAM (Central de Estudos e Pesquisas de Administracao Municipal), which promotes devolution through school meals, community vegetable gardens, fish farming, and soybean milk production units (Cordoba-Novion and Sachs 1987, 123).

Just as devolution from national or state to municipal governments often allows NGOs to enter the local political arena, devolution to NGOs can be strengthened if local governments are included (Toranzo Roca 1992, 105).[16] CEPAM, for example, promotes discussions between municipal authorities and GROs on such topics as health services. In the state of Andhra Pradesh, India, some government officials were "highly involved in working with the NGO [Samakhya] in an unofficial as well as an official capacity . . . [and they] brought knowledge of the government to bear. . . . The actors within and around [Samakhya] found room to maneuver by working in a far broader arena than that offered by the NGO itself" (Biggs and Neame 1996, 40).

Officially sponsored devolution to NGOs can impact national as well as subnational levels of government. In Mexico, the Delegado system, linking government to neighborhood associations in Mexico City, was one of the factors that has weakened the official PRI party over the long run (Ward 1981, 401). And the Lesotho government's previous experience with NGOs is producing a network for change that embodies elements of both deconcentration and devolution. The National Environmental Council makes policy and coordinates activities of the national ministries at the central and local levels, but it also works through GRSOs—for example, the Lesotho Planned Parenthood Association—the private sector, district governments, and village councils (*Brundtland Bulletin* 1990, 35).

Despite such success stories, however, devolution pushed down to NGOs has some negative trade-offs. When Urmul Seemat, a GRSO in Rajasthan, was pressured by the government to rapidly increase primary schools and preschools and comply with demands for monitoring and reporting, it placed great strains on Urmul's capacity to supervise and support the program, leading to serious attendance problems among lower-caste families (Edwards 1996, 80). GROs, in particular, face a number of risks in helping government implement development policies. In Trinidad, for example, village councils have been "subverted by the politics of welfare and patronage," according to Craig (1985, 191). A second type of risk occurs when the political culture of GROs is dominated by partisan infighting and clientalism. In Buenos Aires, Argentina, partisan infighting in neighborhood associations increased after the municipality provided them with funding and new responsibilities (Cavarozzi and Palermo 1995, 44).

Esman and Uphoff's (1984, 166) extensive literature search revealed, however, that GROs are not "spoiled" by connections with governments and that those with no government connection at all did not perform any better. More important, they found that no locally established organization had become totally dominated by the government. Despite their problems, the Trinidadian councils represent, according to Craig (1985, 191), "an undeniable potential case for popular participation in decision-making and policy implementation at the local level . . . [and] it is gratifying to record . . . the subtler aspects of the resistance from below to manipulation from above." Even neighborhood improvement organizations originally created by the Colombian government have become relatively autonomous (Fisher 1984).[17]

The risks involved in government collaboration may also be lessened by networking among GROs. An observer of the African scene, where most cooperatives are creatures of the state, believes that autonomy is enhanced by networking, which, in turn, has an impact on governments (Rouille D'Orfeuille 1985) (see Box 5.3). In Mali as well, a representative of a local cooperative network called the Federacion de Groupement Ruraux meets regularly with the regional political cadre, has had some impact on government policies, and remains independent.

Devolution to NGOs may coexist with NGO advocacy, just as collaboration and advocacy do at the national level. The state of Andhra Pradesh provided $350,000 for a housing program sponsored by AWARE, a GRSO. Meanwhile, AWARE was taking the state government to court to require it

---

Box 5.3   GRO Networking in Ecuador

In Ecuador, as of 1992, there were twenty-six indigenous GRO networks or federations. According to Bebbington and his colleagues (1992, 11, 16), "the area where federations have had real material impact is on leveraging and channeling public resources . . . [and improving] infrastructure." During a cholera outbreak, the indigenous federations collaborated with local public health officials to teach the use of rehydration salts and other basic treatment measures. According to the provincial director for rural health training, "the indigenous organizations are the key factor not only in cholera [control] but in all our work. . . . Without their collaboration, our task would be titanic" (Bebbington et al. 1992, 11). In Zimbabwe as well, according to Farrington and Bebbington (1993, 106–7), GRO federations work jointly with government agricultural technicians and with ORAP, a major GRSO.

---

to implement the laws prohibiting bonded labor. As a result, the state government is exerting pressure on the courts to release and rehabilitate involuntary laborers (Theunis 1992, 27–8). The collaboration between local governments and GRO networks in Ecuador (see Box 5.3) has been buttressed by progressive elements in the church and by GRSOs, such as the Center for Agricultural Services (CESA), which focus specifically on increasing local people's ability to pressure the state for resources.[18]

Pull-Down Devolution through Collaboration

Devolution can also be initiated from below. Subnational governments with no access to the resources of the independent sector may, in theory, assume new functions by themselves in the absence of the effective provision of national governmental services. However, pull-down devolution that includes NGOs appears to be more prevalent.

As GROs and GRSOs become important local political actors, local governments, like their national counterparts, are less and less able to ignore them, although this is not a new phenomenon in countries such as India (see Box 5.4). There is also evidence that in some countries, NGOs may be more likely to form ties with municipal or state authorities than with central governments. A survey of 109 NGOs conducted at the First National Assembly of Brazilian NGOs in 1991 revealed that although 43 percent had collaborated with governments, only 30 percent of those ties were with the federal government, whereas 34 percent were with state governments and 36 percent with municipal governments (Cesar Fernandes and Piguet Carneiro 1995, 80).

Box 5.4   Collaboration in India

Collaborative NGO strategies that avoid co-optation have been evolving for a long time. Autonomous GRSOs are often acutely aware of governmental intentions and are able to cooperate without being swallowed up. In Rajasthan, the Social Work and Research Center's rule was that it would not try to engage in any development activity by itself. A water survey was financed by government irrigation and electrification agencies, which used the results for large-scale government investments that would have been delayed for years in the absence of good data. State agricultural officers worked with SWRC's farmer-training programs and provided the program with seeds and plants for distribution to small farmers. There is no indication that SWRC compromised its independence; rather, it "knew how to find innovative people in government." For example, SWRC's close association with innovators in the state and national ministries of education led to a survey of local educational resources and the creation of three experimental primary schools. (*Source:* Coombs 1980b, 20.)

GROs and their networks often make their presence known to local government through advocacy in the form of direct, organized pressure, which can lead to subsequent collaboration.

- In many parts of Latin America, geographic proximity to the sources of power pushes squatter neighborhood organizations into making demands and obtaining governmental consideration, as well as benefits (Fisher 1984).

- In São Paulo, the grassroots women's movement has demanded and obtained seventy police stations staffed by women who specialize in domestic violence.[19]

- In Maharashtra, India, an anticorruption center, supported by a GRO network of farmer and youth groups, investigates complaints and pursues them through the local courts. Eighteen months of litigation in one case resulted in forty local revenue officers being dismissed. Collaborative relationships have been established with the state government, and the center is training people in other areas to set up similar programs (Ashoka n.d.).

- The Regional Indian Council of Cauca (CRIC), a GRO network of fifty affiliated communities, has had to battle the drug trade, guerrillas, the Colombian military, and the lumber and pulp companies while successfully working with the local court system to help indigenous communities gain land rights.

This strategy can be reinforced when national GRSOs organize local chapters. For example, the Country Women's Association of Nigeria (COWAN) has done this at the local, state, and national government levels.

A second strategy carried out by GRSOs is to promote devolution by acting as brokers between local communities and subnational governments. In Colombia, half of a national sample of GRSOs had been able to persuade governments (national and local) to provide services to the poor in their regions. For example, a business foundation called Fundación Carvajal has lobbied municipal governments to give tax breaks to the small businesses it supports.[20] In Gujarat, India, the Self-Employed Women's Association (SEWA) has negotiated permission for scrap-paper sellers to collect the state government's waste paper. Because of another agreement negotiated by SEWA, the Hariyali vegetable cooperative in Gujarat supplies fruit and vegetables to the jails and state hospitals of Ahmedabad (Krishnaswami 1987, 76; Patel 1992, 13). According to Spodek (1994, 195), "Much of SEWA's growth comes from its ability to work in alliance with different parties at various levels of governments" (see Box 5.5).

Where local governments are hostile to GROs, the role of GRSOs may be merely to provide support until such time as advocacy and/or collaboration becomes possible. In Malaysia in 1987, SAM (Friends of the Earth Malaysia) provided legal assistance and international publicity for villagers arrested by the state of Sarawak for protesting deforestation (Rush 1991, 202).

A third strategy employed by GRSOs is to use training as a way of linking GROs to local governments. In Chile, El Canelo de Nos trains GROs, other GRSOs, and governmental authorities to establish more effective ties with one another. Gram Vikas in Karnataka helps GROs lobby local governmental authorities, although "more militant expressions of discontent, such as threats and demonstrations, are not encouraged" (Viswanath 1991, 88).

The fourth and most innovative strategy, increasingly used by Latin American GRSOs, is to become "mediators for informational exchange" (Caccia Brava and Mullahy 1995, 102). In São Paulo, a GRSO called POLIS initiated a transportation study and proposal that assessed the capacity of the local business sector to pay the costs of expanded bus service. Now that the plan has been adopted and implemented by the municipality, microenterprises with under ten employees are exempt, and discounts are provided for firms that stagger work hours (Caccia Brava and Mullahy 1995). In Lima, a GRSO called Alternativas links poor populations in the Northern Cone section of the city to municipal authorities through other NGOs:

Estimated at approximately 1,520,000 inhabitants, the Northern Cone is a strategic territory for the development of Northern Lima because of its

---

Box 5.5   Insurance for SEWA Members

An insurance policy for pregnant women initiated by the Self-Employed Women's Association (SEWA) is based on a small registration fee. It has built-in family planning incentives (a cash gift to women who undergo sterilization) and is not open to women who already have three children. After SEWA launched its maternity scheme, the Gujarat government followed suit with a similar pilot for agricultural laborers. All SEWA members are now eligible for a national group insurance policy sponsored by the nationalized life insurance company. (*Source:* Patel 1992, 10.)

---

accommodation to population growth. Furthermore, it includes Lima's largest agricultural areas which, along with developing small and medium industrial enterprises, constitute important economic resources. Much of its population lives in acute poverty. The activities of *Alternativas* affect about 10,000 of these residents directly and about 50,000 indirectly. *Alternativas* coordinates its work with the nine local governments of the Northern Cone through the Interdistrict Coordinator of Mayors . . . [and] helps foster coordination among local governments, grassroots social organizations, NGOs, private entities and international support agencies. . . . [It also] serves as a partner in projects addressing production, employment, food and nutrition, health, citizen rights, and democratization of the public agencies in the Northern Cone. Through its participation in working groups . . . *Alternativas* coordinates closely with other NGOs, . . . assists municipal authorities with training, advisory services, policy and programs, assessment and planning, and— most important for democracy and efficiency—advisory services and training for the popular organizations and leaders. . . . [It is also] building a data bank for the use of researchers and professionals as well as local authorities and organizations (Caravedo 1995, 241–2).

Similar networking techniques are being used in rural communities. In Africa, internationally sponsored participatory rural appraisal processes have brought GROs, GRSOs, universities, local governments, and INGOs together to develop a community planning process.[21] In the province of Cochabamba, Bolivia, the Carrasco 2000 project, led by the Instituto de Educación Para el Desarrollo Rural (INEDER), helped organize linkages among GROs, civil authorities, state development projects, churches, and GRSOs to draw up development plans for the region (Theunis 1992, 235) (see also Box 5.6).

Despite the considerable evidence that GRSOs work through GROs to influence local governments, there are also an increasing number of direct power-sharing arrangements between GRSOs and governments,

---

Box 5.6 Bioregionalism and Politics

An Ashoka fellow in Mexico, Rogelio Cova, one of the founders of the Mexican NGO movement, has used his Ashoka support to strengthen the weakest links in the environmental movement, including those between local governments and GROs. By working at the bioregional level, he has been able to develop an integrated education program through a working group of about 200 that includes heads of *ejidos* (cooperatives), NGOs, schools, and municipal authorities. This network developed local radio programs and funded an ecological van and three-day ecological camps for children. (*Source:* Ashoka 1991, 47.)

---

particularly at the provincial or state level. Although power sharing may explicitly include GROs (see Box 5.7), in other cases, GRSOs and GRSO networks work alone (Arruda 1985). Officials in the state of Rajasthan, India, meet monthly with GRSO representatives to review social development programs (Sethi 1983). Also in India, the State Forestry Department in West Bengal works closely with GRSOs, universities, and the Ford Foundation in developing joint management policies for forest reserves and degraded lands (Rush 1991). Whether such collaboration should be considered devolution, co-optation, or some evolving mix of the two is problematic, but worthy of further study.

What accounts for the apparent increase in collaboration between NGOs and subnational governments? Although political protest may catalyze the relationship, the catastrophic dimensions of the poverty-environment-population crisis in the Third World almost force governments into cooperative arrangements that provide NGOs with greater power and responsibility. Local governments, realizing that GROs and GRSOs may be their only significant resource, are often eager for assistance and cooperation.

Nowhere is such "devolution by default" more obvious than in the cities of Brazil. Because of runaway inflation and federal government paralysis, municipal governments in Rio, São Paulo, Boa Esperanca, Santa Catarina, and many other cities are working directly with both neighborhood associations and GRSOs.

- In São Paulo, 1,300 neighborhood associations, with help from GRSOs, work with municipal authorities. Over 400 of these are involved in community fruit and vegetable garden projects, and twenty regularly sell their produce at low prices to almost 200,000 people. Organized grassroots demands for better health

---

Box 5.7 Cooperating with Subnational Governments

On the island of Mindanao in the Philippines, the Development of People Foundation (DPF) was created by a medical school to give students experience in providing health care to nearby villages. DPF members soon realized, however, that the local GROs were concerned about more than health, so they created an enabling environment for other local initiatives by cooperating with GROs and government agencies at various levels in a variety of sectors. A senior DPF representative was asked to join the regional development council—normally restricted to government officials.

In other countries, however, there are more barriers to NGO–local government collaboration. In Indonesia, NGOs need to apply to the *Pemda*, or provincial government, for permits, which are not easily obtained. Even if obtained, such permits may not allow NGOs to work without interference, and this may make NGOs dependent on particular individuals in government. (*Sources:* OECD 1988, 69; Tandon 1989a, 18).

---

care led to neighborhood representatives being elected to health councils with a policy-making role: "No doubt, the mobilizational experiences in São Paulo's peri-urban communities helped pave the way for the municipal government's health reforms in the early 1990s" (Cohn 1995, 93). Garbage collection used to be a major city expenditure, but with neighborhood recycling, garbage is now a source of income (Caccia Brava and Mullahy 1995, 101).

■ The Public Enterprise of the State of Rio de Janeiro uses *mutirão* (self-help) in close cooperation with neighborhood associations to provide sewage, water ducts, garbage collection, and biogas production. Within a short period, such collaboration allowed the state-owned Water and Sewer Company to reach 150,000 more people.

■ In Parana, many cooperatives of the unemployed work for both the city and the private sector and produce basic commodities (Sachs 1986; Aveline 1985). With technical support from Brazilian GRSOs, "Something entirely new is being born . . . self-management, decentralization, local alternatives, mutual help and popular participation" (Aveline 1985, 22).[22]

■ In Curitiba, GRSOs promote recycling and composting to collaborate with a city program exchanging free bus tokens for trash (Caccia Brava and Mullahy 1995, 105).[23]

Such collaboration is happening in many other countries as well, particularly in urban areas, although it is sometimes subject to electoral shifts.[24] Human Settlements of Zambia (HUZA) works closely with the Lusaka Urban District Council on housing policy and helps select advisers to elected ward councils (Rakodi 1990). Lima neighborhood associations are now formally incorporated into urban planning processes on such key issues as water. They have also assisted the municipality in fixing up old tenements and distributing more than 100,000 housing titles (Pease 1988). Bintari, a GRSO in northern Sumatra, has organized squatters in Medan into operating a waste collecting and recycling service for the city (Ashoka 1985).[25]

NGOs sometimes hand over responsibility for projects to their governmental partners. Yet this does not necessarily lead to the end of collaboration. For example, the People's Rural Education Movement (PREM) in Orissa, India, avoided contracting in favor of partnership with the government. When faced with the failure of the schools it had previously handed over to the government, PREM, rather than taking back the schools, worked with GROs to pressure the government to negotiate a solution to the problem (Edwards 1996b, 49).

Pull-Down Devolution through Infiltration

Infiltration is a second, more direct form of pull-down devolution to NGOs. In Peru, between 1984 and 1988, more than 30 percent of municipalities were taken over by GROs (Padron 1988a, 41). This was facilitated by President Alan Garcia's reform legislation providing for the direct election of mayors. Many new municipal officials have also been drawn from GRSOs, and a deputy mayor of Lima sits on the board of DESCO, an important GRSO (Caravedo 1995, 237). In the Philippines, the Coalition for People's Agrarian Reform, which consists of a large number of GROs, encourages its member organizations to help their individual members get elected to local offices. In Bangladesh, organizations of the landless are winning elections to union councils and have formed their own union-level federation of village-level associations, although in some areas there are clear limits on direct challenges to class structure (see Box 5.8).

This trend also seems to be occurring in many parts of India. One GRO-GRSO network near Udaipur has elected forty local associates to village councils: "Most of these people belong to the poorer families and are not typical of the kind of people who normally get elected to village councils" (Seva Mandir 1988–89, 28). Strategic voting by GROs in the 1991 *panchayat* (local council) elections in Orissa meant that their representatives were "able to ensure that more resources from government

---

Box 5.8   Violent Elections in Bangladesh

In Bangladesh, Gono Shahajjo Shangstha (GSS), working among the very poor in Nilphamari, organized a GRO that became strong enough to enter local elections in five unions of the district in 1992. When the GSS group won the first of a staggered series of elections, the local elite reacted with a reign of terror, during which GSS schools were burned; members of the local organization, including women, were beaten up; and house-to-house searches were conducted by armed thugs, who also ensured that GSS members could not reach the remaining four voting sites. The district government, which sided with local elites, arrested some GSS staff members. As a result, GSS has been forced into a new nonconfrontational strategy based on a model of "class harmony." (*Source:* Hashemi 1996, 125–6. For the difficulties with this approach in Bangladesh, see also Edwards 1996, 26.)

---

schemes for infrastructure, credit, etc. are directed toward the interests of the poor" (Edwards 1996, 27). In Madras, the members of Working Women's Forum are pushing their leaders into running for office and want them to consider the forum as a potential player in party politics (Garilao 1987, 119).[26] In Rajasthan, however, the election of one token representative of women's groups did not produce results. Women arriving at the polling station during local elections were told that their votes "had already been cast for them" (Edwards 1996, 26).

Just as GRO leaders are getting elected to local governments, professional "alumni" from the independent sector are entering subnational as well as national governments as professionals. In Peru, one-third of local governments have former staff members of GRSOs as employees, in conjunction with GRO leaders being elected as mayors of municipalities. As the late Mario Padrón, a leader of a major Peruvian GRSO, noted during my 1989 interview with him:

> DESCO has not worked very much with governments, preferring to concentrate on the grassroots, but now we are confronted with the grassroots becoming the local government. DESCO had prepared alternative municipal programs such as how to recycle sixty tons of garbage in Lima that are now really affecting what is implemented.

In a third form of pull-down devolution through infiltration, GRSOs are helping to train local officials, just as they do at the national level. The Arab Urban Development Institute in Saudi Arabia, for example, teaches municipal officials about waste management and urban renewal (Cordoba-Novion and Sachs 1987, 9). In Gadchiroli, India, a destitute tribal area in Southeast Maharashtra, Abhay and Rani Bang organized a national group of medical professionals concerned with the social dimensions of health care. That group is working with local government workers to show how the massive public health system can do a better job (Ashoka 1985). In Gujarat, India, SEWA used video to get the municipal commissioner to view, and reflect upon, his own interactions with market women in a meeting (Stewart 1990, 48).

Although deconcentration is initiated from above, there is evidence that it can positively impact social and economic development. Sometimes it can undermine the vested interests inhibiting local political development. There are also places where local administrators of the national government sponsor and empower potential challengers to local elites. Governments in Taiwan and South Korea, for example, channeled basic-needs assistance through local organizations during the 1960s and 1970s.[27]

However, deconcentration probably has a less consistently powerful impact on political change than devolution. Even devolution pushed down from above can promote sustainable development and empower local actors. And the impact of devolution may be greater when it is directed toward the independent sector.

Pull-down devolution has even more potential for altering local governments. In many cases, NGOs initiate political development processes that force changes in government attitudes and behaviors and advance the processes of power creation and dispersion, as well as interactive learning between the independent and local governmental sectors.

There are contrasts, particularly between the local and national levels, that make this discussion of local governments particularly important. Despite repressive national policies in some countries, GROs and their GRSO allies are often able to overcome local vested interests, particularly if they have the support of the public and of local governments that are dependent on their expertise. Just as elite control has traditionally been tied to the general weakness of local government in many Third World countries, this weakness also exposes them to the influence of growing numbers of GROs and GRSOs that are intent on defeating these same elite interests to promote sustainable local development. Esman and Uphoff (1984, 205), for example, found a number of cases in which local elites had been politically defeated by effective grassroots organizing. In some Latin American countries, decentralization policies adopted at the national level are further advancing this process.

NGOs are both collaborating with subnational governments and infiltrating them in ways that create new forms of power and authoritative decision making. Such collaborations force changes in attitudes and behaviors and promote interactive learning between NGOs and subnational governments. Although African evidence is both more scattered and more problematic than that from Asia and Latin America, and many Middle Eastern countries remain relatively untouched by these developments, political development is occurring in many local spaces in the Third World. Negotiations and bargaining between NGOs and local governments "can be a cause as well as effect of enhanced democratic practice. A product of democracy, such negotiations can also produce it" (Reilly 1995c, 255). Indeed, the local activism of NGOs has certainly contributed to the relatively recent and remarkable fact that "virtually every mayor and council person in the more than 12,000 units of sub-national government in Latin America is elected" (Fiszbein and Crawford 1996, 6).

Notes

An earlier, shorter version of this chapter (Fisher 1992) appeared in McCarthy et al. 1992.

1. Sanyal (1991, 1378), for example, argues that subnational governments in Bangladesh are more responsive to the need for reform than the national government and that the real fate of national policy reform depends on local implementation. See also Abdel Ati (1993, 115), who points out that local governments in the Sudan have had inadequate authority in relief operations. According to Breslin (1991, 7), "The best fit for NGO–State cooperation [in Latin America] may lie on the regional or municipal level." Loveman (1995) points out that during the Pinochet dictatorship in Chile, NGOs collaborated with municipal governments, even though there were no elected mayors after 1973, because municipalities assumed responsibility for previously national welfare programs. Finally, Farrington and Bebbington (1993, 194) note that "mechanisms of coordination [between government and NGOs] are likely to be stronger at sub-national levels."

2. Uphoff (1993, 608), for example, argues that there is little consensus about what constitutes the local level. His comments on Fisher (1992) were instrumental in my use of the term *subnational* instead of *local* (personal communications, fall 1995).

3. See Fisher 1993, chap. 2. Sometimes this pushes them into representation of the established elite. Colchester (1994, 87) points out that in Sarawak, the indigenous village councils are run by elites who often side with loggers. In response to this, more democratic longhouse associations are being created that are challenging the disastrous degradation of natural resources by outside interests.

4. In contrast, interest associations such as women's groups are clearly within the independent sector, whereas cooperatives may be on the conceptual border between the independent and private sectors.

5. A simpler, but less inclusive, definition is "the process through which government or local agencies obtain resources and authority for adapting

to local conditions" (Leonard and Marshall 1982, 4).

6. Rondinelli and Nellis (1986, 5) also add delegation, where line bureaucracies delegate authority to parastatal agencies.

7. Yeager (1989) also points out that the *legotla*, or traditional village meeting, has also declined in importance, thus shifting power away from those with a vested interest in conservation of land rather than livestock commercialization.

8. Unlike most other voluntary action scholars, Uphoff places GRSOs, which he calls "service organizations," in the private sector with businesses, because they have clients; this leaves only GROs, which he calls "local organizations," in the "voluntary sector." I chose, instead, to include both types of organizations in the independent sector (Fisher 1993), since GRSOs are motivated by a shared organizational mission or value rather than political imperatives or economic incentives. (See Brown and Korten 1989, 5.)

9. The South Korean regime in the early 1970s was authoritarian, yet with a strong focus on basic needs implemented through local organizations.

10. Sal is a type of tree that has been rapidly deforested in recent years.

11. One exception to this was in Ceará State, where medical professionals convinced the incoming state government to initiate a highly successful preventive health program based on community participation (Weyland 1995, 1706).

12. Alan Fowler points out that African governments keep a tight rein on the pursestrings and prohibit possibilities for local revenue collection (letter to the author, July 18, 1990).

13. A strong centralized commitment to local empowerment can also pay off when opposition to macro reforms develops. Korten (1987, 151) makes a distinction between "macro" policies that can be implemented with a stroke of the pen—such as the removal of a subsidy from fertilizer imports—and "micro" politics—such as the introduction of a credit policy for small farmers. Unlike the subsidy decision, implementation of a credit policy would require power sharing with local government and GROs. Although the terms *macro* and *micro* can be confusing, because they also imply policy scope, the distinction is useful for potential research on independent-sector impact on policy.

14. Because cost recovery was not immediate, there was also time to ensure that improvements led to increased productivity (see Ludwig and Cheema 1987, 201).

15. This model was based on a pilot project.

16. Eduardo MacLean (in Toranzo Roca 1992, 105) notes that devolution to NGOs is more powerful if accompanied by "political decentralization" (translation).

17. Devolution can also lead to a backlash, as the power of previously unorganized elites is threatened. Thus, even a government intent on devolution may need to depend on GROs to elicit countervailing participation by nonelites (Rondinelli 1983, 134).

18. According to Bebbington (1993, 283–5), GRSOs that work with the federations promote self-management at the community and regional levels, as well as alternative agricultural technologies.

19. Jacqueline Pitanguay, presentation at the fourth Association for Women in Development conference, Washington, D.C., November 17–19, 1989.
20. In contrast, GRSOs in Colombia have faced repression when they severely threaten the local status quo (see Smith 1990).
21. See, for example, Thomas-Slayter (1990) on the use of participatory rural appraisal (PRA) in Kenya. After it was used at the community level, a PRA advisory council was set up to determine the most effective ways to replicate the PRA model through enhancing negotiating, networking, and institution-building skills at the national level among the NGOs, governments, and universities involved in the process.
22. Before the civil war, municipalities in Rwanda were also working with GRSOs and INGOs.
23. Businesses pay fees to the government to support public transportation but receive discounts if they adhere to flextime schedules.
24. In Rosario, Argentina, economic hardship and the deterioration of the local infrastructure have pushed local governments toward cooperation with neighborhood organizations and GRSOs. GRSOs and the neighborhood organization in the Esperanza section coordinated with the municipal government to build a community center, which provides the city staff with strong professional guidance plus a way of avoiding partisan pressures. However, when the Popular Socialist Party came to power in 1989, municipal partisanship and government competition with NGOs increased, even though the government continues to replicate NGO policies (see Martinez Nogueira 1995, 51–2, 61, 65, 68).
25. NGOs cannot always take advantage of decentralization. In Central America, despite devolutionary policies, only a few NGOs have entered into partnerships with municipal governments. According to Sollis (1995, 538), some NGOs project themselves as party entities, and others are small, weak, underfinanced, and need legalization.
26. In India, local-level officials are "invariably apathetic or hostile to voluntary efforts," withhold information or materials, and delay necessary approvals (see Tandon 1989b, 18).
27. See Coombs (1980a, chap. 8) on the Saemaul Undong groups in South Korea. The Taiwanese government worked through the farmers and irrigators associations. The results of the Nepalese government's support for the Small Farmer's Development Groups during the 1980s are less certain.

6

Civil Society, Democracy, and Political Development

■ For several decades we have invested the political process with our hopes and energies only to discover that politics may be more the effect of other social forces than the cause of basic social change. Something has been missing. Put another way, after several decades of "bringing the state back in" to what had become pretty sterile social science, we are now seeing an effort to "reinvent society" from the dual sources of theory and practice.

—Charles Hamilton[1]

■ Building social capital will not be easy, but it is the key to making democracy work.

—Robert Putnam (1993a, 185)

THIS EXPLORATION OF the political impact of NGOs began with their vanguard role in strengthening civil society, followed by a definition of political development that focused on the political commons linking civil society and the state and the rethinking that can occur as a result of this interaction. Chapters 2 through 5 explored the NGO–government relationship from different vistas, all of which underlined the proactive nature of NGOs. Although political context strongly conditions the initial NGO–government relationship, the relationship itself can evolve and reshape political context. Autonomous NGOs with such attributes as technical skills and a mass base, however, probably have more impact on policy and political context than do other NGOs. Although NGOs have significantly impacted local spaces, subnational government policies, and some national policies, they are only beginning, through networking, to use advocacy and collaboration with government to acquire a major ability to promote sustainable development and responsive government.

This final chapter builds on Chapters 1 through 5 by describing how future research could explore the political commons shared by state and civil society in relation to political context. The first section deals with the relationship between the growth of civil society and democratization and assesses the apparent trend toward democracy in the Third World. The second section deals with but does not answer the most difficult question of all: What is the potential for local indicators of political development as a process to ultimately transform the wider context within which it occurs? Finally, I conclude with policy recommendations for supporting NGO–government ties to advance sustainable development and democratization.

Political Development and Democracy

In a wider discussion than is possible in this book, four logical combinations of democratic context and political development can be described, symbolizing a much wider continuum of political realities. (See Box 6.1). Table 6.1 represents a kind of crude first step toward understanding these four possible relationships between political development and democracy. To measure democracy, I used Freedom House's composite measure of both political rights and civil liberties based on extensive checklists that include free elections, protection of civil liberties, multiparty legislatures, and an uncontrolled press.[2] Countries with ratings of 1–2 are considered "free," those rated 3–5 are "part free," and those rated 6 or 7 are considered "not free."

It would be difficult and time-consuming to develop a composite group of indicators for all the countries of the Third World that would measure civil society—as Putnam (1993a) has done for Italy. If civil society could be measured in the Third World, the numbers of variously defined NGOs shown in Table 6.1 would be only one of many necessary indicators. The need for multiple civil society indicators is exemplified by Brazil, whose population is so large (156 million) that even with over 1,500 NGOs (mostly GRSOs) it has a relatively low NGO density, about 9.8 organizations per million people. Yet Brazilian civil society as a whole is stronger than civil society in Paraguay, which has an NGO density of over 50 per million.[3]

There are, of course, other obvious problems with the data on NGOs. Some estimates include only NGOs registered with the government, whereas others include more informal organizations. In a few countries— most notably those from parts of the Middle East and North Africa—the figures include GROs.[4] In some cases, NGOs may be defined to include

---

Box 6.1 Democracy and Political Development

- Political development in an autocratic society.

- Political development in a democratic society.

- No political development in an autocratic society.

- No political development in a democratic society.

---

traditional charities and other kinds of nonprofit organizations. Nonetheless, Table 6.1, with NGO density data from eighty-seven Third World countries, at least suggests one possible hypothesis, which could be tested by a more rigorous study—that societies with high democracy ratings are unlikely to have extremely low NGO densities. Some degree of civil society, in other words, appears to be a necessary if not sufficient condition for democracy (Sullivan 1995, 4). All fourteen countries with democracy ratings of 1, 1.5, or 2 have NGO densities above twenty-two per million. The fact that many of these democracies are small island nations and that high NGO density was therefore easy to achieve should not, by itself, detract from the possible importance of NGO density to democracy.

A more composite measure of civil society might or might not support the hypothesis—introduced by Perez Diaz (1993) in his study of Spain—that an expansion of civil society is likely to precede democracy. Although civil society may grow stronger under a dictatorship, as in Indonesia, conflict and political gridlock remain probable, as evidenced by the mass demonstrations and riots that have occurred in that country in recent years. Fragile democratic governments can be overthrown, even though civil society has grown stronger, and if civil society becomes a target as well, it may be hard to sustain activism. Yet civil society may also persist and circumscribe the range of options available to a new autocratic government. In Thailand, the short-lived democratic government in power between 1973 and 1976 emphasized equality and grassroots democracy and spurred the development of NGOs that outlasted it (Pfirrmann and Kron 1992, 4). As civil society develops, horizontal ties tend to replace vertical bonds of authority, such as patron-client networks, and the democratic habits and values that develop within civil society may begin to influence the state.

The most obvious implication of the data, even without a more rigorous study, is that although organizational density *may* be a necessary condition for democracy, it is surely not a sufficient one.[5] Zimbabwe,

Table 6.1 NGO Density and Democracy

Continent	Country	No. of NGOs	Population (Millions)	NGOs/Million Population	Democracy Rating
South America	Argentina	850	33.8	25.15	2.50
	Bolivia	530	7.1	74.65	3.00
	Brazil	1,533	156.5	9.80	3.00
	Chile	700	13.8	50.72	2.00
	Colombia	1,410	35.7	39.50	4.00
	Ecuador	300	11.0	27.27	2.50
	Paraguay	238	4.7	50.64	3.50
	Peru	950	22.9	41.48	4.50
	Uruguay	103	3.1	33.23	2.00
	Venezuela	351	20.9	16.79	3.00
Central America Mexico, and Caribbean	Belize	11	0.2	55.00	1.00
	Costa Rica	320	3.3	96.97	1.50
	Dominica	26	0.7	37.14	1.00
	Dominican Republic	119	6.4	18.59	3.50
	El Salvador	700	5.5	127.27	3.00
	Grenada	12	0.9	13.33	1.50
	Guatemala	700	10.0	70.00	4.50
	Haiti	146	6.9	21.16	5.00
	Honduras	95	5.3	17.92	3.00
	Jamaica	21	2.4	8.75	2.50
	Mexico	608	90.0	6.76	4.00
	Nicaragua	300	4.1	73.17	4.00
	Panama	30	2.5	12.00	2.50
	St. Lucia	17	0.15	113.33	1.50
	St. Vincent	13	0.11	118.18	1.50
	Trinidad and Tobago	19	1.3	14.62	1.50
Africa	Angola	31	10.3	3.01	6.00
	Benin	113	5.1	22.16	2.00
	Burkina Faso	131	9.8	13.37	4.50
	Burundi	18	6.0	3.00	6.50
	Cameroon	52	12.5	4.16	6.00
	Cape Verde	30	0.37	81.08	1.50

(cont.)

Swaziland, and the Gambia, for example, have high NGO densities and are clearly not democracies.[6]

Nonetheless, 86 of 133 developing countries are now in the free (37) or part free (49) categories.[7] Since most developing countries in the free category have democracy ratings of 2 or 2.5, dynamic civil societies are emerging everywhere within semiauthoritarian political systems (Freedom House 1995–96, 541).[8] Some partially free societies have extremely strong and growing civil societies. One estimate is that in Colombia, one in five people belongs to some type of NGO and, directly or indirectly, NGOs have contacts with half the population (Ritchie-Vance 1991, 33).

Table 6.1 (cont.)

Continent	Country	No. of NGOs	Population (Millions)	NGOs/Million Population	Democracy Rating
	Central African Republic	34	3.2	10.63	3.50
	Congo	44	2.4	18.33	4.00
	Ethiopia	68	51.9	1.31	4.50
	Gabon	5	1.0	5.00	4.50
	Gambia	80	1.0	80.00	6.50
	Ghana	600	16.4	36.59	4.00
	Guinea	69	6.3	10.95	5.50
	Guinea Bissau	37	1.0	37.00	3.50
	Ivory Coast	48	13.3	3.61	5.50
	Kenya	400	25.3	15.81	6.50
	Lesotho	121	1.9	63.68	4.00
	Liberia	41	2.8	14.64	6.50
	Malawi	23	10.5	2.19	2.50
	Mali	120	10.1	11.88	2.50
	Mauritania	7	2.2	3.18	6.00
	Mauritius	48	1.1	43.64	1.50
	Mozambique	27	15.1	1.79	3.50
	Namibia	153	1.5	102.00	2.50
	Niger	64	8.6	7.44	4.00
	Nigeria	233	105.3	2.21	7.00
	Rwanda	64	7.6	8.42	6.50
	São Tomé and Principe	14	0.12	116.67	1.50
	Senegal	72	7.9	9.11	4.50
	Sierra Leone	35	4.5	7.78	6.50
	South Africa	10,000	39.7	251.89	1.50
	Swaziland	55	0.8	68.75	5.50
	Tanzania	130	28.0	4.64	5.00
	Togo	85	3.9	21.79	5.50
	Uganda	250	18.0	13.89	4.50
	Zaire	275	41.2	6.67	6.50
	Zambia	128	8.9	14.38	3.50
	Zimbabwe	1,500	10.7	140.19	5.00

(cont.)

Given the connection between basic-needs policies and ties to GROs explored in Chapter 2, it may be that some authoritarian regimes rated 6 or 7 have extensive but not very autonomous civil societies, at least at the local, grassroots level. Syria may fit this pattern. Not only are its GROs counted as NGOs, but the government confers on local organizations the title of "public utility" and has the power to dissolve any voluntary organization (Kandil 1994, 133).[9] Egypt's high NGO density includes thousands of GRSOs and traditional charities, yet state financial support and control through the Ministry of Social Affairs are pervasive and long-standing. A lack of NGO autonomy, in other words, may allow high density to coexist with authoritarianism indefinitely.

Table 6.1 (cont.)

Continent	Country	No. of NGOs	Population (Millions)	NGOs/Million Population	Democracy Rating
Asia	Afghanistan	148	na	na	7.00
	Bangladesh	1,200	115.2	10.42	3.50
	India	12,000	898.2	13.36	4.00
	Indonesia	1,000	187.2	5.34	6.50
	Nepal	140	20.8	6.73	3.50
	Philippines	6,000	64.8	92.59	3.00
	Sri Lanka	500	17.9	27.93	4.50
	Thailand	200	58.1	3.44	3.50
Middle East	Bahrain	66	0.53	124.53	6.00
	Egypt	13,239	56.4	234.73	6.00
	Jordan	587	4.1	143.17	4.00
	Kuwait	29	1.8	16.11	5.00
	Lebanon	1,300	3.9	333.33	5.50
	Morocco	159	25.9	6.14	5.00
	Oman	16	2.0	8.00	6.00
	Palestine	444	0.7	634.29	5.50
	Qatar	3	0.52	5.77	6.50
	Saudi Arabia	104	17.1	6.08	7.00
	Sudan	262	26.6	9.85	7.00
	Syria	628	13.7	45.84	7.00
	Tunisia	5,186	8.7	596.09	5.50
	United Arab Emirates	89	1.8	49.44	5.50
	Yemen	223	13.2	16.89	5.50

Sources for population and democracy data: UNESCO 1995; World Bank 1995; Freedom House 1995–96.

Sources for NGO data: Fisher 1993, 82–8, except for updates or additions as follows: Fernandes 1994, 326, for Zimbabwe, West Bank, Gaza, Jordan, and Tunisia; Kandil 1994, 119, for Bahrain, Egypt, Jordan, Kuwait, Lebanon, Mauritania, Morocco, Qatar, Saudi Arabia, Sudan, Oman, Syria, United Arab Emirates, and Yemen; Arellano-Lopez and Petras 1994, 562, for Bolivia; Diaz-Albertini 1993, 320, for Peru; Sollis 1995, 525–42, for El Salvador, Guatemala, and Nicaragua; Brautigam 1994, 64, for Gambia; Simukonda 1992, 417–31, for Malawi; Welch 1995, 48, for Namibia; Ndegwa 1996, 20, for Tanzania, Zambia, and Zimbabwe; Jeppe, Theron, and Van Baalen 1992, 4, for South Africa; Navarro 1995, 7, for Venezuela and Costa Rica; Inter-American Foundation 1995, 3–4, 7–8, 18, 21–2, for Brazil, Colombia, Paraguay, Uruguay, and Venezuela; Bennet 1995, 12, for Afghanistan; and Rademacher and Tamang 1993, 34, for Nepal.

The highest Inter-American Foundation figure for Brazil, 1,533, represents only environmental organizations. In a 1988 directory (Landim, 1988a), they represented only one-third of the total. Assuming that the relative position of different types of organizations is the same, there may be as many as 4,000 GRSOs and charities and GROs in Brazil today. See also Reilly (1995b, 12), whose civil society guestimates, based on long years of field experience with the Inter-American Foundation, place Brazil, Chile, and Peru with stronger civil societies than Mexico and Argentina, with Colombia somewhere in the middle.

Because some estimates probably include a few INGOs and other nonprofit organizations such as traditional charities among NGOs, I have chosen to add all three types together, even where data (from the World Bank, cited in Fisher 1993, 82–90) are available that divide the three types of organizations. GROs are generally excluded, except for the figures from North America.

Although the data measure only moments in time, they point to some intriguing contrasts relating to political development, which could be studied longitudinally. For example, Honduras and El Salvador were both given a 3 (part free) rating by Freedom House and are similar in size of population. El Salvador's 700 GRSOs, however, are having a stronger political impact than their 95 counterparts in Honduras (see, for example, Sollis 1995). As Bennett (1995, 153) argues, "[the Salvadoran NGOs] showed a remarkable capacity to take advantage of the peace process and the end of the Cold War." Whether high NGO density will be supported or undermined by other factors might have to be determined over time in both countries.

For one thing, the impact of democratization on civil society can vary dramatically. In Brazil, for example, the transition toward democracy was slow, giving NGOs time to grow in numbers and adjust to a new political context, whereas in Argentina, NGOs had been severely repressed and had little time to adjust to new circumstances with the election of Raul Alfonsin in 1985 (Munck 1990, 32).[10] Even democracies—as shown in Chapter 2—vary in their treatment of NGOs. Some governments practice benign neglect, and a few others, such as the Christian Democratic regime that replaced Pinochet in Chile in 1990, have been actively supportive of civil society.

Thus, political development depends not only on how healthy civil society is but also on what happens to the state. Where democracy is not even an occasional or cyclical phenomenon, institutionalization from below may have its limits. Despite recent democratic trends in a number of countries, democracies—defined as political systems with elections decided by majority rule, as well as the existence of political liberties preserving individual rights and the rights of the opposition—are still in a minority within the Third World. It is important, therefore, to explore the status of democracy in the Third World in more detail.

The Present State of Democracy

The following brief assessment of the status of democracy in the developing countries also uses Freedom House's classifications of countries as "free," "part free," and "not free." Of course, no rating system adequately reflects either the internal complexities or the transitory nature of political systems, particularly those labeled part free. Zimbabwe, for example, has received poor scores of 5 or 6 on civil liberties for many years. Yet in 1982, the convictions of white air force officers who confessed under torture were reversed by the country's high court. The Zimbabwe Congress of Trade Unions is independent and also speaks out against the government. An independent Catholic monthly and a liberal weekly paper are widely read (Sklar 1986; Freedom House 1995–96, 504–5).

Freedom House's rating system is nonetheless useful as a comparative measure between countries and over time.[11] Beginning in 1972 and through most of the 1970s, the number of Third World countries considered democratic by this rating system hovered around 28 out of 129 (including the Gulf states and the Pacific and Caribbean islands). By 1986, the net number of democratic countries had increased to 31, mostly because of changes in Latin America. In 1988, with democratic changes in South Korea and the Philippines, the figure reached 33 (Gastil 1989–90, 50–61). By the end of 1995, there were 37 Third World countries in the free category, including, for the first time, South Africa (Freedom House 1995–96, 541).

Latin America and the Caribbean

In the Americas, with the elections in Haiti, only Cuba remains in Freedom House's not-free category. The southern cone countries, Costa Rica, Panama, Ecuador, Guyana, French Guiana, and many Caribbean nations, including Jamaica, were in the free category as of the end of 1995, with the remainder of countries labeled part free.[12] Unfortunately, some countries that made dramatic shifts toward democracy in the 1970s and 1980s have slid back to the part-free category, and internal trends are sometimes contradictory. Local tyrannies led by drug dealers persist, yet the direct election of municipal officials is increasingly common, and, as noted in Chapter 5, local governments are increasingly collaborating with NGOs. Corruption continues to be a problem almost everywhere, yet Presidents Carlos Andres Perez in Venezuela and Fernando Collar de Mello in Brazil were both successfully removed because of it. Judiciaries are rarely independent, and traditions of civilian control remain weak almost everywhere, yet Colombia recently installed its first civilian defense minister.

The greatest barriers to Latin American democratization are the increasing absolute number of people who live in poverty, the continuing maldistribution of land, and the limited access to economic power. There are, for example, an estimated 40 million street children throughout the hemisphere (Payne 1996, 82). Although the proliferation of GRSOs, now exceeding 10,000, is a particularly crucial long-term trend, it may or may not be able to keep up with an increasing population.[13]

Asia

In Asia, except for one developed country (Japan) and nine of twelve Pacific islands, only Mongolia and South Korea are rated as free. India, Papua New Guinea, and Fiji, rated as free ten years ago, are now rated as part free, along with eleven other countries. In Bangladesh, for example, the freest-ever national assembly elections were held in 1991, and freedoms of speech and the press are generally respected, but key human rights problems center around the army and police. Nine countries are rated as not free, including Indonesia, the Maldives, and Brunei, all rated as part free ten years ago.

Although Asian leaders meeting in Bangkok in 1993 declared that democracy was an alien concept, ordinary Asians have been building civil society for several decades. There are now an estimated 20,000 to 30,000 GRSOs, many of which work directly or indirectly on human rights issues (Fisher 1993, 91). Moreover, as mentioned in Chapter 4, the human rights and sustainable development agendas are increasingly merged in Asia. And, as Graybow (1995–96, 76) noted in writing about Asian NGOs, "In a region of high-flying economies, the most significant developments of all may be taking place on the ground." Unfortunately, as described in Chapter 2, government treatment of NGOs has generally worsened in recent years and has exposed the weakness of the rule of law in many countries.

Africa

In Africa, the end of the Cold War began to erode the remaining support for dictatorship. Africans themselves had already demonstrated their opposition to dictatorship through such events as the long civil war that toppled Idi Amin in Uganda and the student movement that brought down Bokassa in the Central African Republic. Beginning in the early 1990s, national conferences in the Francophone countries helped build national support for moving toward democracy. In Benin and the Congo, sitting presidents have been impeached.

Africa registered the largest number of democratic advances between Freedom House's 1989 and 1995–96 surveys (See Table 6.2). In 1989, Freedom House rated thirty-four countries as not free, fifteen as part free, and only three as free (Welch 1995, 64). By 1995 there were twenty not-free countries, eighteen part-free, and nine free (Freedom House 1995–96, 541).

The most dramatic change was in South Africa, which moved from not

Table 6.2 Democratic Advances in Africa: 1986–96

| Year | Free | —————Number of Countries ————— | | Total* |
		Part Free	Not Free	
1986–87	2	14	30	46
1995–96	10	18	20	48

Sources: Freedom House 1986–87, 1995–96.

*Eritrea and Namibia, which did not exist in 1986–87, are in the part-free and free categories, respectively. Therefore, the 1995–96 country totals are higher by two. I did not include Transkei, which had a part-free rating in 1986–87, since it is now part of South Africa.

free to free. During the same period, Mali moved from part free to free. As of the end of 1995, South Africa, Namibia, Botswana, and Malawi in southern Africa and Benin and Mali in West Africa were in the free category, along with the island nations of Mauritius, Cape Verde, and São Tomé. In 1996 alone there were eighteen multiparty elections in Africa, "more than have ever been held in Africa before in a single year," and those held in Ghana, Madagascar, Benin, Sierra Leone, and Uganda were "generally considered free" (French 1997, 3).

Yet African democracies are considered to be extremely fragile by most specialists,[14] and progress toward democracy was marred by increasing internal violence in some countries. In Chad, Niger, and Gambia, former military leaders managed to transform themselves into elected civilians in 1996, but they did so by "barring major opponents from running, muzzling critics and, in the first two instances, maintaining tight state control over the administration of the elections" (French 1997, 3). In some cases, elections can unleash tribal hatreds, as in the Congo. African democratization continues to confront territorial boundaries imposed under colonialism and the kind of ethnic divisions highlighted by the carnage in Rwanda and Burundi.

Declining foreign assistance and the struggles of new leaders to pay off debts accrued by corrupt former dictators have increased the importance of a still nascent African civil society. Although there are now an estimated 15,000 GRSOs in Africa (an estimated 10,000 of which are in South Africa), most of those outside South Africa were created more recently than their cousins in Asia and Latin America and, like NGOs in the transitional countries, are likely to be heavily dependent on foreign funding. NGOs and other civic organizations may promote patron-client rather than horizontal grassroots ties. Yet there are many signs that civil society is vibrant and growing in strength. Tanzania's tolerance of a relatively free press, including lively weekly newsmagazines, preceded its move from the not-free to the part-free rating. Everywhere, faxes and satellite TV become harder and harder to control.

Middle East

Because most Middle Eastern countries have been under external domination and control by empires and superpowers for over 500 years, people in the Middle East sometimes reject democracy because of where it comes from rather than because of what it is. Although the end of the Cold War has altered this scenario, intraregional issues, often tied to questions of citizenship and flows of stateless people, continue to block political reform. Since the invasion of Kuwait, some Shiite fundamentalists have been willing to unite with non-Islamic organizations and adopt the principles of liberal democracy. Yet no state escapes the impact of an Islamic fundamentalism that paints democracy with the brush of secularism.

Until very recently, civil society has been weak in most of the Middle East; indeed, Kazemi and Norton (1995, 86) call it "stunted." Not only do alternatives to established regimes tend to be expressed as religious fundamentalism, but Islamic fundamentalists continue to benefit from the suppression of secular groups. The worst example of this is in Algeria, where violence on both sides has led to tens of thousands of deaths. In addition, legal systems often impede the formation and functioning of voluntary associations. Although civil society is most developed in Egypt, it is also tightly co-opted and controlled by the Ministry of Social Affairs.

Nonetheless, weak, illegitimate governments, under financial pressure because of declining oil prices, are increasingly contending with obstreperous multiparty parliaments, obstructionist bureaucracies, and the enormous challenge of implementing new legal codes. Hundreds of uncoordinated Western consultants work on everything from Boy Scouts to enterprise development and offer some promise that increased heterogeneity, power diffusion, and grassroots activity will help emerging partial democracies become more deeply rooted. GRSOs in some countries —Israeli-occupied Palestine, Lebanon, and Jordan, for example—have entered independent sectors that already included established charities and thousands of GROs (see Fisher 1993, 91–3).[15] A radio program called "Good Morning Palestine" has become a sounding board for the problems of ordinary Palestinians. In the long run, governments will have "little choice but to reform, because exclusion and repression are losing games" (Kazemi and Norton 1995, 87).

The first steps toward democracy in this political climate are undoubtedly the hardest. Ironically, the ranks of the not free include Saudi Arabia, a very prosperous country. Although Jordan, Lebanon, Kuwait, and Morocco were classified as part free in 1995, Lebanon had regressed to not free by 1996. Iraq and Iran, classified with the remainder of Middle Eastern countries as not free, are nonetheless having to cope with demonstrations and pressures from below. Even in Algeria, the regime gained legitimacy in 1996 "in the Arab world's first ever pluralistic presidential election. As the army pressed its offensive, hundreds of fundamentalist fighters turned themselves in" (Pipes 1995–96, 47).

Overall, there does seem to be a kind of halting, two steps forward, one and a half steps backward progression toward democracy in the Third World. And the broader process of tentative political development that encourages this progress seems to be occurring in a number of countries due to the emergence of NGOs—which I call the vanguard of civil society, and Cesar Fernandes and Piquet Carneiro (1995, 72) call "supercitizens."

Although this book focuses on how NGOs scale up through interactions with governments, scaling up ultimately depends on the ability of NGOs of all types to scale out at the grassroots level through networking with other NGOs, local governments, or local representatives of national governments. In addition to reinforcing local political participation, bottom-up democratization is essential to sustainable development—a process and a change in thinking that must be implemented in hundreds of thousands of local spaces, as well as at the national policy level and in the global commons.

NGOs are strengthening grassroots politics to promote sustainable development in three major ways. First, NGO relationships are filling the void left by governments' failure to reach down to the grassroots. In some countries, grassroots networks play a uniquely powerful role in this respect. Second, particularly in Latin America, subnational governments are beginning to empower themselves and build grassroots ties through their relationships with NGOs. Third, mass-based relationships are crucial to autonomy, and autonomy is related to impact on sustainable development policies at the national level, a conclusion reinforced by Putnam's (1993a) evidence on causal rather than correlational relationships between civil society and long-term economic development in Italy (see Box 6.2).[16]

However, Putnam (1993a, 180) also argues that "with respect to civic community, them that has gets." Indeed, he notes that the reasons that the northern Italians were "already more prone to organize themselves in the year 1100" may be "lost in the mist of the Dark Ages." In response to Putnam's persuasive historical determinism, one is tempted to observe

---

Box 6.2   Civil Society in Italy

Putnam's (1993a) book on Italy provides statistical evidence supporting a causal relationship between civil society and both government performance and economic development. Using a variety of indicators to measure government performance, he found that there was a strong correlation between the success of northern regional governmental performance and the strength of the "civic community." More remarkably, long-term economic development was strongly correlated to the regional differences in an additional civil society index, based on historical data. Putnam and his team have thus been able to move beyond correlation toward causality. "Over the two decades since the birth of the regional governments, civic regions have grown faster than regions with fewer associations and more hierarchy, *controlling for their level of development in 1970*" (176). Equally important was the negative finding that the success or failure of regional governments was "wholly uncorrelated with virtually all measures of political fragmentation, ideological polarization and social conflict" (117). The highly civic community, in other words, is not necessarily free of strife.

---

that guilds were originally organized because a few people voluntarily decided that they were a logical response to a chaotic and threatening environment. By the same token, the dramatic organizational explosion that began in the Third World less than thirty years ago was a conscious response to worsening poverty, high unemployment among educated people, and the increased availability of voluntary foreign assistance. Just as the formation of guilds and the invention of credit were central to the emergence of civil society in northern Italy in the twelfth century, GRSOs have promoted microenterprise development and built economic ties to cooperatives and rotating credit associations.

On the plus side of historical determinism, however, one suspects that Putnam is right when he says that civic traditions "have remarkable staying power" (1993a, 157). To be sure, civil society can be destroyed pretty thoroughly under dictatorial regimes of both the Left and the Right. And, in an article called "Bowling Alone," Putnam (1995) himself noted the apparent decline in social capital in the United States. Yet traditions and something bordering on an associational "collective self-consciousness" persist and can be drawn upon. If civil society in most of the developing and transitional countries is not yet as strong as it is in northern Italy, it is arguably stronger than in Sicily or Calabria.[17] Moreover, unlike Italy, where choral societies and sports clubs are the most common forms of association, NGOs, as noted in Chapter 1, are tied more closely to socioeconomic results.

In some countries, such as Costa Rica and Chile, a "virtuous circle" between democracy and civil society may be in motion. The Costa Rican state has been "remarkably permeable to the demands of the popular sectors. The forms of popular participation which were created may have been primarily symbolic, but even symbolic participation, when successfully institutionalized, can have profound political effects" (Macdonald 1997, 36). And in Chile:

> A relatively higher degree of urbanisation, a stronger political culture and a larger and more influential middle-class were all both cause and consequence of the fact that before 1973, democracy survived for longer and civil society was more developed [than in any other country in Latin America]. This is a virtuous circle. A stronger civil society and middle sectors before 1973 meant that after the 1973 coup the development of NGOs was more substantial which itself meant that after the democratic transition in 1990 civil society emerged more vigorously than elsewhere in Latin America (Hojman 1993, 21, cited in Clarke 1996, 16).

Although the impact of NGOs on political systems differs everywhere and cannot be fully weighed anywhere, NGOs are in the vanguard of an emerging civil society that increasingly interacts with government in many countries. And, as Clarke (1996, 18) points out, the proliferation of NGOs in the Third World has been occurring in a much shorter time frame than the growth of voluntary organizations in the developed countries. Not only are NGOs growing in numbers, promoting grassroots participation, and directly targeting issues of human rights and democratization, they are also, as I argued in the first chapter, at the crux of the relationship between the nonprofit and for-profit sectors in the Third World. Finally, in carving out a political commons within which they interact with governments, they promote, however slowly, empowerment from below and accountability from above. Political development begins, I have argued, when previously excluded groups, organized into associations, enter the political commons and enhance the dimensions available for problem-posing and -solving.

Institutional development has long been considered important to the overall progress of a country. What is happening today, however, has the potential to be tied more closely to sustainable socioeconomic results, because the institutions that are emerging are specifically concerned with local development and national development policies, not just with the advancement of an ideology or economic interest. The extreme dimensions of the global crisis further promote the logic of a "fit" between sustainable development, on the one hand, and sustainable institutional/ political development, on the other. The urgency of the immediate manifestations of this crisis, so visible in the Third World, has also pushed NGOs, through their ties with ordinary people, to the forefront of understanding the public interest.

To argue that political development and socioeconomic development now have the potential to reinforce each other is very different from saying that they have done so historically, despite Putnam's Italian findings.[18] Although they have traditional roots, NGOs, particularly GRO networks and GRSOs, are a new phenomenon. As organizational indicators of political development focused on socioeconomic development, NGOs are consciously promoting and discovering the connections between politics and sustainable development. In some cases, these connections are beginning to influence governments.

Indeed, there are signs that NGOs in many countries are advancing along a path that will cumulatively and eventually lead to major societal as well as governmental changes. For example, one activist argues that Brazilian GRSOs worked with the poor in the 1950s, with the "marginalized" in the 1960s, with the "people" in the 1970s, and with society as a whole in the 1980s (Lopezllera Mendez 1988, 33). A similar evolutionary process is occurring in India. AWARE in Andhra Pradesh, with tens of thousands of grassroots members, has forced the government to implement the land reform laws already on the books. Although AWARE is partially supported through government funds, it is advancing its own candidates for election to 40 out of 200 seats in the state parliament. In Gujarat, another NGO called DISHA works with the landless and has challenged landlords who deny them the right to work for others. This included action in the High Court and the state parliament, which led to an invitation for DISHA to join an all-India government commission on bonded labor (Clark 1991, 5).

When political leaders learn to make conscious use of NGOs, political development from below can reach a critical mass against the leaden weight of poverty and inequality. It is only through increasing this interaction with development from below that they will learn to do so. By increasing and deepening their contacts with NGOs, political leaders can also acquire new resources and enhance their understanding of policy alternatives.

Fortunately, the pressures of a growing civil society are not the only forces propelling top-down democratization. An emerging international civil society—international media, access to the Internet, and publicity about human rights violations promoted by international human rights organizations—is also important. International travel and the communications revolution tend to preclude the possibility of the isolated historical accidents that influenced an Emilia Romagna or a Calabria for a thousand years.

Yet the worldwide advances toward democracy may slow down or even reverse themselves due to the growing dimensions of poverty, population, and environmental degradation. Of these three horsemen of the global apocolypse, the greatest barrier to hope, and the "problem of problems," remains the world's exploding population. Despite encouraging recent news about declining fertility, the relentless momentum of population growth continues, and rapid and continuous fertility reductions are needed just to contain escalating hunger, violence, and environmental devastation. Unless this situation changes, NGOs and governments will have to race ahead with sustainable development just to stay even.

So far, the prospects for policy change on this issue are not encouraging. Although the 1994 Cairo Conference raised the visibility of the relationships between declining fertility and the empowerment of women, and some Third World governments are taking the issue seriously, Third World NGOs, in the vanguard role in so many other issues, remain less likely to focus on population than on environmental degradation or targeted poverty strategies. International funding is still woefully inadequate, although the estimated $17 billion a year needed to provide universal family planning and basic health services is relatively modest.

If the rate of population growth in the developing world were reduced from the current 2.3 percent a year to 1.6 percent, the Third World (excluding China) would have 5.1 billion people in 2025 instead of 6.5 billion (Robey, Rutstein, and Morris 1993, 67).[19] Alternatively, political violence and decay, the exhaustion of basic natural resources such as water, and mass starvation in the Third World will threaten the developed countries as well.

For this reason alone, sustainable development will fail if it does not become politically as well as economically and environmentally sustainable on a global scale. Sustainable development, in this broader sense, will be tough and complicated, requiring enormous persistence and continual learning and adaptation, as well as resources and a certain amount of luck. As the Swiss entrepreneur who created the European Business Council for Sustainable Development argues, "We are at the foot of a steep and rocky path," and it may take generations before human beings are reconciled with nature and with themselves (Smith 1992, 75; see also Chapter 1, note 1).

The potential power of interactions between governments and NGOS provides us with hope that three major trends occurring throughout the developing countries—the proliferation of NGOs, the continuing vitality of the informal for-profit sector, and the human rights and democracy movement—are not just fads. Unless they are overrun by population pressures, they may even have the long-range potential to reinforce one another. As Clark (1995, 593) points out, the possibilities of a favorable climate for poverty reduction are maximized when the three sectors of society—for-profit, nonprofit, and governmental—interact. This process of reinforcement and convergence can be accelerated by autonomous NGOs willing to lobby governments as well as focus on locally sustainable development, by governments willing to facilitate the widespread creation of new wealth rather than protecting economic exploitation, and by political entrepreneurs and ordinary people at the grassroots level who challenge authoritarian governments by enlarging the political commons.

Recommendations

As Southern NGOs and governments struggle to learn from their new relationships, Northern development professionals and donors are increasingly committed to popular participation and partnership with Southern NGOs. Yet Northerners have generally failed to commit time and money to researching local efforts and thereby base their own contributions on who is doing what where. As Bebbington and Riddell (1997, 119) point out, this can raise administrative costs, at least in the short run. Projects are still initiated and partners chosen without regard to whether GROs or GRSOs are active in a particular region. Partnerships are often established with the best-known organizations, which may or may not be doing the best job of grassroots organizing or of changing government policies. Although outside assistance sometimes promotes the creation of NGOs, foreign assistance can also smother indigenous creativity. "Umbrella funding" often organizes NGOs into new networks rather than finding out whether informal NGO networks already exist and could be strengthened. In other words, the subtle assumption that capacity building is a one-way street is still widespread.

Many international development specialists understand the need for long-term institutional support—the much-touted move from project to process. Ndegwa (1996, 25), for example, argues that project-based external dependency is the greatest threat to organizational sustainability and therefore the pluralization of civil society. But the transition is difficult, particularly for large organizations, be they official donors or INGOs. World Neighbors, a small U.S. NGO based in Oklahoma City, has the flexibility to commit $10,000 a year for ten years to a Third World NGO. Yet for large organizations such as CARE or Save the Children, the trade-off between trust for a fledgling organization and accountability to donors is more difficult, particularly when the individual donor might better be described as a taxpayer. Even large organizations, however, could develop "quick and dirty" up-front research techniques with national researchers that would allow the initial selection of a partner to become more important and subsequent monitoring to be easier. This could be supplemented by short-term sabbaticals for national and international field staff to informally explore and research the local institutional terrain.

In addition to developing mapping skills, policy makers in the South and the North need to sharpen their focus on sustainable development and the empowerment of civil society. Most important, they need to cultivate what is already growing from the grassroots. The following recommendations are designed to help them do so.

Sustainable Development

Sustainable development policies should focus on supporting an emerging civil society's efforts to overcome the three horsemen of the global apocalypse—population, poverty, and environmental deterioration.

THE POPULATION CRISIS   One of the conclusions of Chapter 4 was that the impact of NGOs on governments may be long term. But the population crisis narrows choices and makes it more and more difficult, even foolhardy, to assume that civil society will gradually become stronger on its own. Indeed, despite declining fertility in much of the Third World, population momentum is likely to derail, all by itself, the many promising trends described in this book.

By working with university and other researchers in the Third World to map GROs, GRSOs and their networks (to find out who is doing what where), national policy makers, and representatives from the official and voluntary donor community could do the following.

1. Locate and support NGOs of all types that already focus on the population issue as part of their approach to sustainable development. Fortunately, some countries, such as Ghana, have unusually high numbers of family planning NGOs. These could provide guidance for promoting an indigenous family planning movement in other countries through GRSO networks and women's organizations.[20]

2. Support NGOs (including INGOs) already skilled at influencing policy that could enlarge their mandate to include innovative population projects through South-South and South-North partnerships. An excellent current example is Population Communication International's support of population-focused soap operas produced by radio and television stations in the Third World.

3. Support those GRSO networks that have at least one member organization capable of training other GRSOs on a wide range of population

issues, including family planning, family health services, population education, and the education of women. In Nepal, the Philippines, and Ghana, for example, GRSO networks are training their members to provide family planning services. In Malaysia, the Negeri Sembilan Family Planning Association assists other GRSOs in family planning, youth education, and family health and welfare programs through its affiliation with the Federation of Family Planning Associations (Fisher 1994b, 39). Family planning organizations could be helped to improve their capacities for scaling out at the grassroots level through working with GRSOs focusing on poverty and the environment.

4. International support for the thousands of GRSOs already promoting women's enterprise development has undoubtedly increased the demand for family planning, but it might also be redesigned to increase supply. Because of cultural sensitivity and issues of privacy, many women in Africa and elsewhere are buying contraceptives at higher-priced pharmacies rather than going to NGO or government clinics (Caldwell, Orubuloye, and Caldwell 1992, 225). NGOs already involved in enterprise development could be encouraged to promote community-based cooperative pharmacies that could both lower contraceptive prices and provide employment for women.

5. Since not all NGOs are suited to supplying family planning services, much more attention needs to be paid to the role of NGOs in increasing the demand for smaller families. Technical and financial support could be focused on indigenous NGOs that lobby against child labor or early marriage, promote primary education, or develop alternatives to parents being supported by children in old age.[21] Even more important to a demand strategy are NGOs that increase the educational and employment opportunities for women.

6. If international donors were to focus on women's organizations, they could build on the relationship between the demand and the supply sides of strategies to reduce fertility. Moreover, support for existing women's organizations that wish to add clinical services to existing programs may be more cost-effective than creating new organizations. For example, the Zimbabwean National Family Planning Council (a parastatal organization) became so overburdened that it trained 20,000 members of the Association of Women's Clubs to deliver family planning services.

7. The spread of grassroots support functions among many types of voluntary organizations implies that there is also considerable potential for adding family planning to existing health systems such as nonprofit hospitals. Linking hospitals and clinics to GRSO networks as well as women's organizations could rationalize the cost of increasing coverage. The proliferation of indigenous charities and NGOs focusing on AIDS in the 1990s provides another opportunity for institutionalizing

and coordinating reproductive health in the Third World. In Brazil alone, there were seventy-six NGOs focusing on AIDS by 1991 (Landim 1992).

8. Much more concerted attention needs to be paid to the potential for spreading knowledge about family planning through GRO networks. In Burkina Faso, for example, the Naam peasant organizations, "quite spontaneously, started informing their members about birth control," and by 1984, they had initiated training sessions in remote areas (Pradervand 1990, 72).

If such measures were part of an international commitment to provide universal access to family planning, to use the media to strengthen the motivation to keep families small, and to focus on women's productive as well as reproductive roles, a continued lowering of fertility would become probable, and the promising spread of innovative sustainable development strategies through NGOs would continue.

POVERTY   Microenterprise development that includes the provision of credit for the poor is already well accepted and spreading to many countries. Yet there are some changes that could strengthen the impact of microenterprise development on poverty:

1. Through seed capital grants of $100 and partnerships with GRSOs and government departments, Trickle Up, an international NGO based in New York, has been able to reach poor people who are afraid to take out loans, even if they have access to credit. A field study in Ecuador and Guatemala showed that 90 percent of two- and three-year-old Trickle Up businesses are still operating, and many have expanded into new products (Fisher and Peck 1997). With increased international financial support, this approach could be more widely applied to reach the poorest of the poor, who could then graduate to credit programs.

2. GRSOs, international donors, and governments should do more to enhance ties *among* borrower groups rather than focusing exclusively on their own ties with each group. Even donors that assist cooperative federations frequently focus on individual member organizations rather than the ties among them. Facilitating contacts among informal economic networks, cooperative federations, and pre-cooperative federations would strengthen this goal. Donors and GRSOs should also be alert to some disturbing evidence from Bangladesh that microcredit programs are being manipulated by traditional moneylenders.[22]

ENVIRONMENTAL DETERIORATION   The media could do much more to address the environmental crisis on both a national and a global scale. The public awareness of global environmental trends that emerged in the developed countries in the late 1980s has gradually been replaced, at least in the United States, by the desire to avoid confronting global warming, deforestation, species extinction, and resource depletion. Nor does media coverage of international environmental issues make the essential connections among environmental deterioration, population, poverty, and wasteful consumption in the North. Moreover, there has been only scattered television coverage of creative local sustainable development efforts, such as those carried out by NGOs.

Increased publicity should include more attention to "debt swaps," used by international donors to buy discounted debt paper, which is exchanged for governments' local-currency investment in environmental or humanitarian programs, such as the immunization of children. Debt swaps generally have a better track record than other forms of international assistance for empowering local organizations. The Costa Rican government is one of several that have used debt swaps to strengthen partnerships with NGOs and improve environmental policies. Now that debt swaps have been test marketed with relatively small amounts of money, they could be replicated on a larger scale through increased funding and more creative use of NGO networks.

Although GRO networks are already important advocates for the environment, they could become stronger if they were linked, through national or international support, to GRSOs and environmental research programs at Third World universities. Subsidies could be provided that would help GROs and their networks distribute environmentally sustainable technologies. For example, UNITAS, an NGO network in Bolivia with good university ties, collects and distributes sustainable development research results to 3,000 local and national groups, including government ministries (see Chapter 3).

Official international organizations should seek creative ways to involve Third World governments with advanced environmental policies in efforts to support and train other governments. In some cases, this could be done on a South-South basis through the government–NGO environmental commissions established after the Rio Conference. This could include training on how to track the environmental impacts of development projects or managerial reforms that would strengthen governmental programs or departments devoted to the environment. Joint NGO–government project funding could allay government suspicions that too much international support is being channeled to NGOs.

Subnational governments could be drawn into this process most easily in countries undergoing decentralization or devolution to municipalities. Cities such as Curitiba in Brazil have pioneered sustainable development policies and could train officials of other Third World cities or sponsor South-South exchanges, with international support. More support needs to be provided to local networking on the environment, such as that undertaken by Ashoka fellow Rogelio Cova (see Box 5.6).

Both national and multinational business could be encouraged to support this process, partly as a way of preventing environmental conflicts with local communities in the future. The GROs in the Doon Valley of India, for example, were smart enough to include tourist hotel owners in their protests against limestone quarrying (see Chapter 3).

More international attention could be focused on the Philippine NGO experience with the use of "ecoregions" as the focus of NGO–government collaboration. The major purpose of studying this experience would be to explore the possibilities for replication elsewhere (Fisher 1993, 156).

INTEGRATING POPULATION, POVERTY, AND ENVIRONMENTAL DETERIORATION   Finally, to build support for an international sustainable development strategy, there is a need for well-documented and publicized news stories and case studies written by Third World reporters and researchers about those exceptional GRSOs that integrate concern for poverty, population, and environmental deterioration. For example:

- The Federation des Associations Feminines du Senegal (FAFS) is integrating family planning with cookstove development and tree planting to reduce the use of fuelwood and to assist women.

- The Kenyan Family Health Association is cooperating in reforestation efforts and is assisting small cooperatives, as well as training home health visitors, in family planning.

- An even more comprehensive sustainable development model has been implemented by a Thai GRSO, the Population and Community Development Association, in cooperation with Wildlife Fund Thailand, in the village of Sup Tai, near a national park. It includes family health and planning and a low-interest loan fund for income-generating activities such as guiding tourists through the park. A local GRO, the Environmental Protection Society, is engaged in tree planting and road grading. Within one year after the project began, land violations decreased considerably, temporary migration fell, corn and soy production increased significantly, and contraceptive prevalence went from 67 percent to 77 percent (Conservation Foundation 1988, 3).

A strategy of integrating the efforts of donors, governments, and NGOs could help spread such comprehensive approaches to sustainable development. The change in global consciousness needed to implement this strategy must be deeper than alarm about immediate crises, however. We in the North must question not only our consumption patterns but also our ingrained paternalism. To do this, we must learn from and build on what people in the Third World have already achieved. By strengthening women's organizations, GRSO networks, GRO networks, and voluntary health systems, the institutionalization of sustainable development, including family planning, can be accelerated.

Civil Society and Democracy

Policy makers, be they farsighted officials in Southern governments or representatives of international agencies, should also initiate joint efforts to strengthen the relationships between civil society and government that constitute the political commons. The goal, in other words, is to promote political development. How can the role of NGOs as the vanguard of civil society and the promoters of the political development commons be advanced? One strategy would be to work with and support those specific NGOs that, because of their ties with other NGOs and growing autonomy, will have the maximum effect on political development. The more sucessful this strategy becomes, the more spillover effect it will have on a second, parallel strategy, which is to cultivate civil society more generally, including its role in promoting more responsive and accountable governments.[23] This section outlines this double-pronged strategy and then explores the major conceptual barriers that inhibit its implementation.

STRATEGY 1: WORKING WITH NGOs International donors still select indigenous partners based on who they know or the charisma of a particular NGO leader. Even an "objective" bidding process can lead NGOs that previously cooperated with each other at the grassroots level to compete for funding.[24] Perhaps the best overall principle underlying the choice of NGO (and other) partners is that "knowledge and organizational density are interwoven" (David Cooperrider, unpublished memo). Among the "better performing" development linkages that could be used to narrow down the search for partners are the following (Fisher 1993, 196–210):

- GRSOs with ties to preexisting GROs (not GROs created by GRSOs)

- GRO networks with ties to GRSOs

- GRSOs that provide specialized help to large numbers of GROs

- GRSOs that have evolved from a GRO network, with people at the grassroots level hiring their own experts

- GRSOs founded by people who leave their communities, obtain an education, and then return to their original communities

- Informal GRSO networks, particularly those with specialized technical knowledge

- GRSOs with ties to universities or research centers

Using such linkages as indicators would help zero in on the more autonomous NGOs so that support could do double duty—strengthening both NGOs and their impact on governments. In promoting or strengthening autonomy, development professionals (foreign or domestic) would be wise to heed the call of Hippocrates: "First, do no harm." Although it is true that donors are unlikely to be able to promote an internal commitment to autonomy, donors may, by pursuing policies too strongly influenced by Third World governments, end up strengthening precisely those GRSOs or GRSO networks that are the least autonomous.

There are also ways to strengthen the autonomy of promising NGOs:

1. Financial autonomy:

- Northern NGOs skilled in fund-raising and financial management are already focusing on short-term courses for NGO leaders. In Namibia, for example, World Learning designed and implemented assessment tools to determine financial management capability, developed training modules for NGO financial managers, and organized a financial management workshop that simultaneously strengthened NGO networking. Such efforts should be expanded more systematically.

- Country-level clearinghouses of INGOs, donors, and national NGOs could be designed to focus specifically on diversifying foreign funding and on standardizing financial reporting requirements. Government departments not intent on co-optation could be included as well. As Bebbington and Riddell (1997, 122) point out, "the question is not strong state *or* strong NGO sector: it is rather of the need for *strength in both*."

- Instead of merely providing grants for Northern NGOs, Northern foundations should increase their efforts to support philanthropy within the Third World—specifically, to promote community foundations and grant-making foundations.[25] This would not only promote NGO autonomy but also strengthen civil society more generally.

- Much foreign assistance to eastern Europe and the former Soviet Union has focused on creating an "enabling environment for philanthropy" through legal and tax code reforms that promote philanthropy and strengthen the legal autonomy and political advocacy role of NGOs. Similar efforts should be accelerated in the Third World by both governments and foreign donors.

- Regional institutions, such as the European Foundation Center, that could promote the exchange of successful fund-raising techniques should be identified. Matching grant endowments could be used to reward successful fund-raising. This would not only strengthen the autonomy of NGOs but also have a spin-off effect on promoting the philanthropic portion of civil society.

2. A mass base:

- More attention should be focused on horizontal grassroots networking, particularly when it is partially self-financing. The skills already developed by grassroots networks in some countries may be as valuable as those of the highly trained professionals who organize GRSOs.

- Additional attention also needs to be focused on support for three-way ties among GROs, GRSOs, and governments by either governments or foreign donors.

3. Rather than sponsoring training by Northern or international NGOs, international funders should seek out well-managed Third World NGOs and support their efforts to train other organizations, including government departments. Account Aid in India, for instance, already specializes in training other Indian NGOs.[26]

- Focus on specialized or sectoral GRSO networks with good technical, managerial, and strategic knowledge about development. Look for those with a good track record in training their member organizations and/or government bureaucracies instead of general umbrella organizations, which are often created by donors. Care must be taken, however, not to compromise the independence and vitality of informal networks. Shared planning and practice are the keys to unlocking the future potential of GRSO networks to promote interactive learning, to replicate what works, and to challenge the political and societal structures that maintain poverty.

- Support for national administrators, local administrators, and local government officials could also include nonhierarchical skills such as the process of public deliberation, promoted internationally by the Kettering Foundation.

- When NGOs train government officials, they strengthen their own autonomy and political influence. NGO–government collaboration can also be a form of training. International donors therefore need to focus on supporting government–NGO networking within each country as well as among the countries of the South.

- The Internet and other mass communications media provide the global community with unprecedented potential for disseminating the strategic lessons learned about development. More attention needs to be focused, however, on improving the simple communications technologies, such as telephone service, that block access to more advanced technologies in many Third World countries or make them prohibitively expensive (see Fisher forthcoming).

■ Increase support for governmental reforms that include NGOs. In addition to management institutes, Third World NGOs that specialize in training other NGOs might be enlisted in this process. In Guatemala, for example, the Foundation of Financial Consulting to Development and Social Service Agencies (FAFIDESS) assists over forty other organizations in project analysis, proposal writing, fundraising, and administration (FUNDESA 1989). "Service networks" of GRSOs that exchange skill training directly with one another could also be used.[27]

■ Support decentralized approaches to NGO–government coordination through subnational governments or coordination through multiple stratified focus points, as described in Chapter 2. A national NGO office within a government, for example, could convene periodic meetings of the representatives of NGO networks, standardize donor forms, help introduce NGOs to donors, and assist NGOs with proposals; however, it would not be in charge of NGO policies unless a problem could not be solved at a lower level.[28] This would be a particularly useful strategy for big, populous countries such as Brazil, where there are too many NGOs for the government to track.

Carefully planned and targeted collaboration at the local and the national levels could enhance the possibility that positive trends will continue and become more widespread. Such efforts should concentrate on strengthening linkages among local administrators, local governments, GROs, GRSOs, networks, and international donors, as well as with national governments.

STRATEGY 2: CULTIVATING CIVIL SOCIETY   Despite rising international interest in election monitoring, external support for civil society may be more feasible than direct support for democracy. Since authoritarian regimes do not consistently repress NGOs, this international policy shift need not imply a loss of commitment to human rights. Official donors and international NGOs could, for example, focus specifically on those parts of civil society (including media and businesses) that can have the most direct impact on promoting political rights, civil liberties, and the political commons shared by government and civil society.[29]

Small, carefully designed regional workshops on civil society should include both governments and NGOs. Such workshops could be cosponsored by international networks based in the Third World, such as GERDDES-Africa (Study and Research Group on Democracy and Economic and Social Development in Africa), which focuses on building democracy throughout the continent. Where political barriers block assistance to either democracy or civil society, hard choices that exclude certain countries may be necessary.

A political development strategy may also involve some trade-offs between a focus on "the poorest of the poor" and assistance that strengthens the political activism of GRSOs and the middle class (Theunis 1992, 328).[30] Some international donors might concentrate, for example, on mobilizing the national resources of the middle and upper classes in order to strengthen what is now weak national philanthropic support for NGOs.

Support for managerial reforms within national governments of the type described in Chapter 2 could strengthen other components of this strategy, including the initiation of political development at the local level. Bureaucrats can be trained to identify and support local skills and organizations without smothering them and can be rewarded for learning from failure (see, for example, Calavan 1984). Support for local communities could be based on strengthening NGOs as "laboratories of social experimentation, technical assistance and training for local governments" (Reilly 1995b, 25). Decentralization pushed down from above could be strengthened by tax reforms as well as increased cooperation with NGOs. And foreign donors could support the mapping of local institutional resources by local researchers in relation to democratization.

Although GROs and GRSOs are forming vertical and horizontal linkages in many countries, well-targeted international support could also enhance the likelihood that networking will include both local governments and local representatives of national governments. Interactions between NGOs and local governments could become a major focus of the generally recognized need in the development community to move from project to process. As Goodell (1984, 278) writes, "Economic development and foreign aid policies should be founded on the process of building up local and provincial level organization, both public and private, to the principal end that political maturity will gradually take root."

Reilly (1995b, 26) recommends that NGO fund-raising and technical assistance be replicated by local governments through intergovernmental lobbies such as the International Union of Local Authorities, Sister Cities International, or Partners of the Americas. He also recommends that successful NGO–local government collaborations be documented and disseminated widely.

CONCEPTUAL BARRIERS TO IMPLEMENTATION Both of these strategies are based on a shift in consciousness from the idea that outsiders can promote development to the notion that sustainable political and economic development is already under way in many countries, more or less successfully, if unevenly. The logical next step within this shift in thinking is to ask:

- Who is doing what where in the country in question?

- Who is most successful?

- Who is collaborating with whom?

- What are the comparative advantages of existing local actors, including NGOs?

- What are the comparative advantages of the Northern donor?

- What are the comparative advantages of the Southern government?

Capacity building, in other words, should be a two-way street. A Northern NGO may teach fund-raising techniques, but the Southern partner may know more about networking and field collaboration with other NGOs. Whenever possible, it is preferable for Northerners to opt for South-South collaboration in promoting democracy and civil society.[31] Support for South-South training initiatives on advocacy and collaboration can be designed to include both government officials and NGO personnel. For example, World Learning's Democracy Enhancement Project in Haiti links subnational governments and civil society interest groups. In Malawi, SHARED is a network that facilitates communication among the government of Malawi, NGOs, and USAID to improve the effectiveness of development efforts.[32] Such ties can also strengthen human rights and the enabling environment for philanthropy and voluntarism.

International support should also, however, be based on a recognition that the most capable Third World NGOs are spread thin from a programmatic point of view. There are serious trade-offs as well as mutually reinforcing advantages in grassroots organizing, managing sustainable development projects, and impacting governments. Thus, support for collaborative learning processes between governments and NGOs could be based on GRO networks, which strengthen grassroots organizing, and specialized GRSO networks, which strengthen technical and managerial knowledge.

In Chapter 3, I concluded that Northern NGOs, official donors, and even Northern governments can help NGOs strengthen their autonomy. But they can also do more. By asking tough questions, they can promote legal reforms that strengthen civil society and political reforms that enhance pluralism and democracy. Although concerns about political intervention in the affairs of other countries should be taken seriously, policies that push Third World governments to broaden the choices of their citizens should not be viewed in the same light as past or present interventionist policies that strengthen particular elites, such as military establishments. This also implies that foreign support for process reforms (such as strengthening legal codes that pertain to NGOs) may be more effective than support for particular policy initiatives.

International donors, of course, can do only so much. Among the most important elements of the future agenda are the other political changes, mostly within governments, that will make positive responses to the escalating crises of poverty, population, and environmental degradation more likely. How likely is this to happen?

Authoritarianism is not particularly stable and generally doesn't work to promote equitable development.[33] In some cases, such as South Korea in the 1970s, control and support of local organizations led to substantial social and economic gains, but authoritarian governments are far less likely today to be able to afford the top-down development policies that eventually challenge the system that created them. Democracies, still in a minority in the Third World, do not necessarily take advantage of their political assets.

How likely is it that an increasing number of political leaders will begin to build on the mutually reinforcing connections between socio-economic and political development? Given the demographic-resource squeeze, the next group of successful countries to develop will have to devote far more immediate attention to population and environmental policies. Can they also add political development to their crushing agendas? The answer, of course, is that unless they cooperate with "nongovernments," they have little likelihood of achieving any of their goals.

When the sheer necessity of meeting the environmental and resource challenge is bolstered by the demands of GROs and GRSOs, the likelihood of a strong political response will increase. Therefore, the sustainable development role of NGOs, at both the local and the national policy level, remains crucial to political development and, ultimately, to democratization.

Political development has begun to transform the way social and economic policies are planned and implemented in a number of countries, even though many versions of the syncratic coalition remain powerful. This process will, in most countries, be accompanied by continuing violence and instability. In some countries, it may be stalled or defeated. But this is a process that, unlike earlier revolutions, has not substituted a new ruling class for the old, because it depends on political, social, and economic empowerment initiated from below.

Notes

1. I am indebted to my coauthor, Charles Hamilton, for this quotation (see Fisher and Hamilton 1996, 124).
2. For the checklists, see Freedom House 1994–95, 672–3. Coppedge and

Reinicke (1990) developed a scale to measure polyarchy, which they define in terms of real approximations of democracy as an ideal. Their Pearson product-moment correlations with Freedom House's indices of political rights and civil liberties were .938 and .934, respectively, as of 1985.

3. In a cross-national study of the nonprofit sector in eight developed countries, Salamon and Anheier (1996, 5) argue that "the number of nonprofit organizations in a country—either absolutely or per 1,000 population—is a measure of the ubiquity of this sector." Although the one rough indicator used here measures mainly GRSOs per million, it includes other nonprofit organizations. The same authors' (1994, 90–1) study of Brazil found that close to 200,000 nonprofit entities of all types were registered with the Federal Revenue Bureau in Brasilia. "This included 11,076 foundations (almost exclusively operating foundations) and 179,010 associations." Registered GROs would probably be included as associations, but GRSOs might be in either category.

4. Interview with Roslyn Hees of the World Bank, August 1996. In Tunisia, according to Marzouk (1977, 197), "women's organizations and development NGOs represent only 2.5% of the 5186 associations recorded by official statistics."

5. In commenting on Putnam (1993a), Zakaria (1995, 25) points out that "the Italian north has been better run than the Italian south for hundreds of years, during which time the country was, to put it mildly, not always democratic. One might more reasonably conclude from Mr. Putnam's research that social capital makes any regime work, whether monarchical, democratic or facist."

6. The Gambia has a high NGO density because of small population size. The country has suffered democratic reversals in the last several years, according to Freedom House reports.

7. Using Freedom House's 1996 data, I included Mongolia, North Korea, and South Korea in this calculation but left Taiwan and Singapore out of the Third World category. If they are added, the total would be 88 of 135 in the free or part-free category.

8. See also Barkan (1994, 109), who writes that "although Nigeria remains under military rule, civil society is alive, resilient and growing."

9. This practice is also common in Jordan and Lebanon.

10. Mainwaring (1985, 6) points out that Brazilian democratization created new dilemmas and problems for grassroots movements, even as it provided new political space. Cavarozzi and Palermo (1995, 29) note that in Argentina, a weak state and strong civil society may be compatible over the long run.

11. The same might be said about the Carter Center's *Africa Demos*, which has a different democracy rating system. *Africa Demos* listed fifteen democracies in Africa in 1994, compared with seven listed in Freedom House (1994–95).

12. Their political systems were described by Payne (1996, 77) as "market authoritarianism."

13. See Fisher (1993, 81) for an earlier estimate of 6,000, which represented mainly estimates from the late 1980s. Sources available since that time suggest that the figure may now be 10,000. See Arellano-Lopez and Petras

1994 for Bolivia; Diaz-Albertini 1993b, 320, for Peru; Sollis 1995, 525–42, for El Salvador, Guatemala, and Nicaragua; Navarro 1994, 7, for Venezuela and Costa Rica; and Inter-American Foundation 1995 for Brazil.

14. Burundi, for example, was praised by the Clinton administration for "exemplary presidential elections" in June 1993. Yet by October of that same year, the government had been overthrown by a military coup d'état.

15. North Africa, Jordan, and Lebanon already had thousands of grassroots organizations and traditional charities. See Table 6.1.

16. Interestingly, there appears to be little relationship between democracy versus dictatorship and economic development, measured by growth in gross national product per capita (see Bertsch, Clark, and Wood 1982, 458–9, for example). Other studies have concluded that either there is a positive relationship between democracy and growth or the form of government has no statistically significant impact on growth rates. Weede (1984, 309) found that the weak negative correlation between democracy and economic growth disappeared as state control over economic actors weakened. Kohli (1986) concluded that democratic countries as diverse as India, Sri Lanka, Venezuela, and Costa Rica all achieved moderate but steady growth rates between 1960 and 1982. He also found that the slight advantage in growth rates of authoritarian regimes during the same period was purchased at a higher long-term economic cost. During this period, democracies were significantly less likely to have incurred staggering foreign debts, and they were therefore less vulnerable to outside economic shocks. Fortunately, democracies also had more difficulties in crippling their agricultural sectors with price controls and were less likely to overvalue their currency to discourage exports. Moreover, the apparently positive association between authoritarianism and rates of economic growth found in some studies declines at higher income levels, according to Ruttan (1991, 274).

17. In the transitional countries of Europe and the former Soviet Union, the collapse of communism is fueling a similar explosion of the nonprofit sector. Opposition leaders, disillusioned with the political transition, join educated young people to take advantage of increased foreign assistance and create new nonprofit organizations. There are now an estimated 68,000 NGOs in Poland, Slovakia, Bulgaria, Hungary, the Czech Republic, and Romania and thousands in the countries of the former Soviet Union. Although educational levels are higher in the transitional countries than in much of the Third World, the continuing growth of civil society can help people challenge habits of economic and political dependency (see Institute for East West Studies 1995, 99).

18. See, for example, Huntington (1968), who makes a historical case against this relationship.

19. Demographers estimate that even if global fertility were reduced to replacement levels immediately, it would still take fifty to seventy-five years for global population to stabilize.

20. Although fewer Third World NGOs are working on population than on poverty or environmental deterioration, the results of the Cairo Conference, held in September 1994, offer considerable hope that this situation may be changing. The 5,000 NGOs at Cairo, 80 percent of them represented by

women, literally pushed governments toward coming to terms with the connections between fertility and the advancement of women. They were supported in their efforts by a considerable body of research·indicating that combining family planning and health assistance with poverty-focused strategies directed at women has a more dramatic impact on lowering fertility than those projects that merely provide contraceptives.

21. For a discussion of the demand side of reducing fertility, see Demeny (1992).

22. Interview with Jude Fernando, South Asian Studies, University of Pennsylvania, November 11, 1996.

23. For a similar formulation, see Blair (1994, 10).

24. Andrew Le Breton, who works for an environmental NGO in Zimbabwe called Saphire, told me that $26 million of USAID money put up for bid had this effect in his country (personal communication, April 1, 1997).

25. The Charles Stuart Mott Foundation in Flint, Michigan, has helped found community foundations in South Africa and eastern Europe.

26. Oxfam America has used Account Aid to train some of its Indian partners.

27. See Fisher (1993, 143–5) for more on service networks.

28. Brautigam (1994, 65) points out that most NGOs favor coordinating offices over having to coordinate integrated development projects with more than one ministry.

29. For a USAID report on promoting civil society that includes some issues not dealt with here, such as freedom of the press, see Blair (1994).

30. Some civic organizations promoting political participation, such as Conciencia in Argentina, have mainly middle-class members.

31. Northern support for South-South exchanges may be most useful in Africa, where NGOs are younger than in Asia and Latin America and so are more likely to be the creatures of foreign assistance.

32. Clarke (1996, 9) comments on the recent increase in NGO influence over the government of Malawi.

33. Siroway and Inkeles' (1990, 143) data showed that civilian regimes "appear to do better in terms of improving the basic quality of life of the masses of citizens." Among the rare exceptions were the Peruvian generals who held power between 1968 and 1980.

Glossary

Civil society: "Markets, associations and a sphere of public debate" (Perez Diaz 1993, 56).

Counterpart GRSOs: GRSOs founded by Northern NGOs, with all national staffs, that follow a model promoted by the Northern partner.

Decentralization: There are two types of decentralization—deconcentration and devolution. A policy of deconcentration assigns national government employees to local areas but ensures that they remain centrally accountable. A policy of devolution encourages local governments or NGOs to make decisions, thus decentralizing accountability as well as location.

Democratization: "The progressive extension of the citizenship principle to encompass a wider range of eligible participants and a wider scope of domains in which collective choice among equals or their representatives can make binding decisions on all" (O'Donnell and Schmitter 1986, 8).

Grassroots organizations (GROs): Membership organizations that work to improve and develop their own communities; also called people's organizations or base groups. There are three major types of GROs in most countries. Local development associations, such as village councils or neighborhood associations, work on many development issues that concern the entire community. Interest associations are more limited in membership and tend to work on particular issues. These include women's groups, water users associations, and shared work groups. Pre-cooperatives, cooperatives, and other community-based enterprises are the third type of GRO.

Grassroots support organizations (GRSOs): Nationally or regionally based development assistance organizations, usually composed of paid professionals that work with GROs in communities other than their own. Some observers call these intermediary NGOs.

GRO networks: Horizontal linkages among GROs, regionally based.

GRSO networks: Based on horizontal linkages among GRSOs. These include formal umbrella organizations or consortia, informal service networks that exchange expertise and cooperate in the field, and broader support movements that may include individual professionals and activists as well as GROs.

Independent sector: Also called the nonprofit sector, voluntary sector, or third sector, this is often defined as everything except the business and governmental sectors.

International NGOs (INGOs): International nongovernmental organizations must have "national sections" in at least three countries, according to the *Yearbook of International Organizations*. There are an estimated 20,000 of these (example: International Save the Children Alliance).

NGOs: Nongovernmental organizations. The term *NGO* is used in many different ways and has various meanings.

Northern NGOs: Internationally oriented national NGOs, based in the developed world (example: Save the Children–U.S.). In the United States alone there are an estimated 1,000 of these with budgets over $25,000 a year.

Political development: An interactive, public decision-making and learning process within and between government and civil society, based on power creation and dispersion. This process leads to increased individual and group autonomy from below and more responsiveness from above.

Scaling out: Extending the reach of development on the grassroots level, through networking or the expansion of locally based development efforts.

Scaling up: Extending the reach of development through ties to government or other national or international organizations.

Southern NGOs: Indigenous nongovernmental organizations that work on development, relief, education, and human rights in the Third World. As used here, this term includes grassroots organizations (GROs), grassroots support organizations (GRSOs), GRO networks, and GRSO networks. Except for some GROs (pre-cooperatives and cooperatives), most NGOs are nonprofit organizations.

Syncratic alliance: An elite political coalition that preserves inequitable rural landholding patterns and power structures. It usually includes both landowners and industrialists.

References

Abdel Ati, Hassan Ahmed. 1993. The Development Impact of NGO Activities in the Red Sea Province of Sudan: A Critique. *Development and Change* 24: 103–30.

Abzug, Rikki, and Natalie J. Webb. 1996. Another Role for Nonprofits: The Case of Mop-Ups and Nursemaids Resulting from Privatization in Emerging Economies. *Nonprofit and Voluntary Sector Quarterly* 25(2): 156–73.

Accion International. 1987. Accion International's Role in Promoting Policy Initiatives for Microenterprise Development in the Dominican Republic: 1983–1987. Paper for the quarterly meeting of the Advisory Commission on Voluntary Foreign Assistance.

Adams, Richard H. 1986. Bureaucrats, Peasants and the Dominant Coalition: An Egyptian Case Study. *Journal of Development Studies* 22(2): 336–54.

Afonso, Carlos Alberto. 1990. NGO Networking: The Telematic Way. *Development* 2: 51–4.

Ahmed, Hamid Osman. 1994. NGO–State Relationships in East Africa: Development Versus Sovereignty. *Transnational Associations* 3: 170–3.

Alfonso, Felipe. 1983. Assisting Farmer Controlled Development of Communal Irrigation Systems. In *Bureacracy and the Poor,* edited by David C. Korten and Felipe Alfonso. West Hartford, Conn.: Kumarian Press.

Allaghi, Farida. 1995. Women in Poverty in the Arab Region. *The Bulletin* 26: 60.

Alliband, Terry. 1983. Catalysts of Development: Voluntary Agencies in India. West Hartford, Conn.: Kumarian Press.

Allison, Adrienne A., and Lily P. Kak. 1992. NGO/Government Collaboration in Maternal Health and Family Planning Programmes. *Transnational Associations* 3: 163–6.

Allison, Adrienne, and James A. Macinko. 1993. PVOs and NGOs Promotion of Democracy and Health. Paper prepared for the Harvard School of Public Health, Data for Decision Making Project.

Almond, Gabriel A., and G. Bingham Powell. 1966. *Comparative Politics: A Developmental Approach.* New York: Little, Brown.

Alter, C., and J. Hage. 1993. *Organizations Working Together.* London: Sage.

Anang, Frederick T. 1994. Evaluating the Role and Impact of Foreign NGOs in

Ghana. In *The Changing Politics of Non-Governmental Organizations and African States,* edited by Eve Sandberg. Westport, Conn.: Praeger.

ANGOC (Asian NGO Coalition for Agrarian Reform and Rural Development). 1989. *People's Participation and Environmentally Sustainable Development.* Manila: ANGOC.

Anheier, Helmut K. 1987. Private Voluntary Organizations and Development in West Africa: Comparative Perspectives. Draft paper.

———. 1994. Non-Governmental Organizations and Institutional Development in Africa. In *The Changing Politics of Non-Governmental Organizations and African States,* edited by Eve Sandberg. Westport, Conn.: Praeger.

Anheier, Helmut, and Frank P. Romo. 1992. Intendedly Democratic Organizations in Africa: Elite Control, Free Riders and the Social Infrastructure. Unpublished paper.

Annis, Sheldon. 1987. Can Small Scale Development Be a Large Scale Policy? The Case of Latin America. *World Development* 15 (supplement): 129–34.

———. 1992. Evolving Connectedness Among Environmental Groups and Grassroots Organizations in Protected Areas of Central America. *World Development* 20(4): 587–95.

Annis, Sheldon, and Jeffrey Franks. 1989. The Idea, Ideology, and Economics of the Informal Sector: The Case of Peru. *Grassroots Development* 13(1): 9–22.

Apter, David. 1987. *Rethinking Development: Modernization, Dependency and Postmodern Politics.* Newbury Park, Calif.: Sage Publications.

Arbab, Farzzam. 1988. *The Governmental Development Organizations: Report of a Learning Project.* Cali, Colombia: CELATER/PACT.

Arellano-Lopez, Sonia, and James F. Petras. 1994. Non-Governmental Organizations and Poverty Alleviation in Bolivia. *Development and Change* 25: 555–68.

Aremo, James. 1983. Popular Participation in Rural Development. *Ceres* 16(3): 15–8.

Arena-DeRosa, James. 1990. Indigenous Leaders Host U.S. Environmentalists in the Amazon. *Oxfam America News* (summer/fall): 1–2.

———. 1991. Coinca March Forces Bolivian Land Reform. *Oxfam America News,* (winter): 6–7.

Arenson, Karen W. 1995. Charitable Giving Rose 3.6% in 1994, Philanthropy Trust Says. *New York Times,* May 25, A22.

Arruda, Marcos. 1985. *The Role of Latin American Non-Governmental Organizations in the Perspective of Participatory Democracy.* Rome: Third International Consultation, Freedom from Hunger Campaign/Action for Development.

Ashoka. N.d. The Evidence: Profiles of Early Ashoka Fellows. Unpublished paper.

———. 1985. The New Fellows—Early 1985. Changemakers.

———. 1988. Profiles of the Ashoka Fellows.

———. 1990. Ten Years Impact.

———. 1991. Profiles of the Ashoka Fellows.

Attwood, Donald W., Thomas C. Bruneau, and John G. Galaty, eds. 1988. *Power and Poverty: Development and Development Projects in the Third World.* Boulder, Colo.: Westview Press.

Aveline, Carlos. 1985. Communitarian Alternatives for Brazilian Crisis. *IFDA Dossier* 5(45): 19–22.

Bagadion, Benjamin U., and Frances F. Korten. 1985. Developing Irrigators' Organizations: A Learning Process Approach. In *Putting People First: Sociological Variables in Rural Development,* edited by Michael Cernea. New York: Oxford University Press.

Bahuguna, Sunderlal. 1988. Chipko: The People's Movement with a Hope for the Survival of Humankind. *IFDA Dossier* 63: 3–14.

Bailey, Connor. 1986. Government Protection of Traditional Resource Use Rights—The Case of Indonesian Fisheries. In *Community Management: Asian Experience and Perspectives,* edited by David C. Korten. West Hartford, Conn.: Kumarian Press.

Baloyra, Enrique A., and John D. Martz. 1979. *Political Attitudes in Venezuela: Societal Cleavages and Political Opinion.* Austin: University of Texas Press.

Bangladesh Rural Advancement Committee. 1986. Unraveling Networks of Corruption. In *Community Management: Asian Experience and Perspectives,* edited by David C. Korten. West Hartford, Conn.: Kumarian Press.

Baquedano, Manuel. 1989. Socially Appropriate Technologies and Their Contribution to the Design and Implementation of Social Policies in Chile. In *Social Policy from the Grassroots: Nongovernmental Organizations in Chile,* edited by Charles Downs, Giorgio Solimano, Carlos Vergara, and Luis Zuniga. Boulder, Colo.: Westview Press.

Barkan, Joel. 1994. Resurrecting Modernization Theory and the Emergence of Civil Society in Kenya and Nigeria. In *Political Development and the New Realism in Sub-Saharan Africa,* edited by David E. Apter and Carl G. Rosberg. Charlottesville: University of Virginia Press.

Barkan, Joel, and Frank Holmquist. 1989. Peasant-State Relations and the Social Base of Self-Help in Kenya. *World Politics* 16(3): 359–80.

Barnes, J. A. 1968. Networks and Political Process. In *Local Level Politics: Social and Cultural Perspectives,* edited by Marc J. Swartz. Chicago: Aldine.

Barreiro, Fernando, and Anabel Cruz, eds. 1990. *Organizaciónes No Gubernamentales de Uruguay: Analisis y Repertorio.* Montevideo, Uruguay: Institucion de Comunicación y Desarrollo.

Barrig, Maruja. 1990. Women and Development in Peru: Old Models, New Actors. *Community Development Journal* 25(4): 377–85.

Barroso, Carmen. 1987. Innovations in Reproductive Health and Child Survival. Address at the conference of the Association for Women in Development, Washington, D.C., April 16.

Barzetti, Valerie, and Yanina Rovinski. 1992. *Towards a Green Central America.* West Hartford, Conn.: Kumarian Press.

Bebbington, Anthony. 1991. Sharecropping Agricultural Development: The Potential for GSO-Government Cooperation. *Grassroots Development* 15(2): 21–30.

————. 1993. Modernization from Below: An Alternative Indigenous Development? *Economic Geography* 69(3): 274–92.

Bebbington, Anthony, Hernan Carrasco, Lourdes Peralbo, Galo Ramon, Victor Hugo Torres, and Jorge Trujillo. 1992. The Evolution of Indigenous Federations in Ecuador. *Grassroots Development* 16(2): 11–21.

Bebbington, Anthony, and John Farrington. 1993. Governments, NGOs and Agricultural Development: Perspectives on Changing Inter-Organizational Relationships. *Journal of Development Studies* 29(2): 199–219.

Bebbington, Anthony, and Roger Riddell. 1997. Heavy Hands, Hidden Hands, Holding Hands? Donors, Intermediary NGOs and Civil Society Organisations. In *NGOs, States and Donors: Too Close for Comfort?* edited by David Hulme and Michael Edwards. New York: St. Martin's Press.

Bennett, Jon, with Mark Duffield, Monika Kathina Juma, John Borton, Alun Burge, and Charlotte Benson. 1995. *Meeting Needs: NGO Coordination in Practice.* London: Earthscan Publications.

Berg, Robert. 1987. *Non-Governmental Organizations: New Force in Third World Development and Politics.* CASID distinguished speakers series no. 2. East Lansing: Michigan State University, Center for Advanced Study of International Development.

Berg, Robert, and Jennifer Seymour Whitaker, eds. 1986. *Strategies for African Development.* Berkeley: University of California Press.

Berger, Peter L., and Michael Novak. 1985. *Speaking to the Third World: Essays on Democracy and Development.* Washington, D.C.: American Enterprise Institute for Public Policy Research.

Bertsch, Gary, Robert Clark, and David Wood. 1982. *Comparing Political Systems: Power and Policy in Three Worlds.* New York: John Wiley and Sons.

Bhatt, Anil. 1995. Asian NGOs in Development: Their Role and Impact. In *Government-NGO Relations in Asia,* edited by Noeleen Heyzer, James V. Riker, and Antonio Quizon. New York: St. Martin's Press.

Bhatt, Ela. 1989. Towards Empowerment. *World Development* 17(7): 1059–65.

Bianchi, Robert. 1986. Interest Group Politics in the Third World. *Third World Quarterly* 8: 2.

Biggs, Stephen B., and Arthur D. Neame. 1996. Negotiating Room to Maneuver: Reflections Concerning NGO Autonomy and Accountability Within the New Policy Agenda. In *Beyond the Magic Bullet: NGO Performance and Accountability in the Post–Cold War World,* edited by Michael Edwards and David Hulme. West Hartford, Conn.: Kumarian Press.

Binder, Leonard. 1986. The Natural History of Development Theory. *Comparative Studies in Society and History* 28(1): 3–33.

Binder, L., L. W. Pye, J. S. Coleman, S. Verba, J. La Palombara, and M. Weiner. 1971. *Crises and Sequences in Political Development.* Princeton, N.J.: Princeton University Press.

Blackburn, Susan. 1993. *Practical Visionaries: A Study of Community Aid Abroad.* Carlton, Victoria: Melbourne University Press.

Blair, Harry. 1994. *Civil Society and Democratic Development.* A CDIE evaluation design paper. Washington, D.C.: U.S. Agency for International Development.

Booth, John A., and Mitchell A. Seligson. 1979a. Images of Political Participation. In *Political Participation in Latin America,* Vol. 1, edited by John A. Booth and Mitchell A. Seligson. New York: Holmes and Meier.

———. 1979b. Political Participation in Latin America. In *Political Participation in Latin America.* Vol. 2, edited by John A. Booth and Mitchell A. Seligson. New York: Holmes and Meier.

———, eds. 1979c. *Political Participation in Latin America.* 2 vols. New York: Holmes and Meier.

Bossert, Thomas. 1986. The Promise of Theory. In *Promise of Development: Theories of Change in Latin America,* edited by Peter F. Klaren and Thomas J. Bossert. Boulder, Colo.: Westview Press.

Boulding, Elise. 1990. Building a Global Civic Culture. *Development* 2: 39.

Bratton, Michael. 1983. Farmer Organizations in the Communal Areas of Zimbabwe: Preliminary Findings. Paper, Departments of Land Management and Political and Administrative Studies, University of Zimbabwe, Harare.

———. 1989. Poverty, Organization and Public Policy: Towards a Voice for Africa's Rural Poor. Unpublished paper.

———. 1994a. Civil Society and Political Transition in Africa. *IDR Reports* 11(6).

———. 1994b. Non-Governmental Organizations in Africa: Can They Influence Public Policy? In *The Changing Politics of Non-Governmental Organizations and African States,* edited by Eve Sandberg. Westport, Conn.: Praeger.

Bratton, Michael, and Aji Baldo. 1989. Poverty, Organization and Public Policy: Towards a Voice for Africa's Rural Poor. Paper presented at the Conference on the Voluntary Sector Overseas, Center for the Study of Philanthropy, City University of New York, April 26.

Brautigam, Deborah. 1994. State, NGOs and International Aid in the Gambia. In *The Changing Politics of Non-Governmental Organizations and African States,* edited by Eve Sandberg. Westport, Conn.: Praeger.

Breslin, Patrick. 1991. Democracy in the Rest of the Americas. *Grassroots Development* 15(2): 3–7.

Brienes, Wini. 1989. *Community and Organization in the New Left 1962–1968: The Great Refusal.* New Brunswick, N.J.: Rutgers University Press.

Brown, L. David. 1990. *Bridging Organizations and Sustainable Development.* IDR working paper no. 8. Boston: Institute for Development Research and Boston University School of Mangement.

———. 1993. Social Change Through Collective Reflection with Asian Nongovernmental Development Organizations. *Human Relations* 46(2): 249–73.

Brown, L. David, and Darcy Ashman. 1995. *Intersectoral Problem-Solving and Social Capital Formation: A Comparative Analysis of African and Asian Cases.* Boston: Institute for Development Research.

Brown, L. David, and David C. Korten. 1989. *The Role of Voluntary Organizations in Development.* Boston: Institute for Development Research.

Brown, L. David, and David Winder. 1996. Civil Society, Sector Institutions, and Civil Society Resource Organizations. Conference of the Association for Research on Nonprofit Organizations and Voluntary Action (ARNOVA), Boston, November.

Brown, Stephen J. 1984. The Logic of Problem Generation: From Morality and Solving to De-Posing and Rebellion. *For the Learning of Mathematics* 4(1): 9–20.

Brundtland Bulletin, Number 7 (March), 1990.

Bryant, Coralie, and Louise G. White. 1980. *Managing Rural Development: Peasant Participation in Rural Development.* West Hartford, Conn.: Kumarian Press.

Burnell, Peter. 1991. *Charity, Politics and the Third World.* New York: Harvester Wheatsheaf.

Caccia Brava, Silvio, and Laura Mullahy. 1995. Making Cities Liveable: Local Initiatives in Solid Waste and Public Transportation Management in Brazil. In *New Paths to Democratic Development in Latin America: The Rise of NGO-Municipal Collaboration,* edited by Charles Reilly. Boulder, Colo.: Lynne Rienner.

Calavan, Michael. 1984. Appropriate Administration: Creating a "Space" Where Local Initiative and Voluntarism Can Grow. In *Private Voluntary Organizations as Agents of Development,* edited by Robert F. Gorman. Boulder, Colo.: Westview Press.

Caldwell, J. C., I. O. Orubuloye, and P. Caldwell. 1992. Fertility Decline in Africa: A New Type of Transition? *Population and Development Review* 18(2): 211–42.

Camara, Gabriel. 1993. Sociedad en Diálogo con el Estado. *La Otra Bolsa de Valores* 6(24): 1–2.

Canadian Centre for International Studies and Cooperation (CECI), Asia Regional Office. 1992. *The Potentials of Nepali NGOs.* Vol. 1. Kathmandu, Nepal: CECI.

Cantori, Louis J., and Iliya Harik, eds. 1984. *Local Politics and Development in the Middle East.* Boulder, Colo.: Westview Press.

Carapico, Sheila. 1995. Yemen Between Civility and Civil War. In *Toward Civil Society in the Middle East? A Primer,* edited by Jillian Schwedler. Boulder, Colo.: Lynne Rienner.

Caravedo, Baltazar M. 1995. NGOs, State and Society in Peru: Anchors of the Utopian Vision. In *New Paths to Democratic Development in Latin America: The Rise of NGO-Municipal Collaboration,* edited by Charles Reilly. Boulder, Colo.: Lynne Rienner.

Cavarozzi, Marcelo, and Vicente Palermo. 1995. State, Civil Society, and Popular Neighborhood Organizations in Buenos Aires: Key Players in Argentina's Transition to Democracy. In *New Paths to Democratic Development in Latin America: The Rise of NGO-Municipal Collaboration,* edited by Charles Reilly. Boulder, Colo.: Lynne Rienner.

Cernea, Michael, ed. 1985. *Putting People First: Sociological Variables in Rural Development.* New York: Oxford University Press.

———. 1988. Non-Governmental Organizations and Local Development. World Bank discussion papers no. 40.

Cesar Fernandes, Rubem. 1994. Threads of Planetary Citizenship. In *Citizens Strengthening Civil Society,* edited by Miguel Darcy de Oliveira and

Rajesh Tandon. Washington, D.C.: CIVICUS (World Alliance for Citizen Participation).

Cesar Fernandes, Rubem, and Leandro Piquet Carneiro. 1995. Brazilian NGOs in the 1990s: A Survey. In *New Paths to Democratic Development in Latin America: The Rise of NGO-Municipal Collaboration,* edited by Charles Reilly. Boulder, Colo.: Lynne Rienner.

Chapin, Mac. 1992. The View from the Shore: Central America's Indians Encounter the Quincentenary. *Grassroots Development* 16(2): 2–10.

Checci and Company Consulting, Inc. 1989. Final Report: Evaluation of Experience of USAID Missions with PVO Umbrella Groups in Costa Rica, Guatemala, Honduras and Haiti. Submitted to Office of Development Programs, Latin American Caribbean Bureau, U.S. Agency for International Development.

Chilton, Stephen. 1988. *Defining Political Development.* Boulder, Colo.: Lynn Rienner.

Chitiga-Machingauta, Rudo. 1995a. East and Southern Africa. *IRED Forum* 53: 11–2.

———. 1995b. NGOs Not Active in Policy Issues. *IRED Forum* 53: 15.

Clapham, Christopher. 1985. *Third World Politics: An Introduction.* Madison: University of Wisconsin Press.

Clark, John. 1991. *Democratizing Development: The Role of Voluntary Organizations.* West Hartford, Conn.: Kumarian Press.

———. 1993. *Initiating Memorandum—Proposed Study Series on the Relationship Between the State and the Voluntary Sector.* Washington, D.C.: World Bank.

———. 1995. The State, Popular Participation and the Voluntary Sector. *World Development.* 23(4): 593–601.

Clarke, Gerard. 1995. Non-Governmental Organisations (NGOs) and the Philippine State: 1986–93. *South East Asia Research* 3(1): 67–91.

———. 1996. *Non-Governmental Organisations (NGOs) and Politics in the Developing World.* Papers in international development no. 20. Swansea: Centre for Development Studies, University of Wales.

Clement, Charles. 1993. SatelLife: Strategic Health Initiative. *Development* 3: 60.

Cohen, John M., and Norman T. Uphoff. 1980. Participation's Place in Rural Development: Seeking Clarity Through Specificity. *World Development* 8(2): 215–35.

Cohn, Amelia. 1995. NGOs, Social Movements and the Privatization of Health Care: Experiences in São Paulo. In *New Paths to Democratic Development in Latin America: The Rise of NGO-Municipal Collaboration,* edited by Charles Reilly. Boulder, Colo.: Lynne Rienner.

Colchester, Marcus. 1994. Sustaining the Forests: The Community-Based Approach in South and South-East Asia. *Development and Change* 25: 69–100.

Commuri, Chandrasekhar. 1995. State Repression and the Limits of Voluntary Action: Case Study of the "Save Narmada" Movement in India. Conference of the Association for Research on Nonprofit Organizations and Voluntary Action (ARNOVA), Cleveland, Ohio, November 2–4.

Conservation Foundation. 1988. *Conservation Foundation Letter* 3: 3.

Constantino-David, Karina. 1992. The Philippine Experience in Scaling Up. In *Making a Difference: NGOs and Development in a Changing World,* edited by Michael Edwards and David Hulme. London: Earthscan Publications.

Coombs, Philip H., ed. 1980a. *Meeting the Basic Needs of the Rural Poor.* New York: Pergamon Press.

———. 1980b. What It Will Take to Help. In *Meeting the Needs of the Rural Poor,* edited by Philip Coombs. New York: Pergamon Press.

Cooperrider, David, ed. Forthcoming. *The Human Dimensions of Global Change.* San Francisco: Sage Publications.

Cooperrider, David, and Suresh Srivastva. 1987. Appreciative Inquiry in Organizational Life. *Research in Organizational Change and Development* 1: 129–69.

Coppedge, Michael, and Wolfgang H. Reinicke. 1990. Measuring Polyarchy. *Studies in Comparative International Development* 25(1): 51–72.

Cordoba-Novion, Cesar, and Celine Sachs. 1987. *Urban Self-Reliance Directory.* Nyon, Switzerland: International Foundation for Development Alternatives.

Court, David, and Kabiru Kinyanjui. 1986. African Education: Problems in a High Growth Sector. In *Strategies for African Development,* edited by Robert Berg and Jennifer Seymour Whitaker. Berkeley: University of California Press.

Covey, Jane. 1996. Accountability and Effectiveness in NGO Policy Alliances. In *Beyond the Magic Bullet: NGO Performance and Accountability in the Post–Cold War World,* edited by Michael Edwards and David Hulme. West Hartford, Conn.: Kumarian Press.

Cox, Elizabeth. 1987. Networking Among the Rural Women in the South Pacific. *Ideas and Action* 175: 18–23.

Craig, Susan. 1985. Political Patronage and Community Resistance: Community Councils in Trinidad and Tobago. In *Rural Development in the Caribbean.* New York: St. Martin's Press.

Crossette, Barbara. 1989. Shiny Tomorrow Meets Ragged, Hungry Today. *New York Times,* July 3.

Cruz, Anabel. 1990. La incorporación de las Nuevas Tecnologias de Información por las Organizaciones No Gubernamentales Uruguayas. In *Organizaciónes No Gubernamentales de Uruguay: Análisis y Repertorio,* edited by Fernando Barreiro and Anabel Cruz. Montevideo, Uruguay: Institucion de Comunicación y Desarrollo.

Danoewidjojo, Soenarjono. 1980. IPPA Youth Projects: An Indonesian Experiment in Population Education. In *Meeting the Needs of the Rural Poor,* edited by Philip Coombs. New York: Pergamon Press.

Darcy de Oliveira, Miguel, and Rajesh Tandon, eds. 1995. *Citizens Strengthening Civil Society.* Washington, D.C.: CIVICUS (World Alliance for Citizen Participation).

Dasgupta, S., S. Tilakaratna, and Poona Wignaraja. 1984. Why Can the U.N. System Not Do More? *Development* 2: 80–1.

DAWN Informs. 1989. No. 7/8.

Dawson, Elsa. 1993. NGOs and Public Policy Reform: Lessons from Peru. *Journal of International Development* 5(4): 401–14.

De Coninck, John. 1992. *Evaluating the Impact of NGOs in Rural Poverty Alleviation: Uganda Country Study.* Working paper 51. London: Overseas Development Institute.

De Graaf, Martin. 1987. Context, Constraint or Control? Zimbabwean NGOs and Their Environment. *Development Policy Review* 5(3): 277–301.

Delpino, Nena. 1991. Las organizaciones femininas por la alimentacion: un menu Sazonado. In *La Otra Cara de la Luna,* edited by Luis Pasara, Nena Delpino, Ricio Vandeavellano, and Alonso Zarzar. Buenos Aires: Manatial S.R.L.

Delpino, Nena, and Luis Pasara. 1991. El otro actor en escena: Las ONGDs. In *La Otra Cara de la Luna,* edited by Luis Pasara, Nena Delpino, Ricio Vandeavellano, and Alonso Zarzar. Buenos Aires: Manatial S.R.L.

Demeny, P. 1992. Policies Seeking a Reduction of High Fertility: A Case for the Demand Side. *Population and Development Review* 18(2): 321–32.

Desai, Vandana, and Mick Howes. 1996. Accountability and Participation: A Case Study from Bombay. In *Beyond the Magic Bullet: NGO Performance and Accountability in the Post–Cold War World,* edited by Michael Edwards and David Hulme. West Hartford, Conn.: Kumarian Press.

de Soto, Hernando. 1989. *The Other Path: The Invisible Revolution in the Third World.* New York: Harper and Row.

De Tocqueville, Alexis. 1969. *Democracy in America.* Garden City, N.Y.: Anchor, Doubleday.

Diaz-Albertini, Javier. 1989. Development as Grassroots Empowerment: The Case of NGOs in Lima, Peru. Submitted to the Yale Program on Non-Profit Organizations.

———. 1993a. Ideology and Social Change: The Process of Non-Governmental Planning and Activism in Lima, Peru. Ph.D. dissertation, State University of New York at Stony Brook.

———. 1993b. Nonprofit Advocacy in Weakly Institutionalized Political Systems: The Case of NGDOs in Lima, Peru. *Nonprofit and Voluntary Sector Quarterly* 22(4): 317–37.

Dichter, Thomas W. 1986a. Demystifying "Policy Dialogue." How Private Voluntary Organizations Can Have an Impact on Host Country Policies. In *Findings '86.* Norwalk, Conn.: Technoserve.

———. 1986b. The Neglected Middle Scale. Implications of Size. In *Findings '86.* Norwalk, Conn.: Technoserve.

———. 1989. NGOs and the Replication Trap. In *Findings '89.* Norwalk, Conn.: Technoserve.

Dick, G. William. 1974. Authoritarian vs. Non-Authoritarian Approaches to Economic Development. *Journal of Political Economy* 82: 817–27.

Diong, Ibrahim Cheikh. 1994. *African Regional NGOs: An Overview of*

Institutions. Washington, D.C.: U.S. Forest Service, Office of International Forestry.

Doulaye Maiga, Issaka. 1995. West Africa/Sahel. *IRED Forum* 54: 15–9.

Downs, Charles, and Giorgio Solimano. 1989. Toward an Evaluation of the NGO Experience in Chile: Implications for Social Policy and Future Investigation. In *Social Policy from the Grassroots: Nongovernmental Organizations in Chile,* edited by Charles Downs, Giorgio Solimano, Carlos Vergara, and Luis Zuniga. Boulder, Colo.: Westview Press.

Downs, Charles, Giorgio Solimano, Carlos Vergara, and Luis Zuniga, eds. 1989. *Social Policy from the Grassroots: Nongovernmental Organizations in Chile.* Boulder, Colo.: Westview Press.

Duncan, Graeme, ed. 1983. *Democratic Theory and Practice.* Cambridge: Cambridge University Press.

Durning, Alan. 1989. People Power and Development. *Foreign Policy* 76: 66–83.

Eberlee, John. 1995. Computer Networks: A Democratic Tool for NGOs. *IDRC Reports* 23(1): 16–7.

Eckstein, Susan. 1990. Poor People Versus the State and Capital: Anatomy of a Successful Community Mobilization for Housing in Mexico City. *International Journal of Urban and Regional Research* 14(2): 274–96.

Edwards, Michael. 1996. *NGO Performance–What Breeds Success? A Study of Approaches to Work in South Asia.* Working paper no. 14. London: Save the Children.

Edwards, Michael, and David Hulme, eds. 1992a. *Making a Difference: NGOs and Development in a Changing World.* London: Earthscan Publications.

———. 1992b. Scaling Up the Developmental Impact of NGOs: Concepts and Experiences. In *Making a Difference: NGOs and Development in a Changing World,* edited by Michael Edwards and David Hulme. London: Earthscan Publications.

———, eds. 1996a. *Beyond the Magic Bullet: NGO Performance and Accountability in the Post–Cold War World.* West Hartford, Conn.: Kumarian Press.

———. 1996b. Introduction: NGO Performance and Accountability. In *Beyond the Magic Bullet: NGO Performance and Accountability in the Post–Cold War World,* edited by Michael Edwards and David Hulme. West Hartford, Conn.: Kumarian Press.

El-Baz, Shahida. 1992. Historical and Institutional Development of Arab NGOs. Conference of the Association for Research on Nonprofit Organizations and Voluntary Action (ARNOVA), Indiana University, March 11–13.

Eldridge, Philip. 1984–85. The Political Role of Community Action Groups in India and Indonesia: In Search of a General Theory. *Alternatives: A Journal of World Policy* 10 (winter): 401–34.

———. 1988. Non-Government Organizations and the Role of the State in Indonesia. Paper presented to the Conference on the State and Civil Society in Contemporary Indonesia, Centre for Southeast Asian Studies, Monash University, Melbourne, Australia, November 25–27.

Engardio, Pete. 1994. Third World Leapfrog. *Business Week* (special issue on the information revolution), 47–9.

Esman, Milton J., and Norman T. Uphoff. 1984. *Local Organizations: Intermediaries in Local Development*. Ithaca, N.Y.: Cornell University Press.

Esteva, Gustavo. 1986. Mexico: Self-Help Network. *IFDA Dossier* 51: 73–5.

Eyoh, Ndumbe. 1985–86. The Kumba Workshop on Theatre for Integrated Rural Development. *Ideas and Action* 165: 12–8.

Fals Borda, Orlando. 1990. Social Movements and Political Power: Evolution in Latin America. *International Sociology* 5(2): 115–27.

FAO/FFHC. 1987. NGOs in Latin America: Their Contribution to Participatory Democracy. *Development: Seeds of Change* 4: 100–5.

Farrington, John, and Anthony Bebbington, with Kate Wellard and David J. Lewis. 1993. *Reluctant Partners? Non-Governmental Organizations, the State and Sustainable Agricultural Development*. London: Routledge.

Farrington, John, and Anthony Bebbington. 1994. From Research to Innovation: Getting the Most from Interaction with NGOs in Farming Systems Research and Extension. Gatekeeper Series no. 43. London: International Institute for Environment and Development.

Fernandes, Rubem Cesar. 1994. Threads of Planetary Citizenship. In *Citizens: Strengthening Global Civil Society*. Washington, D.C.: CIVICUS.

Fernandez, Aloysius P. 1987. NGOs in South Asia: People's Participation and Partnership. *World Development* 15 (supplement): 39–49.

Finkle, Jason L., and Richard W. Gable, eds. 1966. *Political Development and Social Change*. New York: John Wiley and Sons.

Finquelievich, Susana. 1987. Interactions of Social Actors in Survival Strategies: The Case of the Urban Poor in Latin America. *IFDA Dossier* 59: 19–30.

Fisher, Julie. 1977. Political Learning in the Latin American Barridas: The Role of the Junta de Vecinos. Ph.D. dissertation, Johns Hopkins University, School of Advanced International Studies, Washington, D.C.

———. 1984. Development from Below: Neighborhood Improvement Associations in the Latin American Squatter Settlements. *Studies in Comparative International Development* 19(1): 61–85.

———. 1986. Colombia: When Women Are United. In *Already I Feel the Change: Lessons from the Field 1*. Westport, Conn.: Save the Children.

———. 1992. Local Governments and the Independent Sector. In *The Nonprofit Sector in the Global Community*, edited by Kathleen McCarthy, Virginia Hodgkinson, Russy Sumariwalla, and associates. San Francisco: Jossey-Bass.

———. 1993. *The Road from Rio: Sustainable Development and the Nongovernmental Movement in the Third World*. Westport, Conn.: Praeger.

———. 1994a. Is the Iron Law of Oligarchy Rusting Away in the Third World? *World Development* 22(2): 129–43.

———. 1994b. NGOs: The Missing Piece of the Population Puzzle. *Environment* 36(7): 6–11, 37–41.

———. Forthcoming. International Networking: The Role of Southern NGOs.

In *The Human Dimensions of Global Change,* edited by David Cooperrider. San Francisco: Sage Publications.

Fisher, Julie, and Charles Hamilton. 1996. Review of *Making Democracy Work: Civic Traditions in Modern Italy,* by Robert Putnam. *Nonprofit and Voluntary Sector Quarterly* 25(1): 124–35.

Fisher, Julie, and Richard Peck. 1997. *Before Credit: An Evaluation of Trickle Up's Seed Capital Grants in Guatemala and Ecuador.* New York: Trickle Up.

Fiszbein, Ariel, and Susan Crawford. 1996. Beyond National Policies: Partnerships for Poverty Reduction. Paper, Human Resources and Poverty Division, Economic Development Institute, World Bank, Washington, D.C.

Foweraker, Joe, and Ann L. Craig. 1990. *Popular Movements and Political Change in Mexico.* Boulder, Colo.: Lynne Rienner.

Fowler, Alan. 1988. Non-Governmental Organizations in Africa: Achieving Comparative Advantage in Relief and Micro-Development. Discussion paper no. 249, Institute of Development Studies, Sussex.

———. 1990. Political Dimensions of NGO Expansion in Eastern and Southern Africa and the Role of International Aid. Paper, Ford Foundation.

———. 1991. The Role of NGOs in Changing State-Society Relations: Perspectives from Eastern and Southern Africa. *Development Policy Review* 9: 53–84.

———. 1996. Assessing NGO Performance: Difficulties, Dilemmas and a Way Ahead. In *Beyond the Magic Bullet: NGO Performance and Accountability in the Post–Cold War World,* edited by Michael Edwards and David Hulme. West Hartford, Conn.: Kumarian Press.

Fox, Jonathan, and John Butler. 1987. Research Project Preview: Membership Organization Dynamics: Lessons from the Inter-American Foundation Experience. *IAF Memorandum,* May 18.

Fox, Jonathan, and Luis Hernandez. 1992. Mexico's Difficult Democracy: Grassroots Movements, NGOs and Local Government. *Alternatives* 17: 165–208.

Foxley, Alejandro, Michael D. McPherson, and Guillermo O'Donnell, eds. Reflections from the Recent Argentine Experience. In *Development, Democracy and the Art of Trespassing: Essays in Honor of Albert O. Hirschman,* Notre Dame, Ind.: University of Notre Dame.

Frantz, Telmo Rudi. 1987. The Role of NGOs in the Strengthening of Civil Society. *World Development* 15 (supplement, autumn): 121–8.

Freedom House. 1994–95. *Freedom in the World: The Annual Survey of Political Rights and Civil Liberties.* New York: Freedom House.

———. 1995–96. *Freedom in the World: The Annual Survey of Political Rights and Civil Liberties.* New York. Freedom House.

French, Howard W. 1997. Despite Setbacks, Democracy Gains in Africa. *New York Times,* January 11, 3.

Friedmann, John. 1989. Collective Self-Empowerment and Social Change. *IFDA Dossier* 69: 3–14.

Fruhling, Hugo. 1985. Non-Profit Organizations as Opposition to Authoritarian Rule: The Case of Human Rights Organizations and Private Research Centers in Chile. Program on Non-Profit Organizations, working paper no.

96. Institution for Social and Policy Studies, Yale University.

FUNDESA (Guatemalan Development Foundation). 1989. *Directory of Private Voluntary Organizations Serving the Guatemalan Community.* Guatemala City: FUNDESA.

Furet, Francois. 1983. La revolution dans l'imaginaire politique francais. *Le Debat* 26.

Gadgil, Madhav, and Ramachandra Guha. 1994. Ecological Conflict and the Environmental Movement in India. *Development and Change* 25: 101–36.

Gamer, Robert E. 1982. *The Developing Nations: A Comparative Perspective.* Boston: Allyn and Bacon.

Garilao, Ernesto. 1987. Indigenous NGOs as Strategic Institutions: Managing the Relationship with Government and Resource Agencies. *World Development* 15 (supplement): 113–20.

Gariyo, Zie. 1996. NGOs and Development in East Africa. In *Beyond the Magic Bullet: NGO Performance and Accountability in the Post–Cold War World,* edited by Michael Edwards and David Hulme. West Hartford, Conn.: Kumarian Press.

Garrison, John. 1989. Computers Link NGOs Worldwide. *Grassroots Development* 13(2): 48–9.

———. 1991. An Alternative Approach to Saving Amazon Rainforest. *Grassroots Development* 15(2): 43.

Garrison, John, and Leilah Landim. 1995. Harvesting the Bounty of Citizenship: The Fight Against Hunger and Poverty in Brazil. *Grassroots Development* 19(2): 38–48.

Gastil, Raymond D. 1988–89. *Freedom in the World: Political Rights and Civil Liberties: 1988–89.* Westport, Conn.: Greenwood Press.

Germaine, Adrienne, and Jane Ordway. 1989. Population Control and Women's Health: Balancing the Scales. New York: International Women's Health Coalition.

Gibbons, Michael. 1994. Capacity-Building for Human Development in Cooperative Self-Organizing Networks. Conference on Children of Urban Families in Asia, Save the Children, Westport, Conn.: September 5–9.

Gifford, C. Anthony. 1993. TIPS: Developing a Strong South-South Bridge. *Development,* 3: 62.

Glagow, M., and H. D. Evers, eds. 1986. *Unbürokratische Entwicklungshilfe? Universität Bielefeld.* Fakultät fur Soziologie/Entwicklungssoziologie. Materialien 20.

Goertzen, Donald. 1991. Sweet and Sour: Planters and Peasants Battle It Out. *Far Eastern Economic Review,* August 8.

Goff, Brent. 1994. Reviving Crafts and Affirming Culture: From Grassroots Development to National Policy. In *Cultural Expression and Grassroots Development,* edited by Charles David Kleymeyer. Boulder, Colo.: Lynne Rienner.

Gohlert, Ernest W. 1992. Thai Democracy and the May 1992 Crisis: The Role of Private Non-Profit Organisations. Paper presented to the Western Conference of the Association for Asian Studies, University of Arizona, Tucson, October 23–24.

Gomez, Henry, and Richard A. Myers. 1983. The Service Module as a Social Development Technology. In *Bureaucracy and the Poor,* edited by David C. Korten and Felipe Alfonso. West Hartford, Conn.: Kumarian Press.

Goodell, Grace. 1984. Political Development and Social Welfare: A Conservative Perspective. In *People Centered Development: Contributions Toward Theory and Planning Frameworks,* edited by David C. Korten and Rudi Klaus. West Hartford, Conn.: Kumarian Press.

Gorman, Robert F., ed. 1984. *Private Voluntary Organizations as Agents of Development.* Boulder, Colo.: Westview Press.

Goulet, Denis. 1986. Three Rationalities in Development Decision-Making. *World Development* 14(2): 301–17.

Graham, Laura. 1987. Constitutional Lobbying in Brazil: Indians Seek Expanded Role. *Cultural Survival Quarterly* 11(2): 61–2.

Graybow, Charles. 1995–96. South and East Asia: A Raw Deal for the Masses. In *Freedom in the World: 1995–96,* edited by Roger Kaplan. New York: Freedom House.

Greenberger, Robert S. 1995. Developing Countries Pass Off Tedious Job of Assisting the Poor. *Wall Street Journal,* June 5, 1.

Grimshaw, Richard G. 1993. The Vetvier Network. *Development* 3: 64.

Grindle, Merilee, ed. 1980. *Politics and Policy Implementation in the Third World.* Princeton, N.J.: Princeton University Press.

Grzybowski, Candido. 1990. Rural Workers and Democratisation in Brazil. *Journal of Development Studies* 6(4): 19–43.

Guedan, Manuel. 1991. Las ONGs en la Perspectiva de la Politica Ibero-americana de España. Centro Español de Estudios de America Latina (CEDEAL).

Gueneau, Marie Christine. 1988. L'Emergence des O.N.G. du Sud. *Croissance de Juenes Nations* 310: 16–8.

Gupta, Anil. 1993. Honey Bee: An Accountable Global Network of Grassroots Innovators and Experimenters. *Development* 3: 64–5.

Gupta, Ranjit. 1983. The Poverty Trap: Lessons from Dharampur. In *Bureaucracy and the Poor,* edited by David C. Korten and Felipe Alfonso. West Hartford, Conn.: Kumarian Press.

Hadden, Susan G. 1980. Controlled Decentralization and Policy Implementation: The Case of Rural Electrification in Rajasthan. In *Politics and Policy Implementation in the Third World,* edited by Merilee Grindle. Princeton, N.J.: Princeton University Press.

Hall, Anthony. 1992. From Victims to Victors: NGOs and Empowerment at Itaparica. In *Making a Difference: NGOs and Development in a Changing World,* edited by Michael Edwards and David Hulme. London: Earthscan Publications.

Hall, Bud L. 1993. Global Networks, Global Civil Society? Lessons from International Non-Governmental Organizations. Conference of the Association for Research on Nonprofit Organizations and Voluntary Action (ARNOVA), Toronto, October 28–29.

Hamilton, Charles H. 1994. Citizenship and Philanthropy: On the Vitality of Civil Society. Association for Research on Nonprofit Organizations and

Voluntary Actions, Berkeley, Calif. October 20–22.

Handem, Alfredo. 1991. Creating a Legal Framework for the Emergence of NGOs in Guinea Bissau. In *Initiatives* (summer). Washington, D.C.: Datex.

Harik, Iliya. 1984. Continuity and Change in Local Development Policies in Egypt: From Nasser to Sadat. In *Local Politics and Development in the Middle East,* edited by Louis J. Cantori and Iliya Harik. Boulder, Colo.: Westview Press.

Hashemi, Sayed. 1996. NGO Accountability in Bangladesh: Beneficiaries, Donors and the State. In *Beyond the Magic Bullet: NGO Performance and Accountability in the Post–Cold War World,* edited by Michael Edwards and David Hulme. West Hartford, Conn.: Kumarian Press.

Hauzeair, Rene F. 1984. FEPEC-Colombia. *ICVA News* 118: 1–2.

Healy, Kevin. 1996. Ethnodevelopment of Indigenous Bolivian Communities: Emerging Paradigms. In *Tiwanaku and Its Hinterland: Archeology and Paleoecology of an Andean Civilization,* edited by Alan L. Kolata. Washington, D.C.: Smithsonian Institution Press.

Hernando, Soledad A. 1982. Village Immersion: An Approach in Reorienting Career Civil Servants. *Philippine Journal of Public Administration* 26(3, 4): 309–18.

Heyzer, Noeleen. 1995. Toward New Government-NGO Relations for Sustainable and People-Centered Development. In *Government-NGO Relations in Asia,* edited by Noeleen Heyzer, James V. Riker, and Antonio Quizon. New York: St. Martin's Press.

Heyzer, Noeleen, James V. Riker, and Antonio Quizon, eds. 1995. *Government-NGO Relations in Asia.* New York: St. Martin's Press.

Hiremath, S. R. 1991. Synopsis of Work of Samaj Parivartana Samudaya (SPS), Dharwad, India. Asia Society conference, New York, April 24–26.

Hirschman, Albert O. 1963. *Journeys Toward Progress: Studies of Economic Policy-Making in Latin America.* New York: Twentieth Century Fund.

———. 1984. *Getting Ahead Collectively: Grassroots Experiences in Latin America.* New York: Pergamon Press.

Hojman, David E. 1993. Non-Governmental Organisations (NGOs) and the Chilean Transition to Democracy. *European Review of Latin American and Caribbean Studies* 54 (June).

Holloway, Richard. 1989a. Afterword. Where to Next? Governments, NGOs and Development Practitioners. In *Doing Development: Government, NGOs and the Rural Poor in Asia,* edited by Richard Holloway. London: Earthscan Publications.

———, ed. 1989b. *Doing Development: Government, NGOs and the Rural Poor in Asia.* London: Earthscan Publications.

———. 1989c. Partners in Development? The Government and NGOs in Indonesia. In *Doing Development: Government, NGOs and the Rural Poor in Asia,* edited by Richard Holloway. London: Earthscan Publications.

Hovde, Robert L. 1992. Nongovernmental Organizations in Ethiopia: The Role of the Christian Relief and Development Association. Third International Conference of Research on Voluntary and Nonprofit Organizations (ARNOVA), Indiana University, March 11–13.

Howe, Elizabeth A. 1986. A Contingent Analysis of Social Development Programmes in Seven Countries. *Regional Development Dialogue* 7(1): 186–201.

Hulme, David, and Michael Edwards. 1997a. NGOs, States and Donors: An Overview. In *NGOs, States and Donors: Too Close for Comfort?* edited by David Hulme and Michael Edwards. New York: St. Martin's Press.

———, eds. 1997b. *NGOs, States and Donors: Too Close for Comfort?* New York: St. Martin's Press.

Huntington, Richard. 1988. Memories of Development: The Rise and Fall of a Participatory Project Among the Dinka, 1977–1981. In *Power and Poverty: Development and Development Projects in the Third World,* edited by Donald W. Attwood, Thomas C. Bruneau, and John G. Galaty. Boulder, Colo.: Westview Press.

Huntington, Samuel P. 1965. Political Development and Political Decay. *World Politics* 17: 384–430.

———. 1968. *Political Order in Changing Societies.* New Haven, Conn.: Yale University Press.

Huntington, Samuel P., and Joan M. Nelson. 1976. *No Easy Choice: Political Participation in Developing Countries.* Cambridge: Harvard University Press.

Hyden, Goran. 1983. *No Shortcuts to Progress: African Development Management in Perspective.* Berkeley: University of California Press.

———. 1987. Ethnicity and State Coherence in Africa. *Development* 1: 82–6.

Ickes, John C. 1983. Structural Responses to New Rural Development Strategies. In *Bureaucracy and the Poor,* edited by David C. Korten and Felipe Alfonso. West Hartford, Conn.: Kumarian Press.

Ilchman, Warren, and Norman Uphoff. 1969. *The Political Economy of Change.* Berkeley: University of California Press.

Infante, Antonio. 1989. Primary Health Care in a Local Community. In *Social Policy from the Grassroots: Nongovernmental Organizations in Chile,* edited by Charles Downs, Giorgio Solimano, Carlos Vergara, and Luis Zuñiga. Boulder, Colo.: Westview Press.

Institute for East West Studies. 1995. *Assistance to Transition.* Washington, D.C.: Institute for East West Studies.

Inter-American Foundation. 1993. Grassroots Development Framework: The Cone. Memo, September 17, Arlington, Va.

———. 1995. *A Guide to NGO Directories: How to Find over 20,000 Nongovernmental Organizations in Latin America and the Caribbean.* Washington, D.C.: Inter-Hemispheric Education Resource Center.

International Tree Project Clearinghouse. 1987. *A Directory: NGOs in the Forestry Sector,* 2d Africa ed. New York: Non-Governmental Liaison Service, United Nations.

Ireland, Emilienne. 1991. Neither Warriors nor Victims, the Wauja Peacefully Organize to Defend Their Land. *Cultural Survival Quarterly* 15(1): 56–7.

IRED. 1987. *IRED Forum,* no. 22. Geneva: Innovations et Reseaux pour le Developpement.

Jaguaribe, Helio. 1973. *Political Development: A General Theory and a Latin American Case Study.* New York: Harper and Row.

James, Estelle. 1987. The Nonprofit Sector in Comparative Perspective. In

The Nonprofit Sector: A Research Handbook, edited by Walter Powell. New Haven, Conn.: Yale University Press.

Jason, Karen. 1992. The Role of Non-Governmental Organizations in International Election Observing. *International Law and Politics* 24: 1795–1843.

Jenkins, Craig. 1987. Nonprofit Organizations and Policy Advocacy. In *The Nonprofit Sector: A Research Handbook,* edited by Walter Powell. New Haven, Conn.: Yale University Press.

Jenkins, Karen. 1994. The Christian Church as an NGO in Africa: Supporting Post-Independence Era State Legitimacy or Promoting Change? In *The Changing Politics of Non-Governmental Organizations and African States,* edited by Eve Sandberg. Westport, Conn.: Praeger.

Jeppe, W. J. O., F. Theron, and J. P. V. Van Baalen, eds. 1992. *NGOs in Development.* Stellenbosch: Department of Development Adminstration, University of Stellenbosch.

Jiggins, Janice. 1983. Poverty-Oriented Rural Development: Participation and Management. *Development Policy Review* 1(2): 219–30.

Johnson, John J. 1966. The Political Role of the Latin American Middle Sectors. In *Political Development and Social Change,* edited by Jason L. Finkle and Richard W. Gable. New York: John Wiley and Sons.

Johnson, Willard R., and Vivian Johnson. 1990. *West African Governments and Volunteer Development Organizations.* Lanham, Md.: University Press of America.

Kabarhuza, Hamuli. 1990. Development NGOs in Zaire: Experiences and Challenges. *Voices from Africa* 2: 29–37.

Kaimowitz, David. 1993. The Role of Nongovernmental Organizations in Agricultural Research and Technology Transfer in Latin America. *World Development* 21(7): 1139–50.

Kale, Pratima, and Philip H. Coombs. 1980. Social Work and Research Centre: An Integrated Team Approach in India. In *Meeting the Needs of the Rural Poor,* edited by Philip Coombs. New York: Pergamon Press.

Kandil, Amani. 1994. The Status of the Third Sector in the Arab World. In *Citizens Strengthening Civil Society,* edited by Miguel Darcy de Oliveira and Rajesh Tandon. Washington, D.C.: CIVICUS (World Alliance for Citizen Participation).

Karim, M. Bazlul. 1985–86. Rural Development Projects—Comilla, Puebla, and Chilalo: A Comparative Assessment. *Studies in Comparative International Development* 20(4): 3–41.

Karim, Mahbubul. 1996. NGOs in Bangladesh: Issues of Legitimacy and Accountability. In *Beyond the Magic Bullet: NGO Performance and Accountability in the Post–Cold War World,* edited by Michael Edwards and David Hulme. West Hartford, Conn.: Kumarian Press.

Kautsky, John H. 1972. *The Political Consequences of Modernization.* New York: Wiley.

Kazemi, Farhad, and Augustus Richard Norton. 1995. Conclusion: Civil Society and Political Reform in the Middle East. In *Toward Civil Society in the Middle East? A Primer,* edited by Jillian Schwedler. Boulder, Colo.: Lynne Rienner.

Khan, Mafruza. 1991. *Participatory Management of Local Resources: Proshika's Initiatives in Forest Management.* Dhaka, Bangladesh: Proshika.

Klaren, Peter F., and Thomas J. Bossert, eds. 1986. *Promise of Development: Theories of Change in Latin America.* Boulder, Colo.: Westview Press.

Kleymeyer, Charles David. 1994. *Cultural Expression and Grassroots Development.* Boulder, Colo.: Lynne Rienner.

Klinmahorm, Somthavil, and Kevin Ireland. 1992. NGO-Government Collaboration in Bangkok. In *Making a Difference: NGOs and Development in a Changing World,* edited by Michael Edwards and David Hulme. London: Earthscan Publications.

Kohli, Athol. 1986. Democracy and Development. In *Development Strategies Reconsidered: U.S. Third World Policy,* edited by John P. Lewis and Valeriana Kallab. Perspectives no. 5, Overseas Development Council. New Brunswick, N.J.: Transaction Books.

Korten, David C. 1983. Social Development: Putting People First. In *Bureaucracy and the Poor,* edited by David C. Korten and Felipe Alfonso. West Hartford, Conn.: Kumarian Press.

———. 1986a. Community Based Resource Management. In *Community Management: Asian Experience and Perspectives,* edited by David C. Korten. West Hartford, Conn.: Kumarian Press.

———, ed. 1986b. *Community Management: Asian Experience and Perspectives.* West Hartford, Conn.: Kumarian Press.

———. 1987. Third Generation NGO Strategies: A Key to People-Centered Development. *World Development* 15 (supplement): 145–59.

———. 1990. *Getting to the 21st Century: Voluntary Action and the Global Agenda.* West Hartford, Conn.: Kumarian Press.

———. 1995. *When Corporations Rule the World.* West Hartford, Conn.: Kumarian Press; San Francisco: Berrett-Koehler Publishers.

Korten, David C., and Felipe Alfonso, eds. 1983. *Bureaucracy and the Poor.* West Hartford, Conn.: Kumarian Press.

Korten, David C., and Rudi Klaus, eds. 1984. *People Centered Development: Contributions Toward Theory and Planning Frameworks.* West Hartford, Conn.: Kumarian Press.

Korten, Frances F. 1983. Community Participation: A Management Perspective on Obstacles and Options. In *Bureaucracy and the Poor,* edited by David C. Korten and Felipe Alfonso. West Hartford, Conn.: Kumarian Press.

Kothari, Rajni. 1986. NGOs, the State and World Capitalism. *Economic and Political Weekly* (December 13).

Kramer, Ralph. 1981. *Voluntary Agencies in the Welfare State.* Berkeley: University of California Press.

Krasner, Stephen D. 1985. *Structural Conflict: The Third World Against Global Liberalism.* Berkeley: University of California Press.

Krishnaswami, Lalita. 1987. The SEWA Experience. *IRED Forum* 24: 69–78.

La Forgia, Gerard. 1985. *Local Organizations for Rural Health in Panama: Community Participation, Bureaucratic Reorientation and Political Will.* Ithaca, N.Y.: Rural Development Committee, Cornell University.

La Gra, Jerry, Larry Leighton, and Susan Oechsle. 1989. *Profiles of Farmers Organizations in Saint Lucia.* Castries, St. Lucia: Interamerican Institute for Co-Operation on Agriculture.

Landim, Leilah. 1987. Non-Governmental Organizations in Latin America. *World Development* 15 (supplement): 29–38.

———, ed. 1988a. *Sems Fins Lucrativos: As organizacoes não-governamentais no Brasil.* Rio de Janeiro: Instituto de Estudos da Religião.

———. 1988b. A Servico do Movimento Popular: As organizacões nãogovernamentaís no Brasil. In *Sems Fins Lucrativos: As organizacoês não-governamentaís no Brasil,* edited by Leilah Landim. Rio de Janeiro: Instituto de Estudos da Religião.

———. 1992. What Is an NGO? Notes on the Nonprofit Organizations in Brazil. Third International Conference of Research on Voluntary and Nonprofit Organizations, Center on Philanthropy, Indiana University, March 11–13.

Leach, Mark, Jeanne McCormack, and Candace Nelson. 1988. The Tototo Home Industries Rural Development Project. Case study prepared for the Synergos Institute.

Leach, Melissa. 1988. Becoming a People Sector: Indian Voluntary Agencies at a Crossroads. *Community Development Journal* 23(2): 86–93.

Lecomte, Bernard J. 1986. *Project Aid: Limitations and Alternatives.* Paris: OECD Development Center Studies.

Ledesma, Cesar R., and Cesar Decena. 1992. Political Science Activism among NGOs in the Philippines. Paper submitted to the Third International Conference of the Association for Research on Voluntary and Nonprofit Action (ARNOVA), Indiana University, Center on Philanthropy, March 11–13.

Lee, Robin. 1992. Remarks. In *NGOs in Development,* edited by W. J. O Jeppe, F. Theron, and J. P. V. Van Baalen. Stellenbosch, South Africa: Department of Development Adminstration, University of Stellenbosch.

Leonard, David K. 1982. Choosing Among Forms of Decentralization and Linkage. In *Institutions of Rural Development for the Poor: Decentralization and Organizational Linkages,* edited by David K. Leonard and Dale Rogers Marshall. Berkeley: Institute of International Studies, University of California.

Leonard, David K., and Dale Rogers Marshall, eds. 1982. *Institutions of Rural Development for the Poor: Decentralization and Organizational Linkages.* Berkeley: Institute of International Studies, University of California.

Lernoux, Penny. 1984. *Fear and Hope: Towards Political Democracy in Central America.* New York: Field Foundation.

Lesch, Ann Moseley. 1995. The Destruction of Civil Society in the Sudan. In *Toward Civil Society in the Middle East? A Primer,* edited by Jillian Schwedler. Boulder, Colo.: Lynne Rienner.

Levitt, Peggy. 1996. Transnationalizing Community Development: The Case of Migration Between Boston and the Dominican Republic. Conference of the Association for Research on Nonprofit Organizations and Voluntary Action (ARNOVA), New York.

Levy, Daniel C. 1987. The Mexican Government's Loosening Grip? *Current History* 86(518): 113–6, 132–3.

———. 1992. From Private Philanthropy to Mixed Public and Private Funding: Latin America's Private Research Centers. Conference of the Association for Research on Nonprofit Organizations and Voluntary Action (ARNOVA), Yale University, New Haven, Conn.

———. 1996. *Building the Third Sector: Latin America's Private Research Centers and Nonprofit Development*. Pittsburgh, Pa.: University of Pittsburgh Press.

Levy, Marc. 1994. Review of *The Road from Rio: Sustainable Development and the Nongovernmental Movement in the Third World*. *Environment* 36(8): 26.

Lewis, John P., and Valeriana Kallab, eds. 1986. *Development Strategies Reconsidered. U.S. Third World Policy*. Perspectives no. 5, Overseas Development Council. New Brunswick, N.J.: Transaction Books.

Liamzon, Tina. 1990. Strategizing for Relevance: Trends and Roles for NGOs in the 1990s. *Phildhrra Notes* 6(4): 3–5.

Livernash, Robert. 1992. The Growing Influence of NGOs in the Developing World. *Environment* 34(5): 12–20, 41–3.

Livezey, Lowell W. 1988. *Nongovernmental Organizations and the Ideas of Human Rights*. Occasional paper no. 15. Princeton, N.J.: World Order Studies Program, Center of International Studies, Princeton University.

Logan, Kathleen. 1990. Women's Participation in Urban Protest. In *Popular Movements and Political Change in Mexico,* edited by Joe Foweraker and Ann L. Craig. Boulder, Colo.: Lynne Rienner.

Lopezllera Mendez, Luis. 1988. Sociedad Civil y Pueblos Emergentes: Las Organizaciones Autónomas de Promoción Social y Desarrollo en México. Mexico City: Promoción del Desarrollo Popular.

———. 1990. The Struggle of the Indigenous People and the New "Reservations." *Fenix* 00: 6–7.

Louckey, James, and Robert Carlsen. 1991. Massacre in Santiago Atitlán. *Cultural Survival Quarterly* 15(3): 65–70.

Lovell, Catherine. 1987. Social Mobilization in Development: Scaling up in BRAC. Paper, University of California, Riverside.

———. 1992. *Breaking the Cycle of Poverty: The BRAC Strategy*. West Hartford, Conn.: Kumarian Press.

Loveman, Brian. 1991. NGOs and the Transition to Democracy in Chile. *Grassroots Development* 15(2): 8–19.

———. 1995. Chilean NGOs: Forging a Role in the Transition to Democracy. *New Paths to Democratic Development in Latin America: The Rise of NGO-Municipal Collaboration,* edited by Charles Reilly. Boulder, Colo.: Lynne Rienner.

Ludwig, Richard L., and G. Shabbir Cheema. 1987. Evaluating the Impact of Policies and Projects: Experience in Urban Shelter and Basic Urban Services. *Regional Development Dialogue* 8(4): 190–209.

Macdonald, Laura. 1997. *Supporting Civil Society: The Political Role of Non-Governmental Organizations in Central America*. New York: St. Martin's Press.

Macdonald, Theodore. 1987. Grassroots Development: Not Just Organic Farming and Good Faith. *Cultural Survival Quarterly* 11(1): 41–5.

Mackie, James. 1992. Multiplying Micro-Level Inputs to Government Structures. In *Making a Difference: NGOs and Development in a Changing World,* edited by Michael Edwards and David Hulme. London: Earthscan Publications.

Maeda, Justin. 1983. Creating National Structures for People Centered Agrarian Development. In *Bureaucracy and the Poor,* edited by David C. Korten and Felipe Alfonso. West Hartford, Conn.: Kumarian Press.

Mainwaring, Scott. 1985. Grassroots Popular Movements and the Struggle for Democracy: Nova Iguacu, 1974–1985. Working paper no. 52. Helen Kellogg Institute for International Studies, University of Notre Dame.

Mainwaring, Scott, and Edward Viola. 1984. New Social Movements, Political Culture, and Democracy: Brazil and Argentina. Working paper no. 33. Helen Kellogg Institute for International Studies, University of Notre Dame.

Maren, Michael Paul. 1987. Kenya: The Dissolution of Democracy. *Current History* 86(520): 209–12, 228–9.

Marklein, Mary Beth. 1991. Putting the World Rightside Up: The Grassroots Perspective. *Grassroots Development* 15(1): 8–15.

Marris, Peter. 1982. *Community Planning and Conceptions of Change.* London: Routledge and Kegan Paul.

Martinez Nogueira, Roberto. 1987. Life Cycle and Learning in Grass Roots Organisations. *World Development* 15 (supplement): 169–78.

———. 1995. Negotiated Interactions: NGOs and Local Government in Rosario, Argentina. In *New Paths to Democratic Development in Latin America: The Rise of NGO-Municipal Collaboration,* edited by Charles Reilly. Boulder, Colo.: Lynne Rienner.

Marzouk, Mohsen. 1997. The Associative Phenomenon in the Arab World: Engine of Democratisation or Witness to the Crisis? In *NGOs, States and Donors: Too Close for Comfort?* edited by David Hulme and Michael Edwards. New York: St. Martin's Press.

Mayberry-Lewis, David. 1989. Indians in Brazil: The Struggle Intensifies. *Cultural Survival Quarterly* 13(1): 2–5.

McBeth, John. 1991. A New People-Power. *Far Eastern Economic Review,* August 8, 22.

McCarthy, Kathleen D. 1989. The Voluntary Sector Overseas: Notes from the Field. Working papers, Center for the Study of Philanthropy, City University of New York.

McCarthy, Kathleen D., Virginia A. Hodgkinson, Russy D. Sumariwalla, and associates, eds. 1992. *The Nonprofit Sector in the Global Community.* San Francisco: Jossey-Bass.

McClelland, David C. 1970. The Two Faces of Power. *Journal of International Affairs* 24(1): 29–47.

McClintock, Cynthia. 1981. *Peasant Cooperatives and Political Change in Peru.* Princeton, N.J.: Princeton University Press.

Meyer, Carrie. 1995. Opportunism and NGOs: Entrepreneurship and Green North-South Transfers. *World Development* 23(8): 1277–89.

————. 1996. NGOs and Environmental Public Goods: Institutional Alternatives to Property Rights. *Development and Change* 27: 453–74.

Michels, Robert. [1915] 1959. *Political Parties.* New York: Dover Publications.

Millet, Richard. 1987. The Honduran Dilemma. *Current History* 86(524): 409–12, 435–6.

Moen, Elizabeth. 1991. *Voluntary Sector Grass Roots Development in Tamil Nadu.* Gandhigram Rural Institute, Deemed University, Tamil Nadu, India.

Moguel, Julio. 1995. Local Power and Development Alternatives: An Urban Popular Movement in Northern Mexico. In *New Paths to Democratic Development in Latin America: The Rise of NGO-Municipal Collaboration,* edited by Charles Reilly. Boulder, Colo.: Lynne Rienner.

Montague, Joel, and Ava Kabouchy Clough. 1995. The Efficiency and Effectiveness of Tropical African Private Voluntary Agency Development Consortia. Paper, Aspen Institute Grant 93-NSR-12.

Montgomery, John D. 1972. The Allocation of Authority in Land Reform Programs: A Comparative Study of Administrative Process and Outputs. *Administrative Science Quarterly* 17(1): 62–75.

————. 1987. How African Managers Serve Development Goals. *Comparative Politics* 19(3): 347–60.

Morales, Danilo A. Q., ed. 1995. Meio ambiente, desenvolvimento e cidadania: Desafios para as Ciencias Sociais. São Paulo: Cortez Editora.

Moreira, Betina. 1993. Giving Brazil's Street Children a Voice. *Grassroots Development* 17(1): 39.

Morgan, Elizabeth A., Grant Power, and Van B. Weigel. 1993. Thinking Strategically About Development: A Typology of Action Programs for Global Change. *World Development* 21(12): 1913–30.

Morgan, Lynn M. 1990. International Politics and Primary Health Care in Costa Rica. *Social Science and Medicine* 30(2): 211–19.

Morgan, Mary. 1990. Stetching the Development Dollar: The Potential for Scaling-Up. *Grassroots Development* 14(1): 2–11.

Morgenthau, Ruth. N.d. International Liaison Committee for Food Corps Programs. Waltham, Mass.: Brandeis University.

Mowlana, Hamid. 1993. Information Hunger and Knowledge Affluence: How to Bridge the Gap? *Development* 3: 23–26.

Muller, Jean-Daniel. 1989. *Les ONG Ambigues: Aides aux Etats, Aides aux Populations?* Paris: L'Harmattan.

Mulyungi, Josphat. 1990. On the Role of African NGOs. *Voices from Africa* 2: 45–58.

Munck, Geraldo. 1990. Identity and Ambiguity in Democratic Struggles. In *Popular Movements and Political Change in Mexico,* edited by Joe Foweraker and Ann L. Craig. Boulder, Colo.: Lynne Rienner.

Myrdahl, Gunnar. 1970. *The Challenge of World Poverty.* New York: Pantheon Books.

Najam, Adil. 1996a. NGO Accountability: A Conceptual Framework. *Development Policy Review* 14(4): 339–53.

————. 1996b. *Nongovernmental Organizations as Policy Entrepreneurs: In*

Pursuit of Sustainable Development. PONPO working paper no. 231. Program on Non-Profit Organizations, Yale University.

Narkwiboonwong, Werachai, and Walter E. J. Tipps. 1989. Project Identification, Formulation and Start-Up by Voluntary Organizations (NGOs) in Thailand's Rural Development. *Public Administration and Development* 9: 201–14.

Navarro, Juan Carlos, ed. 1994. *Community Organizations in Latin America.* Washington, D.C.: Inter-American Development Bank.

Ndegwa, Stephen N. 1996. *The Two Faces of Civil Society: NGOs and Politics in Africa.* West Hartford, Conn.: Kumarian Press.

Nielsen, Waldemar. 1979. *The Endangered Sector.* New York: Columbia University Press.

Nishimura, Kunio. 1993. The New Volunteerism: Japanese NGOs, Helping Hands. *Transnational Associations* 1: 13–6.

O'Donnell, Guillermo. 1986. On the Fruitful Convergences of Hirschman's "Exit, Voice and Loyalty" and "Shifting Involvements": Reflections from the Recent Argentine Experience. In *Development, Democracy and the Art of Trespassing: Essays in Honor of Albert O. Hirschman,* edited by Alejandro Foxley, Michael D. McPherson, and Guillermo O'Donnell. Notre Dame, Ind.: University of Notre Dame.

O'Donnell, Guillermo, and Philippe Schmitter. 1986. *Tentative Conclusions About Uncertain Transitions.* Vol. 4 of *Transitions from Authoritarian Rule.* Baltimore: Johns Hopkins University Press.

OECD (Organization for Economic Cooperation and Development), Development Centre. 1988. Voluntary Aid for Development: The Role of the Secretariat. Note by the Secretariat, September 14.

Organski, A. F. K. 1965. *The Stages of Political Development.* New York: Knopf.

Oxby, Clare. 1983. Farmer Groups' in Rural Areas of the Third World. *Community Development Journal* 18(1): 50–9.

Padrón, Mario. 1988a. Los Centros de Promoción y la cooperación internacional en América Latina: El caso Peruano. In *Las organizaciones no gubernamentales en el Perú,* edited by Mario Padrón. Lima: DESCO (Centro de Estudios y Promoción del Desarrollo).

————, ed. 1988b. *Las organizaciónes no gubernamentales en el Peru.* Lima: Desco (Centro de Estudios y Promoción del Desarrollo).

Pare, Luisa. 1990. The Challenges of Rural Democratisation in Mexico. *Journal of Development Studies* 26(4): 79–95.

Parsons, Talcott. 1963. On the Concept of Political Power. *Proceedings of the American Philosophical Society* 3: 232–62. Reprinted in Talcott Parsons. 1969. *Politics and Social Structure.* New York: Free Press.

Pasara, Luis, Nena Delpino, Ricio Vandeavellano, and Alonso Zarzar, eds. 1991. *La Otra Cara de la Luna.* Buenos Aires: Manatial S.R.L.

Patel, Rohini. 1992. The Role of Voluntary Associations in Civic Society and Democracy: A Case Study of the Self-Employed Women's Association, Ahmedabad, India. Paper prepared for the Third International Conference of Research on Voluntary and Nonprofit Organizations, Center for Philanthropy, Indiana University, March 11–13.

Payne, Douglas W. 1996. Latin America and the Caribbean: Storm Warnings. In *Freedom in the World,* edited by Roger Kaplan. New York: Freedom House.

Pease, G. H. 1988. Experiencias de Democracia Local y ONGD. In *Las organizaciónes no gubernamentales en el Perú,* edited by Mario Padrón. Lima: DESCO (Centro de Estudios y Promoción del Desarrollo).

Peng, Khor Kok. 1983. Whose Felt Needs? *Ceres* 16(3): 28–32.

Perez Diaz, Victor. 1993. *The Return of Civil Society: The Emergence of Democratic Spain.* Cambridge: Harvard University Press.

Pfirrman, Claudia, and Dirk Kron. 1992. *Environment and NGOs in Thailand.* Bangkok: Thai NGO Support Project, Friedrich-Naumann-Stiftung.

Pipes, Daniel. 1995–96. The Middle East: Between Peace and Jihad. In *Freedom in the World: The Annual Survey of Political Rights and Civil Liberties, 1995–1996,* edited by Roger Kaplan. New York: Freedom House.

Population Institute. 1987a. Bangladesh Determined to Lower Its Fertility. *Popline* 9(7).

―――. 1987b. World Bank Turning to NGOs for Support. *Popline* 9(2).

Powell, Walter W., ed. 1987. *The Nonprofit Sector: A Research Handbook.* New Haven, Conn: Yale University Press.

PRADAN (Professional Assistance for Development Action). 1988. *On Enhancing Capabilities of Voluntary Agencies.* A report submitted to the Council for the Advancement of People's Action and Rural Technology, New Delhi.

Pradervand, Pierre. 1990. *Listening to Africa: Developing Africa from the Grassroots.* New York: Praeger.

Pratton, David T., and Suliman Ali Baldo. 1996. Return to the Roots: Processes of Legitimacy in Sudanese Migrant Associations. In *Beyond the Magic Bullet: NGO Performance and Accountability in the Post-Cold War World,* edited by Michael Edwards and David Hulme. West Hartford, Conn: Kumarian Press.

Prijono, Onny S. 1992. Voluntarism and Voluntary Organizations in Indonesia. In *The Nonprofit Sector in the Global Community,* edited by Kathleen D. McCarthy, Virginia A. Hodgkinson, Russy D. Sumariwalla, and associates. San Francisco: Jossey-Bass.

Puliatti, Enzo. 1990. Computer Mediated Communication—Systems and Developing Countries. *Development* 2: 60–5.

Putnam, Robert D. 1993a. *Making Democracy Work: Civic Traditions in Modern Italy.* Princeton, N.J.: Princeton University Press.

―――. 1993b. Social Capital and Public Affairs. *American Prospect* 13 (spring): 1–8.

―――. 1995. Bowling Alone. *Journal of Democracy* 6(1): 65–78.

Pye, Lucian W. 1966. *Aspects of Political Development.* Boston: Little, Brown.

Quick, Stephen. 1980. The Paradox of Popularity: "Ideological" Program Implementation in Zambia. In *Politics and Policy Implementation in the Third World,* edited by Merilee Grindle. Princeton: Princeton, N.J. Princeton University Press.

Qureshi, Moeen A. 1988. The World Bank and NGOs: New Approaches. Remarks Before the Washington Chapter of the Society for International

Development Conference, April 22.

Rademacher, A., and D. Tamang. 1993. *Democracy, Development and NGOs.* Kathmandu: SEARCH.

Rakodi, Carole. 1990. After the Project Has Ended: The Role of a Non-Governmental Organisation in Improving the Conditions of the Urban Poor in Lusaka. *Community Development Journal* 25(1): 9–20.

Randall, Vicky, and Robin Theobald. 1985. *Political Change and Under-development.* Durham, N.C.: Duke University Press.

Rees, William E. 1996. Revisiting Carrying Capacity: Area-Based Indicators of Sustainability. *Population and Environment* 17(3): 195–215.

Reilly, Charles. 1989. The Democratization of Development: Partnership at the Grassroots. In *Inter-American Foundation, Annual Report,* 16–20.

———. 1990. Helping the Poor to Save the Planet. *Grassroots Development* 14(2): 42–4.

———. 1993. NGO Policy Makers and the Social Ecology of Development. *Grassroots Development* 17(25): 25–35.

———, ed. 1995a. *New Paths to Democratic Development in Latin America: The Rise of NGO-Municipal Collaboration.* Boulder, Colo.: Lynne Rienner.

———. 1995b. Public Policy and Citizenship. In *New Paths to Democratic Development in Latin America: The Rise of NGO-Municipal Collaboration,* edited by Charles Reilly. Boulder, Colo: Lynne Rienner.

———. 1995c. Topocrats, Technocrats and NGOs. In *New Paths to Democratic Development in Latin America: The Rise of NGO-Municipal Collaboration,* edited by Charles Reilly. Boulder, Colo: Lynne Rienner.

Renard, Robrecht. 1987. *Le Role des ONG au Zaire.* Brussels: Centre Nacion de Cooperation au Developpement.

Rigg, Jonathan. 1991. Grass-Roots Development in Rural Thailand: A Lost Cause? *World Development* 19(2/3): 199–211.

Riggs, Fred W. 1964. *Administration in Developing Countries.* New York: Houghton Mifflin.

———. 1966. Bureaucrats and Political Development: A Paradoxical View. In *Political Development and Social Change,* edited by Jason L. Finkle and Richard W. Gable. New York: John Wiley and Sons.

Riker, James V. 1995a. Contending Perspectives for Interpreting Government-NGO Relations in South and Southeast Asia: Constraints, Challenges and the Search for Common Ground in Rural Development. In *Government-NGO Relations in Asia,* edited by Noeleen Heyzer, James V. Riker, and Antonio Quizon. New York: St. Martin's Press.

———. 1995b. From Cooptation to Cooperation and Collaboration in Government-NGO Relations: Toward an Enabling Policy Environment for People-Centered Development in Asia. In *Government-NGO Relations in Asia,* edited by Noeleen Heyzer, James V. Riker, and Antonio Quizon. New York: St. Martin's Press.

———. 1995c. Reflections on Government-NGO Relations in Asia: Prospects and Challenges for People-Centered Development. In *Government-NGO Relations in Asia,* edited by Noeleen Heyzer, James V. Riker, and Antonio Quizon. New York: St. Martin's Press.

Ritchie-Vance, Marion. 1991. *The Art of Association: NGOs and Civil Society in Colombia.* Country Focus Series 2. Rosslyn, Va.: Inter-American Foundation.

Rivera Franco, Jorge Eliecer. 1986. Colombia's National Association of Artisanal Fishermen. *Ideas and Action* 169(4): 3–7.

Robey, B., S. O. Rutstein, and L. Morris. 1993. The Fertility Decline in Developing Countries. *Scientific American,* December, pp. 60–7.

Robinson, Mark A. 1992. Assessing the Impact of NGO Rural Poverty Alleviation Programmes: Evidence from South India. *Journal of International Development* 4: 397–417.

———. 1997. Privatising the Voluntary Sector: NGOs as Public Service Contractors? In *NGOs, States and Donors: Too Close for Comfort?* edited by David Hulme and Michael Edwards. New York: St. Martin's Press.

Romm, Jeff. 1986. Frameworks for Governmental Choice. In *Community Management: Asian Experience and Perspectives,* edited by David C. Korten. West Hartford, Conn.: Kumarian Press.

Rondinelli, Dennis A. 1983. *Development Projects as Policy Experiments: An Adaptive Approach to Development Administration.* London: Methuen.

Rondinelli, Dennis A., and John R. Nellis. 1986. Assessing Decentralization Policies in Developing Countries: The Case for Cautious Optimism. *Development Policy Review* 4(1): 3–23.

Ronen, Dov, ed. 1986. *Democracy and Pluralism in Africa.* Boulder, Colo: Lynne Rienner.

Rood, Steven. 1992. *The State and Non-Government Organisations.* Paper presented at the fourth International Philippine Studies Conference, Australian National University, Canberra, July 1–3.

Rothenberg, Irene Fraser. 1980. Administrative Decentralization and the Implementation of Housing Policy in Colombia. In *Politics and Policy Implementation in the Third World,* edited by Merilee Grindle. Princeton, N.J.: Princeton University Press.

Rouille D'Orfeuille, Henri. 1985. *Cooperer Autrement: L'engagement des organisations non gouvernementales aujourd'hui.* Paris: L'Harmatton.

Rubin, Jeffrey W. 1990. Popular Mobilization and the Myth of State Corporatism. In *Popular Movements and Political Change in Mexico,* edited by Joe Foweraker and Ann Craig. Boulder, Colo. Lynne Rienner.

Rush, James. 1991. *The Last Tree.* New York: Asia Society.

Ruttan, Vernon W. 1991. What Happened to Political Development? *Economic Development and Cultural Change* 39(2): 265–92.

Sabanes, Carlos. 1988. Experiencias de Cooperación: El Caso Argentino. In *Cooperación Internacional al Desarrollo* 3. Santiago: Taller de Cooperación al Desarrollo.

Sabatier, Paul A. 1986. Top Down and Bottom-Up Approaches to Implementation Research: A Critical Analysis and Suggested Synthesis. *Journal of Public Policy* 6: 21–48.

Sabur, M. Abdus. 1986. Asia: Grassroots and Transnational Networking. The AFCOD Experience. *IFDA Dossier* 55: 67–70.

Sachs, Celine. 1986. Mutirão in Brazil: Initiatives for Self-Reliance. *Development* 4: 65–9.

Salamon, Lester M. 1987. Of Market Failure, Voluntary Failure, and Third-Party Government: Toward a Theory of Government–Non-Profit Relations in the Modern Welfare State. *Journal of Voluntary Action Research* 16(1, 2): 29–49.

Salamon, Lester M., and Helmut K. Anheier. 1994. *The Emerging Sector: The Nonprofit Sector in Comparative Perspective—An Overview.* Baltimore: Johns Hopkins University Institute for Policy Studies.

——— 1996. Social Origins of Civil Society: Explaining the Nonprofit Sector Cross-Nationally. Paper prepared for the second annual conference of the International Society for Third Sector Research, Mexico City, July 18–21.

Samoff, Joel. 1989. Popular Initiatives and Local Government in Tanzania. *Journal of Developing Areas* 24(2): 1–18.

Sandberg, Eve, ed. 1994a. *The Changing Politics of Non-Governmental Organizations and African States.* Westport, Conn.: Praeger.

———. 1994b. Introduction: The Changing Politics of Non-Governmental Organizations and the African State. In *The Changing Politics of Non-Governmental Organizations and African States,* edited by Eve Sandberg. Westport: Praeger.

Sandberg, Eve, and Carol L. Martin. 1994. Namibia: An Institutional Analysis of a Consultative Model of Decision Making by a Democratizing State and Its NGOs. In *The Changing Politics of Non-Governmental Organizations and African States,* edited by Eve Sandberg. Westport, Conn.: Praeger.

Santana Rodriguez, Pedro. 1995. Local Governments, Decentralization and Democracy in Colombia. In *New Paths to Democratic Development in Latin America: The Rise of NGO-Municipal Collaboration,* edited by Charles Reilly. Boulder, Colo.: Lynne Rienner.

Santuc Laborde, Vicente. 1988. De un programa conyuntural a una institución estructural: El CIPCA. In *Las organizaciónes no gubernamentales en el Peru,* edited by Mario Padrón. Lima: DESCO (Centro de Estudios y Promoción del Desarrollo).

Sanyal, Bikas. 1991. Antagonistic Cooperation: A Case Study of Non-governmental Organizations, Government and Donor's Relationships in Income-Generating Projects in Bangladesh. *World Development* 19(10): 1367–79.

Saouma, Edouard. 1985. Issues in Rural Poor Organizing. *Ideas and Action* 162: 18–21.

Satia, J. K. 1983. Development Tasks and Middle Management Roles in Rural Development. In *Bureaucracy and the Poor,* edited by David C. Korten and Felipe Alfonso. West Hartford, Conn.: Kumarian Press.

Sawadogo, Alfred. 1990. The State Counter-Attacks: Clearly Defined Priorities for Burkina Faso. *Voices from Africa* 2: 59–64.

Scherer-Warren, Ilse. 1995. ONGs na América Latina: Trajectoria e perfíl. In *Meio ambiente, desenvolvimento e cidadania: Desafios para as Ciencias Sociaís,* edited by Danilo A. Q. Morales. São Paulo: Cortez Editora.

Schneider, Bertrand. 1985. *La Revolution des Pieds Nus—Rapport au Club de Rome.* Paris: Fayard.

Schrader, Peter. 1994. Elites as Facilitators or Impediments to Political

Development? Some Lessons from the "Third Wave" of Democratization in Africa. *Journal of Developing Areas* 29 (October): 69–90.

Schuurman, Frans J., and Ellen Heer. 1992. *Social Movements and NGOs in Latin America: A Case Study of the Women's Movement in Chile.* Nijmegen Studies in Development and Cultural Change no. 11. Saarbrücken, Germany: Verlagbreitbach Publishers.

Schwedler, Jillian, ed. 1995. *Toward Civil Society in the Middle East? A Primer.* Boulder, Colo.: Lynne Rienner.

Schweitz, Martha L. 1993. Indigenous Environmental NGOs and International Law: A Reconstruction of Roles and Possibilities. *University of British Columbia Law Review* 27(1): 133–51.

———. 1995. NGO Participation in International Governance: The Question of Legitimacy. Remarks delivered at the American Society of International Law annual meeting, April 8.

Semmes, Rafael. 1987. Field Office Communication, Save the Children, April 5. Presented at sustainable development conference, London, April 28–30.

Sen, Siddhartha. 1994. Government and the Nonprofit Sector: India. Paper prepared for the inaugural conference of the International Society for Third Sector Research, Pecs, Hungary, July 4–7.

———. 1996. State-NGO Relationship in India: An Overview of the Post-Independence Era. Paper.

Serrano, Isagani R. 1994. Civil Society in the Asia-Pacific Region. In *Citizens Strengthening Civil Society,* edited by Miguel Darcy de Oliveira and Rajesh Tandon. Washington, D.C.: CIVICUS (World Alliance for Citizen Participation).

Sethi, Harsh. 1983. Development Is Not a Politically Neutral Task. *Ceres* 16(3): 19–22.

Seva Mandir. 1988–89. *Annual Report.* Udaipur, India: Seva Mandir.

Shaw, Timothy. 1994. Beyond any New World Order: The South in the 21st Century. *Third World Quarterly* 15(1): 137–46.

Sheth, D. L. 1983. Grass-Roots Stirrings and the Future of Politics. *Alternatives* 9(1): 1–24.

Simukonda, H. P. M. 1992. Creating a National NGO Council for Strengthening Social Welfare Services in Africa: Some Organizational and Technical Problems Experienced in Malawi. *Public Administration and Development* 12: 417–31.

Siroway, Larry, and Alex Inkeles. 1990. The Effects of Democracy on Economic Growth and Inequality: A Review. *Studies in Comparative International Development* 25(1): 126–57.

Skinner, R. J. 1983. Community Participation: Its Scope and Organization. In *People, Poverty and Shelter,* edited by R. J. Skinner and M. J. Rodell. London: Methuen.

Skinner, R. J., and M. J. Rodell, eds. 1983. *People, Poverty and Shelter.* London: Methuen.

Sklar, Richard L. 1986. Reds and Rights: Zimbabwe's Experiment. In *Democracy and Pluralism in Africa,* edited by Dov Ronen. Boulder, Colo: Lynne Rienner.

Smith, Brian H. 1990. *More Than Altruism: The Politics of Private Foreign*

Aid. Princeton, N.J.: Princeton University Press.

Smith, Carol. 1996. Development and the State: Issues for Anthropologists. In *Transforming Societies, Transforming Anthropology,* edited by Emilio Moran. Ann Anbor: University of Michigan Press.

Smith, Emily. 1992. Growth vs. Environment. *Business Week,* May 11, 66–75.

Smith, Jackie, Ron Pagnucco, and Winnie Romeril. 1994. Transnational Social Movement Organizations in the Global Political Arena. *Voluntas* 5(3): 121–54.

Society for Participatory Research in Asia. 1991. *Voluntary Development Organisations in India.* New Delhi: Society for Participatory Research in Asia.

Soedjatmoko. 1986. Social Energy as a Development Resource. In *Community Management: Asian Experience and Perspectives,* edited by David C. Korten. West Hartford, Conn.: Kumarian Press.

Sollis, Peter. 1995. Partners in Development? The State, Nongovernmental Organisations and the UN in Central America. *Third World Quarterly* 16(3): 525–42.

Sommer, John G. 1977. *Beyond Charity: U.S. Voluntary Aid for a Changing Third World.* Washington, D.C.: Overseas Development Council.

Spodek, Howard. 1994. Review Article: The Self-Employed Women's Association (SEWA) in India: Feminist, Gandhian Power in Development. *Economic Development and Cultural Change* 43(1): 193–222.

Stein, Alfredo. 1990. Critical Issues in Community Participation in Self-Help Housing Programmes. The Experience of FUNDASAL. *Community Development Journal* 25(1): 21–30.

Stevenson, Hugh C. 1994. NGOs in Chaipas: Nongovernmental and Proud of It. *The Other Stock Exchange* (Mexico), June 30.

Stewart, Sarah. 1990. Video as a Tool in Training and Organizing: Experiences of Video SEWA. *Development* 2: 48.

Stremlau, Carolyn C. 1987. NGO Coordinating Bodies in Africa, Asia and Latin America. *World Development* 15 (supplement, autumn): 213–26.

Sudan Council of Voluntary Agencies. 1988. Conference on the Role of Indigenous NGOs in African Recovery and Development, Khartoum, January 10–15.

Sullivan, William M. 1995. The Infrastructure of Democracy: From Civil Society to Civic Community. Paper.

Swartz, Marc J., ed. 1968. *Local Level Politics: Social and Cultural Perspectives.* Chicago: Aldine.

Swartzendruber, J. F., and Bernard Berka Njovens. 1993. *African NGO Participation in Natural Resource Policy Reform.* Washington, D.C.: World Resources Institute, Center for International Development and Environment.

Tandon, Rajesh. 1987. The State and Voluntary Agencies in India. Paper prepared for the Society for Participatory Research in Asia.

———. 1988. The State and Voluntary Agencies in Asia. Society for Participatory Research in Asia. Unpublished paper.

———. 1989a. *NGO Government Relations: A Source of Life or a Kiss of Death.* New Delhi: Society for Participatory Research in Asia.

———. 1989b. The State and Voluntary Agencies in Asia. In *Doing*

Development: Government, NGOs and the Rural Poor in Asia, edited by Richard Holloway. London: Earthscan Publications.

———. 1993. NGO Regulation: South Asian Scenario. *Transnational Associations* 4: 200–6.

Tendler, Judith. 1987. What Ever Happened to Poverty Alleviation? Report prepared for the mid-decade review of the Ford Foundation's Programs on Livelihood, Employment and Income Generation.

Terrant, James, and Hasan Poerbo. 1986. Strengthening Community-Based Technology Management Systems. In *Community Management: Asian Experience and Perspectives,* edited by David C. Korten. West Hartford, Conn.: Kumarian Press.

Theunis, Sjef, ed. 1992. *Non-Governmental Development Organizations of Developing Countries: And the South Smiles. . . .* Dordrecht: Martinus Nijhoff.

Thomas-Slayter, Barbara. 1990. *Implementing Effective Local Management of Natural Resources: New Roles for NGOs in Africa.* Working papers in African studies, no. 148. Boston: African Studies Center, Boston University.

———. 1992. Implementing Effective Local Mangement of Natural Resources: New Roles for NGOs in Africa. *Human Organization* 51(2): 136–43.

———. 1994. Structural Change, Power Politics, and Community Organizations in Africa: Challenging the Patterns, Puzzles and Paradoxes. *World Development* 22(10): 1479–90.

Thompson, Andres. 1990. *Philanthropy and Ecology in South America: The Role of Nonprofits and Their Funding Strategies in Buenos Aires, Santiago and São Paulo.* New York: Center for the Study of Philanthropy, City University of New York.

——— 1992. Democracy and Development: The Role of NGOs in the Southern Cone (Argentina, Chile and Uruguay). In *The Nonprofit Sector in the Global Community,* edited by Kathleen McCarthy, Virginia Hodgkinson, Russy Sumariwalla, and associates. San Francisco: Jossey-Bass.

Thoolen, Hans. 1990. Information and Training in an Expanding Human Rights Movement. *Development* 2: 86–90.

Tinker, Hugh. 1968. Local Government and Politics, and Political and Social Theory in India. In *Local Level Politics: Social and Cultural Perspectives,* edited by Marc J. Swartz. Chicago: Aldine.

Tongsawate, Maniemai, and Walter E. J. Tipps. 1985. *Coordination Between Governmental and Non-Governmental Organizations in Thailand's Rural Development.* Monograph no. 5. Bangkok: Division of Human Settlements Development, Asian Institute of Technology.

Toranzo Roca, Carlos F., ed. 1992. *La Relación entre Estado y ONG's.* La Paz, Bolivia: Cotesu, Ildis, Cooperación Holandesa.

Towle, Judith, and Bruce G. Potter. 1989. *Organizational Profiles of Who Is Doing What in Support of Programs for Sustainable Development and Environmental Management in the Eastern Caribbean: A Guide to Donor Assistance Agencies.* St. Thomas: Island Resources Foundation.

Tripp, Aili Mari. 1994. The Impact of Crisis and Economic Reform on Tanzania's Changing Associational Life. In *The Changing Politics of Non-*

Governmental Organizations and African States, edited by Eve Sandberg. Westport, Conn.: Praeger.

UNESCO (United Nations Educational, Scientific, and Cultural Organization). 1995. *Statistical Yearbook.* Paris: UNESCO.

Union of International Associations. 1993. *Relationships Between International Non-Governmental Organizations and the United Nations System.* Geneva: Union of International Associations.

United Nations. 1988. *Africa: Four Years On.* Final Report, UN-NGO Conference, April 23–27.

United Nations, Department for Economic and Social Information and Policy Analysis. 1996. *World Population Prospects: The 1996 Revision,* annex II and III. New York.

United Nations, Non-Govermental Liaison Service. 1988. *Non-Governmental Organizations and Sub-Saharan Africa.* Geneva: UN Non-Governmental Liaison Service.

United Nations Development Programme. 1993. *Human Development Report.* New York: UNDP.

Uphoff, Norman. 1986a. Activating Community Capacity for Water Management in Sri Lanka. In *Community Management: Asian Experience and Perspectives,* edited by David C. Korten. West Hartford, Conn.: Kumarian Press.

––––––. 1986b. *Local Institutional Development: An Analytical Sourcebook with Cases.* West Hartford, Conn.: Kumarian Press.

––––––. 1992. *Learning from Gal Oya: The Possibilities for Participatory Development and Post-Newtonian Social Science.* Ithaca, N.Y.: Cornell University Press.

––––––. 1993. Grassroots Organizations and NGOs in Rural Development: Opportunities with Diminishing States and Expanding Markets. *World Development* 21(4): 607–22.

Uvin, Peter. 1995. Fighting Hunger at the Grassroots: Paths to Scaling Up. *World Development* 23(6): 927–39.

Uvin, Peter, and David Miller. 1994. *Scaling Up: Thinking Through the Issues.* Paper, Brown University, Providence, R.I.

Valarelli, Moema. 1996. *Acao Cidadania Contra a Miseria e Pela Vida.* Second Inter-American Conference of Mayors: IAF/OAS Consultation on Local Development. Washington, D.C.: Inter-American Foundation.

Van der Heijden, Hendrik. 1987. *Economic Development and Poverty Alleviation Efforts of the Private Voluntary Sector.* Paper prepared for an international symposium on the non-profit sector and the welfare state, Bad Honeff, Germany, June 10–13

Velarde, Federico. 1988. Las ONGs en el Peru: Algunas Notas. *Coorperación Internacional al Desarrollo* (Santiago) 3: 15–8

––––––. 1989. Peru: Algunas Notas sobre Las ONGs. *IFDA Dossier* 69: 63–6.

Verma, M. C., and P. G. Menon. 1993. Role of NGOs: UN and Bilateral Aid. Proceedings of the International Conference on Sustainable Village-Based Development, Colorado State University, September 27–October 1.

Viola, Eduardo. 1987. O Movimento Ecológico no Brasil (1974–1986) do

Ambientalismo à Ecopolítica. Working paper no. 93. Helen Kellogg Institute for International Studies, University of Notre Dame.

Viswanath, Vanita. 1991. *NGOs and Women's Development in Rural South India: A Comparative Analysis*. Boulder, Colo.: Westview Press.

Wali, Alaka. 1990. Living with the Land: Ethnicity and Development in Chile. *Grassroots Development* 14(9): 12–20.

Walsh, Mary Williams. 1986. Stoic Masses: Poor People of Mexico, Afraid of Protesting, Endure Much Injustice. *Wall Street Journal,* December 29.

Walters, Shirley. 1993. Non-Governmental Organisations and the South African State. *Community Development Journal* 28(1): 1–10.

Waltz, Susan E. 1995. *Human Rights and Reform: Changing the Face of North African Politics*. Berkeley: University of California Press.

Walzer, Michael. 1991. The Idea of Civil Society. *Dissent* (spring): 293–304.

Wanyande, Peter. 1987. Women's Groups in Participatory Development: Kenya's Development Experience Through the Use of Harambee. *Development* 2/3: 94–102.

Ward, Peter. 1981. Political Pressure for Urban Services: The Response of Two Mexico City Administrations. *Development and Change* 12: 379–407.

Weber, Ron. 1995. Local Leaders, Global Heroes. *Grassroots Development* 19(1): 41–2.

Weede, Erich. 1984. Political Democracy, State Strength and Economic Growth in LDCs: A Cross National Analysis. *Review of International Studies* 10: 297–312.

Welch, Claude. 1995. *Protecting Human Rights in Africa: Role and Strategies of Non-Governmental Organizations*. Philadelphia: University of Pennsylvania Press.

Weyland, Kurt. 1995. Social Movements and the State: The Politics of Health Reform in Brazil. *World Development* 23(10): 1699–712.

Wiarda, Howard. 1989–90. Rethinking Political Development: A Look Backward over Thirty Years, and a Look Ahead. *Studies in Comparative International Development* 24(4): 65–82.

Williams, Aubrey. 1990. A Growing Role for NGOs in Development. *Finance and Development* (December): 31–3.

Williams, Carlos, and Gustavo Riofrio. 1987. Squatters and Shantytowns in Lima. *Regional Development Dialogue* 8(4): 166–89.

Williams, Paula. 1989a. Despite Many Voices, African Women Unite. Letter to the Institute for Current World Affairs, Hanover, N.H. February 13.

———. 1989b. Zimbabwean Women's Groups. Letter to the Institute for Current World Affairs, Hanover, N.H. February 28.

Wils, Frits. 1996. Scaling Up, Mainstreaming, and Accountability. In *Beyond the Magic Bullet: NGO Performance and Accountability in the Post–Cold War World,* edited by Michael Edwards and David Hulme. West Hartford, Conn.: Kumarian Press.

Woldemarian, Habte. 1992. Indigenous Non-Governmental Organizations in Africa: Issues and Challenges. In *The Nonprofit Sector in the Global Community,* edited by Kathleen D. McCarthy, Virginia A. Hodgkinson, Russy D. Sumariwalla, and associates. San Francisco: Jossey-Bass.

World Bank. 1984. *World Development Report.* Washington, D.C.: World Bank.

———. 1995. *Social Indicators for Development.* Washington, D.C.: World Bank.

World Resources Institute. 1992. The World Conservation Union and the United Nations Environment Programme. Global biodiversity strategy. Washington, D.C.: World Resources Institute.

Yeager, Roger. 1989. Democratic Pluralism and Ecological Crisis in Botswana. *Journal of Developing Areas* 23: 385–404.

Zakaria, Fareed. 1995. Bigger than the Family, Smaller than the State (a review of *Trust* by Francis Fukuyama). *New York Times Book Review,* August 13, 1.

Zambrano, Angel Enrique. 1989. Las Asociaciones de Vecinos en Venezuela. *IFDA Dossier* 72: 25–36.

Zeuli, Kim. 1991. Solving the Problems of the Third World Through Women. *Thesis,* Vassar College, Poughkeepsie, N.Y.

Zubaida, Sami. 1992. Islam, the State and Democracy: Contrasting Conceptions of Society in Egypt. *Middle East Report* (November–December): 2–10.

Zuevkas, Charles Jr. 1986. Political Democracy and Economic Growth in Latin America, 1980–1985. *LASA Forum* 18(3) (fall).

Index

Specific nongovernmental organizations are found under country name.

About the Author

Julie Fisher is a Program Officer at the Kettering Foundation and a former scholar in residence at the Program on Non-Profit Organizations at Yale University. As an independent consultant she has worked for UNICEF, Save the Children, Lutheran World Relief, Technoserve, Trickle Up, and CIVICUS, among many other organizations. She has a doctorate in international studies from the Johns Hopkins School of Advanced International Studies.

 Kumarian Press is dedicated to publishing and distributing books and other media that will have a positive social and economic impact on the lives of peoples living in "Third World" conditions no matter where they live.

As well as books on Nongovernmental Organizations,
Kumarian Press also publishes books
on Peace and Conflict Resolution,
the Environment, International Development,
International Health,
Government, Gender and Development

To receive a complimentary catalog, request writer's
guidelines, or to order books, call or write:

Kumarian Press, Inc.
14 Oakwood Avenue
West Hartford, CT 06119-2127
USA

Inquiries: 860-233-5895
Fax: 860-233-6072
Order toll free: 800-289-2664

e-mail: kpbooks@aol.com